D1450894

Unlocking the Past

Published in cooperation with the Society for Historical Archaeology

Florida A&M University, Tallahassee
Florida Atlantic University, Boca Raton
Florida Gulf Coast University, Ft. Myers
Florida International University, Miami
Florida State University, Tallahassee
University of Central Florida, Orlando
University of Florida, Gainesville
University of North Florida, Jacksonville
University of South Florida, Tampa
University of West Florida, Pensacola

Unlocking the Past

Celebrating Historical Archaeology in North America

Edited by Lu Ann De Cunzo and John H. Jameson Jr.

University Press of Florida
Gainesville/Tallahassee/Tampa/Boca Raton
Pensacola/Orlando/Miami/Jacksonville/Ft. Myers

10 09 08 07 06 05   6 5 4 3 2 1

Library of Congress Cataloging-in-Publication Data
Unlocking the past : celebrating historical archaeology in North
America / edited by Lu Ann De Cunzo and John H. Jameson, Jr.
p. cm.
"Published in cooperation with the Society for Historical Archaeology."
Includes bibliographical references and index.
ISBN 0-8130-2796-9 (alk. paper)
1. Archaeology and history--United States. 2. United States--Antiquities.
3. Historic sites--United States. 4. United States--History, Local. 5. Ar-
chaeology and history--North America. 6. North America--Antiquities.
I. De Cunzo, Lu Ann. II. Jameson, John H. III. Society for Historical Archaeology.
E159.5.U55 205
973--dc22   2004066138

The University Press of Florida is the scholarly publishing agency
for the State University System of Florida, comprising Florida A&M
University, Florida Atlantic University, Florida Gulf Coast University,
Florida International University, Florida State University, University
of Central Florida, University of Florida, University of North Florida,
University of South Florida, and University of West Florida.

University Press of Florida
15 Northwest 15th Street
Gainesville, FL 32611-2079
http://www.upf.com

Contents

Acknowledgments   ix

Introduction: The Stuff of Histories and Cultures   1
    Lu Ann De Cunzo

Part 1. Cultures in Contact: Melting Pots or Not?   15
    Lu Ann De Cunzo

1. Spaniards and Native Americans at the Missions of La Florida   19
    Jerald T. Milanich
2. Bioarchaeology of the Spanish Missions   25
    Clark Spencer Larsen
3. African Americans on Southern Plantations   30
    Leland Ferguson, from *Uncommon Ground*,
    adapted by Lu Ann De Cunzo
4. Black Seminole Freedom Fighters on the Florida Frontier   36
    Terrance Weik
5. The Chinese in the Cities of the West   45
    Roberta S. Greenwood

**Part 2. Challenging and Changing Environments: Exploring New Lands
and Exploiting New Environments   51**
    Lu Ann De Cunzo

6. Early Encounters with a "New" Land: Vikings and Englishmen
    in the North American Arctic   53
    William Fitzhugh
7. Jamestown, Virginia   62
    Andrew Edwards
8. The Shipwreck of La Salle's *La Belle*   68
    James E. Bruseth
9. Mining the West   72
    R. Scott Baxter and Rebecca Allen

Part 3. Building Cities: Tales of Many Cities 79
    Lu Ann De Cunzo

10. Quebec City, Canada 82
    William Moss
11. New York City 89
    Diana diZerega Wall and Nan A. Rothschild
12. Community Archaeology in Alexandria, Virginia 97
    Pamela J. Cressey
13. Urban Life in Colonial Charleston, South Carolina 102
    Martha Zierden
14. "A Place to Start From": West Oakland, California 110
    Lu Ann De Cunzo and Mary Praetzellis

Part 4. Making a Living in Rural America: The Archaeology of Work 117
    Lu Ann De Cunzo

15. The Archaeology of Agricultural Life 119
    Sara Mascia
16. The Archaeology of Rural Industry 134
    David R. Starbuck

Part 5. Cultures in Conflict: Contests on Land and at Sea 149
    Lu Ann De Cunzo

17. The Archaeology of America's Colonial Wars 151
    David R. Starbuck
18. The Civil War Under Water 160
    Sarah McDowell, with contributions by Mark Wilde-Ramsing
19. Native and "Newcomer": Battle of Little Bighorn 166
    Richard A. Fox
20. A Global Contest: World War II 174
    Daniel Lenihan, Gary Cummins, James Delgado, David Clark,
    and Lu Ann De Cunzo

Part 6. Unlock the Past for the Future: From the Past in the Present to the Future 183
    Lu Ann De Cunzo

21. Conserving Our Past 185
    Lisa Young
22. Historical Archaeology That Matters Beyond Academics 189
    Maria Franklin

23. The Past Belongs to Us All   195
    John Triggs
24. Does Historical Archaeology Really Matter in Today's World?   200
    Audrey Horning

Epilogue   205
    John H. Jameson Jr.

For Further Reading and Viewing   213
Contributors   225
Index   229

Acknowledgments

The editors gratefully acknowledge the assistance, support, and patience of all those who have worked with us over the years on the *Unlocking the Past* project of the Society for Historical Archaeology (SHA). We extend our thanks and appreciation to:

All the contributors, who graciously endured several rounds of writing, rewriting, and rethinking the entire project;

SHA Public Education and Information Committee chairs Martha Williams, Diana diZerega Wall, and Kim McBride, who shepherded the project through the SHA Board;

SHA presidents Glenn Farris, Henry Miller, Pamela Cressey, Teresita Majewski, Susan Henry Renaud, Douglas Armstrong, Vergil Noble, and Julia King, who ensured that we had the needed resources and support from the Society;

SHA editor Ronald Michael, associate editor William Turnbaugh, reviewers Glenn Farris, James Gibb, Paul Shackel, Karolyn Smardz, and anonymous reviewers, who encouraged us to know our audience and to represent the breadth and diversity that characterizes our discipline;

John E. Ehrenhard, director of the Southeast Archeological Center, U.S. National Park Service, Tallahassee, for administrative support and for donation of the oil painting *Unlocking the Past* by Martin Pate, and Center staff member Seth Johnstone, who assisted John Jameson in the collection, scanning, and editing of images and World Wide Web postings;

University Press of Florida (UPF) editor Meredith Morris-Babb, who saw the value of the project and challenged us to write not for ourselves but for our audience, and UPF editor John Byram, who has guided the manuscript through the review and publication process with skill and patience;

SHA members who contributed ideas, critiques, and essays during the planning stages of the project, especially Julia Costello, Kathleen Deagan, Robin Denson, Lynn Evans, and Judy Tordoff;

Our authors and these individuals and organizations who graciously provided images and granted permission to publish them: Kathleen Deagan, Pierre Lahoud, Bonnie McEwan, Jack McIlroy, Roberto Osti, Brigitte Ostiguy, Douglas Scott, and Sue Wilkinson; Anthropological Studies Center, Sonoma State University; Archives Nationales du Québec à Québec; Arctic Studies Center, Smithsonian Institution; Arkansas Archeological Survey;

Charleston Museum; Colonial Williamsburg Foundation; Department of Anthropology, William Duncan Strong Museum, Columbia University; Friends of the *Hunley*; Historic St. Mary's City; Kentucky Archaeological Survey; Mackinac State Historic Parks; Mariners' Museum, Newport News, Virginia; Nebraska State Patrol; Phoebe Apperson Hearst Museum of Anthropology and the Regents of the University of California; Seaver Center for Western History Research, Los Angeles County Museum of Natural History; South Street Seaport Museum, New York; U.S. Library of Congress; U.S. National Archives; and U.S. National Park Service;

Sarah McDowell, University of Delaware Summer Social Science Scholar, who authored essays and assisted with editing and images as an apprentice in historical archaeology;

And, finally, to all our colleagues in North American historical archaeology whose fine work has made it at once easy and difficult to write this book.

Introduction

The Stuff of Histories and Cultures

Lu Ann De Cunzo

What comes to mind when you think of archaeology? Pith-helmeted adventurers traversing jungles and deserts in search of great treasures? The thrill of first peering through the dimly lit entrance to a tomb? But how about a white-haired gentleman in a fedora steering an old Volkswagen bus full of students through a picturesque cemetery, stopping to scrutinize marble lambs and praying hands? Or a tall, lanky man with an infectious sense of humor lecturing about clipped poodles and Medusa-headed gravestones? Or a petite blond woman leading a team through the wet heat of Hispaniola's sugarcane fields and banana gardens in search of the places where Spanish and Native American peoples first encountered each other? Doesn't sound familiar? Are you wondering what new Hollywood release or *New York Times* bestseller you have missed? None—at least not if you were looking for these three real-life archaeologists.

Fifteen years before I ever met that white-haired archaeologist in a fedora, I learned on my own what he spent a lifetime advocating: archaeology has a fundamental role in education, to galvanize kids' interest in *discovery*. For me the epiphany came when I was eight, as I crept along in a cotton field in search of arrowheads. I was with a family friend who was a collector, not an archaeologist, but the distinction meant nothing to me then. I cared only about discovering those bits of stone that lie scattered on the ground. Someone had shaped them into tools centuries ago, and then broken them and thrown them away. No one had touched them since. I was hooked.

In 1978 I had the good fortune to be among the students in that Volkswagen bus. The gentleman was John Cotter, and the course was one he had introduced to American universities, American historical archaeology.

We were on the legendary Halloween tour of Philadelphia's cemeteries, learning how death could help us understand life, asking why eighteenth-century Quakers marked graves with small stones carved with the person's

1

John L. Cotter, 1911–1999
Lu Ann De Cunzo

John L. Cotter developed his interest in archaeology at the University of Denver, where he earned his B.A. in 1934. During his entire career he lived an archaeologist's dream, excavating at some of the most important sites in the United States. In the 1930s he worked at Clovis and at Lindenmeier, sites left by some of the first Americans—called by archaeologists the Paleo-Indians—who arrived here eleven thousand years ago. In 1940 Cotter joined the National Park Service. World War II interrupted his career, like those of so many other young men. Cotter served proudly in the army infantry and was wounded at Normandy. After the war he became chief archaeologist at Jamestown, Virginia, the oldest permanent British settlement in North America, overseeing excavations in preparation for its 350th anniversary in 1957 (see chapter 7). Later that year he was named regional archaeologist of the Northeast Region and moved to Philadelphia, birthplace of the nation. During his twenty-year tenure in this post, he worked at Independence National Historical Park and throughout the core of colonial Philadelphia, as well as at Valley Forge and other historical parks in the region.

In 1959 Cotter completed his Ph.D. in anthropology at the University of Pennsylvania, and the following year he introduced the first course devoted to North American historical archaeology there. A founding member and first president of the Society for Historical Archaeology (SHA), Cotter also held the positions of adjunct associate professor and curator for American historical archaeology at the University of Pennsylvania. In 1984 he received the SHA's J. C. Harrington Medal in recognition of his lifelong contributions to the field. The SHA later created the John L. Cotter Award to recognize outstanding contributions by historical archaeologists at the start of their professional careers. Of his contributions to archaeology Cotter said, with characteristic humility, "I have simply tried to say what is there, but in doing so, I couldn't help but observe and comment just a little bit, and if that involves a certain amount of wit, I'm happy about it because I see things as being awfully funny very often."

> Old archaeologists don't fade away like some old generals I can recall, by golfing and garnering big bucks on the lecture circuit. Nor do they fade away like most politicians I have read about, men of high office who endow presidential libraries while enriching themselves with fat consultant fees, unless detoured by jail. Old archaeologists don't seem to fade away at all. Many of us would rather publish than perish.
>
> Cotter, "Antique Archaeologists," *Archaeology* 50 (1)

John Cotter *(left)* and Patrick Malone examining a redware handled trivet, recovered with other eighteenth-century ceramics from a subbasement pit dug by bottle and pot hunters in 1970 on the north side of Market Street between Fourth and Fifth Streets in Philadelphia. (Collection of the late John L. Cotter; photographer unknown.)

names or initials, and why Victorian Philadelphians created romantic land-scaped parks for their dead, complete with classical obelisks and towering mausoleums. By the time we took that tour, the last semester he taught the course, John Cotter had trained a generation of American historical archaeologists. He taught us a historical archaeology fundamentally simple in concept, profoundly difficult to accomplish. Archaeologists worth a damn try to evoke enough of the past to make it a semblance of life. Archaeology worth a damn is *relevant*. "There is an archaeology of everything. Computers have an archaeology beginning, of course, with your ten fingers."

I had already learned that the best archaeologists want to know the *people* of the past, not just the *things* they left behind. James Deetz taught me that in his lectures on poodles and gravestones, what archaeologists and others call *material culture*. What do we mean by material culture? Well, Deetz ex-

2

James J. F. Deetz, 1930–2000
Lu Ann De Cunzo

James J. F. Deetz directed historical archaeological projects across the United States and in South Africa. At his death in 2000, he was the David A. Harrison Professor of Historical Archaeology at the University of Virginia. A native of western Maryland, Deetz began his career as a student at Harvard University as what he called "an early case of affirmative action, providing for the admission of hillbillies to Ivy League institutions." He earned a Ph.D. in anthropology in 1960. Soon after, he became intrigued by the idea of the archaeology of the Pilgrims, and bringing the past to life at Plimoth Plantation. Then in the summer of 1963 Deetz discovered gravestones in the colonial cemeteries of New England. The rest, as they say, is history. As his career took him from Brown University to the College of William and Mary, the University of California at Berkeley, the University of Cape Town, and finally the University of Virginia, Deetz uncovered two hundred years of tobacco plantations in Tidewater Virginia, the coal-mining town of Somersville, California, and colonial outposts in South Africa. In recognition of his accomplishments, the SHA awarded him the J. C. Harrington Medal in Historical Archaeology in 1997.

plained, it is fishhooks, office buildings, banjos, Freaky cereal and the little band of plastic Freakies that dwell in the box, the box, standing rib roast, apple pies, jumbo jets, stepladders, borders of perennial flowers, tattoos, a knotted rope, clipped poodles, and everything else people have made or done to their environment inspired by their culture. All these things carry messages from their makers and users. Archaeologists try to decode the messages, because you can understand people only if you understand these things that people made.

The year I studied American material culture with James Deetz, his classic book *In Small Things Forgotten: An Archaeology of Early American Life* had just been published. It opens with a series of brief vignettes. Set along the eastern seaboard between Virginia and Massachusetts, spanning the years 1658 to 1932, and featuring an enslaved African American pastry chef, a carpenter, a gravestone carver, a banjo picker, a tobacco planter, and an estate appraiser, the vignettes captured many of Deetz's wide-ranging research interests. His stories of these Americans related them to their material world. Together with the written documents people left behind and the oral stories they passed from one generation to the next, these material remains tell us about people's everyday experiences, and what they thought of their lives and their world.

3

What Is It? What Does It Mean?
Lu Ann De Cunzo

What is it? What does it mean? These deceptively simple questions belie the complexity and fundamental importance of material culture studies to historical archaeology. Archaeologists build our interpretations of past peoples, cultures, and histories on the foundation of these studies of what people made and threw out, lost, or otherwise left behind as a record of their existence. Many archaeologists devote their careers to learning from ceramic pots, glass bottles and beads, clay tobacco pipes, and every other thing that we find.

From our first questions flow a host of others that hint at the challenge posed by every excavated object. What is it made of? Why does it look like that? How does it work? When was it made? How was it made? Where was it made? Who made it? Who used it, and for what purposes? What did it mean to its users? How did it get to the place where it was found? You get the picture.

We begin by identifying and classifying artifacts on the basis of comparisons with others. Here we face our first challenge. On what do we base our classification—physical features that the archaeologist thinks are important, or those that the people who made and used the artifact thought were important? Careful physical and, sometimes, chemical analysis of the artifact reveals details of form, color, design, and composition that allow us to group artifacts into standard descriptive categories. A crucial goal of these archaeologists' classifications, or typologies, is to tell time.

Roderick Sprague and Karlis Karklins, for example, detailed typologies of the tiny glass beads that have adorned European, Native American, and African American clothing and other objects for centuries. Iain Walker crafted typologies of Dutch and English tobacco smoking pipes that allow archaeologists to determine their place of origin and estimate their production date based on the shape of the bowl, length and bore diameter of the stems, and molded and stamped markings. And a well-worn copy of Ivor Noël Hume's *A Guide to Artifacts of Colonial America* anchors the bookshelf of every self-respecting historical archaeologist. Otherwise known as the "colonial artifact bible," this guide by Colonial Williamsburg's emeritus archaeological director covers everything from armor to wig curlers, including the finer points of dating a chamber pot by the shape of its rim.

Artifacts are more than tools to tell time for archaeologists. Through our studies of manufacturing technique, we write the history of technology from bricks and toys and buttons. Following the travels of objects as commodities from producers to consumers, we write the history of trade and exchange from ceramics and bottles. George L. Miller has led our studies of these industrial commodities, unraveling the complexities of how innovative technologies, availability, price, form and decorative style, marketing, and fashion came together to shape choice during the "consumer revolution." He has computed indices for analyzing consumers' economic investment in nineteenth-century ceramics and applied today's economists' "market basket" to evaluate the significance of those investments. These economists' tools open a window into the meanings people gave to objects and why they made the choices they did. Ivor Noël Hume named his recent book *If These Pots Could Talk*. The title alludes to the passion he shares with all historical archaeologists to know the people behind the pots, and the world those people knew. That's what we mean by "unlocking the past."

James Deetz at work at Flowerdew Hundred, Virginia, in the mid-1980s. (Photograph by Gene Prince, courtesy of the Phoebe Apperson Hearst Museum of Anthropology and the Regents of the University of California.)

This is what defines historical archaeology: an attention to the everyday world of all peoples, approached from multiple perspectives. The existence of written historical records distinguishes our method from that of prehistoric archaeology, the archaeology of peoples who communicated and transmitted their cultural heritage without a means of translating their language into writing. Historical archaeology is at once history and anthropology; historical archaeologists seek to understand the cultural processes and human experiences that produced the world we live in today. In North America, it is the archaeology of the modernizing world. The earliest written records document European exploration, colonization, and conquest beginning with Norse voyagers. These records, when read in the context of material culture and oral traditions, tell the stories of peoples from the Americas, Europe,

Africa, and Asia encountering each other and the North American environment over the course of many centuries. They tell the "big" stories of immigration, contact, contest, capitalism, racism, slavery, and ethnicity, viewed from the perspectives of individual lives lived locally. Archaeological remains teach us what historical documents cannot about these things, enhancing and amplifying history and making it more meaningful to people.

James Deetz thought and wrote most extensively about a dramatic change that occurred in Anglo-Americans' view of the world beginning in the eighteenth century, one that still shapes our views today. In the "old" world, many families ate, slept, worked, and entertained together in one- or two-room houses. They didn't worry that the front windows in the house didn't match. They shared plates and spoons and mugs, they tossed trash wherever it was most convenient. In contrast, order and control, balance, mechanics, science, and individuality marked this new way of thinking about oneself, others, and the world.

But *why* did it happen? As a result of what we know as the Scientific Revolution, religion became less and less the central, integrating factor of many people's lives. Accumulating wealth and material possessions took on a new and powerful meaning in a free-enterprise economy. By the opening of the eighteenth century, the framework of beliefs that had given comfort and support to society was cracking, and Anglo-Americans saw a world becoming more complex. They compensated by making dramatic changes to their material culture, imposing balance and order on a world spinning out of their control. The results? New houses with central doors flanked by matching windows to create visual symmetry. Behind the façade, a central hall lined with closed doors and a stairway to the second floor. Parlors for entertaining downstairs in the front, kitchen and other work areas hidden from public view in the back, bedchambers—one for each family member—upstairs for privacy. Gardens planned according to precise geometric formulae to make the house seem larger, and planted with carefully clipped trees and hedges signifying human control over nature. Sets of dining wares with ever-growing numbers of special forms, like oyster forks and dishes for butter pats. Trash buried out of sight far from the house, not scattered about the yard. Gravestones with Medusa-like heads shaped by carvers trying new images to represent new ideas about death and God.

To a baby boomer who grew up in the sixties, studies of such "cultural revolutions" held a certain attraction. At a time when the GIRLS LOVE DIRT t-shirt I now wear would have appalled mothers like mine, women weren't an especially welcome sight on an archaeological site in North America. That's how Kathleen Deagan, "girl archaeologist," became my role model. She

4

Kathleen A. Deagan, 1948–
Lu Ann De Cunzo

Kathleen A. Deagan specializes in historical archaeology of the Spanish colonies. She is Distinguished Research Curator of historical archaeology at the Florida Museum of Natural History, adjunct professor of anthropology and history at the University of Florida, and a past president of the SHA. She earned a Ph.D. in anthropology, beginning her studies in precontact Native American archaeology, but was drawn, as she has said, "unavoidably" into historical archaeology. She has studied the interactions among people of different backgrounds in colonial St. Augustine, Florida, and on the island of Hispaniola in the Caribbean. She began research on Hispaniola in 1979, seeking the places that witnessed the first century of contact and conquest. Her search led to an Indian town occupied in the late 1400s; La Navidad, established by Christopher Columbus's shipwrecked crew in 1492; La Isabela, established the following year by colonists who joined Columbus's second voyage from Spain; and Puerto Real, a Spanish city occupied from 1503 to 1578.

knew about being denied jobs on excavations because men assumed she wouldn't know how to deal with the bulldozers and because her presence would mean having to dig a separate latrine.

Historical archaeology for the boomer generation wasn't just about getting women into the field. The civil rights and feminist movements made an impression on our thinking and our work (see part 1, "Cultures in Contact"). Deagan agrees that the best historical archaeology deals with the daily lives of all classes and all races of people in America and the ways they shaped the world in which they lived. This means we often deal with the underside of American history. The stories of voluntary and forced immigrants excluded from the American dream are as much a part of our history as the stories of those men and women who created the dream and, indeed, believed they lived it. We are in a unique position to help understand the history of slavery, imperialism, our class system and consumer culture, and the accelerating rate at which North Americans are degrading the environment, among many other topics. To do so, however, requires that we work with written records and oral histories as well as material culture, food remains, and environmental evidence from our excavations.

Deagan has tried to explain what happened when Native American, Spanish, and African men, women, and children came into contact with one another in Spanish Florida and the Caribbean. At the early-sixteenth-century Spanish town of Puerto Real on Hispaniola, for example, she has uncovered

Kathleen Deagan and James Deetz indulging their shared passion for music.
(Courtesy of Kathleen Deagan.)

the origins of many processes that ultimately created the modern Americas. The Spanish government purposely sited Puerto Real and other towns so as to control and exploit the island's native peoples and natural resources and to firmly establish Spanish town life as an institution on the colonial frontier. Here the Spanish first experimented with a colonial system in the New World. As European diseases struck down the native people, the Spanish replaced them with other Indians and Africans brought to the town against their will to live and work in bondage. Their interactions created a biological and cultural heritage reflecting both the European presence and the persistence and influence of Indians and Africans. Women—particularly Indian and African women—served as a primary link between the three peoples and their cultures. As wives, concubines, and servants to Spanish men, they produced the multiracial population and multicultural identity that defines much of Latin America today. They interwove their own traditions with those of the Spanish to create new ones suited to the environment and economy of colonial Hispaniola. Most critically, they developed a cuisine combining locally available foods with meat from European animals able to adapt to the tropical environment. Their innovations literally ensured the survival of Puerto Real's residents.

Across America, other archaeologists are also devoted to helping people take back their history. Suzanne Spencer-Wood's commitment to women's history led her to research the impact of women's reform movements on material culture in Boston. Her work has challenged us to rethink the impact women had on the public landscapes of nineteenth-century cities. Many of the sites she documented, such as working women's homes, playgrounds, kindergartens, and domestic science schools, are now included on the Boston Women's Heritage Trails. Similar projects across the continent are bringing alive women's material accomplishments in the past. In the West, a group of archaeologists involved in the Colorado Coal Field War Archaeology Project with Randall McGuire of Binghamton University are also pursuing clear political goals. In 1914, Colorado National Guard troops killed twenty striking coal miners and family members in what became known as the Ludlow Massacre. The massacre marked a turning point in United States labor history, and historians have mined the rich collection of documents and photos that recorded the strike and the culminating catastrophe. But none of the studies explored the miners' lives, the conditions that led them to strike, or their living and working conditions during or after the strike. Archaeologists have. Perhaps the most important question their project has posed is "How could this have happened in America?" The reality of class conflict is widely ignored in the history we learn in our classrooms. The Colorado Coal Field War project is dedicated to changing that, and to assisting union laborers and their families in remembering this past.

These North American historical archaeologists share a common goal of creating a sharper, richer image of the forces and the people that influenced North American history. We all start with individual places like Puerto Real, and the unique array of objects, building foundations, and plant and animal remains that make up the archaeological site. We agree these things are meaningless except in contexts that range from the local to the global. But how do we move from the local to the global in our studies? Which groups of people should receive our greatest attention? The Native American women who married Spanish craftsmen in Puerto Real? The European immigrant men who imposed the Spanish vision in the Caribbean? The enslaved African men who replaced native laborers? And on what should we focus as we try to unravel their complex interactions? The opportunities and limitations of the Caribbean environment? The different cultural traditions of Native American, African, Spaniard? The role that gender played in organizing life? The

Map showing locations
discussed in text.

1 Spanish Florida
2 Spanish missions along Georgia
  and Florida coast
3 African American residence
* on South Carolina plantations
4 African American residence
  on Virginia plantations
5 Abraham's Old Town,
  Black Seminole town, Florida
6 California Chinatowns
7 Greenland
8 L'Anse aux Meadows, Newfoundland
9 Frobisher's landing places on Kodlunarn
  and Baffin Islands
10 Jamestown Island, Virginia
11 Matagorda Bay, Texas
12 Mining areas of California and Nevada
13 Quebec City
14 New York City
15 Alexandria, Virginia
16 Charleston, South Carolina
17 West Oakland, California
18 New England sites of agriculture,
   rural industry, and colonial wars
19 Arkansas

20 Western ranches
21 Little Rapids, Minnesota
22 Delaware
23 Pleasant Hill, Kentucky
24 Mississippi River
25 Sugarcane mills in southern Florida
   and Caribbean
26 Ironmaking sites in Pennsylvania,
   New Jersey, and Maryland
27 Chattanooga, Tennessee
28 Old Fort St. Joe Point, Ontario
29 Fortress of Louisbourg,
   Cape Breton Island
30 Fort Michilimackinac, Michigan
31 USS *Monitor*
32 *Maple Leaf*
33 Little Bighorn Battlefield, Montana
34 Santa Rosa Island, Florida
35 Camp Hearn, Texas
36 Pearl Harbor, Hawaii

colonial economy? On these points we don't agree, and that provides historical archaeology with its richness. Indeed, many would add other issues to this
list if given the chance.

In this book, we gave that chance to a team of thirty North American
historical archaeologists working in different parts of the continent studying
different time periods from different perspectives. And many others offered
their ideas as the book developed. We don't all agree about how to explain the
past, or how and what to present about what we learn and how to make the
history of our cultures useful in the present. We spent a lot of time discussing
these issues, and this book is the result. *Unlocking the Past* represents a sub-
jective view of a field characterized by a diversity of approaches, experiences,
and opinions about the most significant contributions our work makes to
historical and anthropological scholarship. Our selections do not attempt to
establish a canon of most important people, places, and studies in our field,
and we have deliberately not thought about the book as a historical archaeology textbook. Our goal is to introduce our readers to the fascinating "underground" world of historical archaeology, and to guide you to other sites,
books, films, and Web pages where you may learn more. The Society for
Historical Archaeology, the international professional association for historical archaeologists, has sponsored this project. The society's Web site,
www.sha.org, contains an online changing exhibit on North American historical archaeology that complements this book and an expanded guide to
internet sources.

The next five chapters present cultural themes on which much North
American historical archaeology has focused, thanks to the pioneering work
of John Cotter, James Deetz, Kathleen Deagan, and many others. The voluntary and forced immigration of peoples from around the world and their
interaction with native peoples in many ways *is* the story of North America.
"Cultures in Contact" introduces studies of Spanish and Native Americans,
African Americans, and Chinese sojourners in America. Colonization by
nonnative peoples dramatically reshaped North America. "Challenging and
Changing Environments" considers the archaeology of environmental change
wrought by early colonization and industrial-scale mining. In "Building Cities" we see how urban archaeologists have dug up the past of huge cities like
New York and World Heritage cities like Quebec. Yet for centuries most
North Americans lived in farming and manufacturing communities; we look
into their world in "Making a Living in Rural America." The interaction of
so many diverse peoples in North America inevitably sparked conflict. In
"Cultures in Conflict" we have studied colonial wars, the American Civil

War (here we discuss the war fought on and under water), Custer's mythic last stand at Little Bighorn, and even World War II.

For North Americans in the past as in the present (Unlock the Past for the Future), seemingly little and insignificant things accumulated across lifetimes encode the essence of life. Don't forget these things and the people who made and used them. Through them, we can gain a new appreciation for what life is today, and was in the past. Perhaps James Deetz said it best. Reading what people wrote is not enough. Look at what they have done, he urged. And so, in this book, we will.

In all our work, despite differences in the questions we ask and the perspectives we take, historical archaeologists share a crucial goal. We want you to discover this complex history and preserve the places in which Americans forged our multicultural heritage. Look around you. Get involved. Help save our past for the future.

Part 1

Cultures in Contact

Melting Pots or Not?

Lu Ann De Cunzo

We have all heard America referred to as a melting pot of cultures from around the world. Each group of immigrants contributed customs and traditions to the ever-changing American culture and slowly or quickly lost their distinctiveness as they became American. Yet Americans today honor a multicultural heritage in ethnic celebrations held across the continent, in the varied foods that we all enjoy, and in the value systems we embrace. We see signs of this diversity everywhere. Is America a melting pot or not? Is there one American culture or many? What does it mean to be, or to become, an American? These questions lead to more general ones about what happens when people of different cultures come in contact with each other, and why. Anthropologists, historians, and archaeologists write of assimilation, acculturation, ethnicity, and the creation of creole cultures. But these terms have acquired a confusing array of meanings, particularly because of differences in the nature of these contacts. Some people immigrated to America voluntarily, others came forcibly. Some were enslaved, others conquered, and most expected women and children to submit to men's authority. All faced decisions, and factors that limited their choices, as they proceeded to redefine themselves and others in a new world. Historical archaeologists have the rare chance to explore these contacts, choices, and identities through time, from the unique perspective of material culture.

The heritage we study began when Europeans sailed west and met with diverse peoples living on the vast continent and island chains of North America. Beyond the mythic history of Christopher Columbus's "discovery" of America with support from the Spanish crown, Spain's important role in colonizing North America is an oft-slighted chapter of American history. The Spanish and their Catholic missions introduced new ideas and ways of life to the peoples of North America, but they also brought new perils. We still live with the mix of Spanish and Native cultures in our southern borderlands, where corn tortillas and earthen pueblos coexist with Spanish place-names and Catholic churches. Archaeologists like Jerald Milanich have teamed with bioarchaeologists like Clark Spencer Larsen to learn more about those fateful encounters between Catholic clerics and Native villagers. Others have looked back to Spain, to understand the people, culture, and objects that traveled the Atlantic to New Spain. Florence and Robert Lister took an object-centered approach, studying the Spanish-tradition pottery used in the New Spain colonies. Florence Lister describes the ceramics as "fissured with global history." The Listers' efforts to tell the story of these ceramics and their makers spanned several decades and led them around the world to observe archaeological sites and contemporary potters at work in Morocco, Italy, Panama, Peru, the Caribbean, Taiwan, and the southern United States.

The spirit of the civil rights movement in the 1960s inspired other archaeologists, like Charles Fairbanks, to probe beneath the ground for a deeper understanding of slavery and the creation of African American cultures. Heading to the heart of the southern plantation—its slave quarters—Fairbanks began to write the story of the work and lives of enslaved Africans. The story emphasized enslaved people drawing upon their African heritage to make their way in a new and, for them, especially difficult world. A decade later, other archaeologists like Leland Ferguson were drawn to the task, bringing a humanistic perspective to a historical archaeology increasingly devoted to a scientific view of the world. Ferguson and a younger generation of scholars like Terrance Weik continue to help us see and come to terms with the pain, the inhumanity, and the creative cultural power intertwined in the institution of slavery. Their task has led them to plantations across the South, to colonial cities like Annapolis, New York, Charleston, and St. Augustine, and to the maroon communities built by escaped captives.

Other archaeologists like Roberta Greenwood have pioneered the study of immigrants arriving in North America across the Pacific rather than the Atlantic Ocean. Chinese sojourners helped East meet West as they laid mile after mile of railroad track and built the cities of the West. Greenwood recognized that the physical remains of past Chinese and other ethnic communities often survive just below city pavements. She has spent much of her career connecting these archaeological remains with the people who left them behind, then linking the specific stories of these places to larger historical concerns. Her work and that of the urban archaeologists she has trained and inspired revealed a continentwide trend in the siting of immigrant communities on land of low value or high hazard, often nearest the place of first arrival. The sequence of ethnic groups moving into and out of these communities does not tell a happy story, chronicling as it does the history of the most economically and politically scapegoated groups. We cannot always celebrate the history that archaeology offers us, but neither can we ignore it.

I

Spaniards and Native Americans
at the Missions of La Florida

Jerald T. Milanich

Few Americans know much about Spain's role in colonizing the United States. From Florida to Chesapeake Bay and west across the southern third of the country into California, Spanish soldiers and settlers sought to extend Spain's American empire northward from Mexico and the Caribbean, beginning in the 1560s.

To help in this endeavor Spanish state and church officials sent Catholic priests—first Jesuits and later Franciscans—into the land they called La Florida to establish missions among the original inhabitants. At the time, these Native Americans numbered in the hundreds of thousands. By controlling minds, bodies, and souls, colonial officials sought to turn the native people into loyal Catholic subjects of the crown. As such, they posed no threat to Spanish interests and would toil to support the colony.

Researchers have undertaken a number of projects to learn about life at these missions. Across northern Florida and in southern and coastal Georgia, excavations have uncovered clues to the impact of colonialism on the native people. The evidence gathered so far is remarkable. Archaeologists have excavated entire churches burned in rebellions. We have even discovered small religious medallions associated with *cofradías* (Catholic confraternities) and worn by Christian Indians to display their piety. Changes in foodways accompanied these changes in native beliefs. We have found numerous examples of those dietary changes, including chicken bones and grains of wheat, both introduced from Spain. We now understand the economic contributions made to the colonies by the mission Indians. These important contributions, reflected in things as innocuous as tiny charred corncobs, tell a story of crops planted, harvested, shucked, ground into meal, and transported to St. Augustine at the behest of colonial officials and native chiefs, then exported to produce a profit. We have learned that the Spanish established more than 150 churches, mostly in Florida and Georgia, before 1763.

In that year the politics of colonial expansion forced Spain to cede what was left of its La Florida colony to Great Britain.

Mission Mysteries

In 1999 I published a book about the missions of La Florida, *Laboring in the Fields of the Lord*. It followed by more than two decades my entry into mission archaeology, an entry largely unplanned. In 1976, when I was a new assistant curator at the University of Florida's Florida Museum of Natural History, two of our undergraduate students were looking for archaeological sites north of the Suwannee River in northern Florida. There in a newly planted pine field beside Baptizing Spring, a small spring-fed sinkhole, they found mission-period Spanish and Indian pottery.

Later that year I excavated the site with a student field crew, finding the remains of a small clay-floored mission church or chapel with a wooden-post framework and wattle-and-daub walls. Fire had destroyed the building. Nearby had stood an even smaller, earthen-floored building with a central hearth, most likely a *convento* where a Franciscan friar lived. Inside this second building we found Spanish majolica, a type of tin-glazed earthenware, as well as ceramics shaped like Spanish bowls but made by native potters for use by the friar. The two mission buildings had stood across a small plaza from a Timucua village laid out in the shape of a crescent. There we recovered native pottery decorated with crosses. Two radiocarbon dates and the types of majolica we found indicated that the Spanish and Timucua used the mission in the early seventeenth century.

Though Baptizing Spring (named by a religious group in the twentieth century) was an exciting discovery, it also created consternation. What mission had we just excavated? The Baptizing Spring site lay near the Spanish *camino real*, the "royal road" or main road that ran more than two hundred miles from St. Augustine west through the mission district across northern Florida. Parts of the road are visible today. In 1674–75 a Franciscan bishop from Cuba traveled the *camino real* and recorded the names of twenty-four missions, listing them in the order he arrived at each, and recording distances. His report, translated and published by Lucy L. Wenhold, contains the following passage regarding the Timucua missions between the St. Johns River and the Suwannee in northern Florida:

> On the bank of the river Corrientes [the St. Johns], is the village and mission of San Diego de Salamototo. It [the river] is very turbulent and almost a league and a half in width. From there to the village and

mission of Santa Fe there are some 20 uninhabited leagues. Santa Fe is the principal mission of this province. Off to the side [from Santa Fe] toward the southern border, at a distance of 3 leagues, is the deserted mission and village of San Francisco. Twelve leagues from Santa Fe is the mission of Santa Catalina, with Ajohica 3 leagues away and Santa Cruz de Tarihica 2. Seven leagues away, on the bank of the large river Guacara [the Suwannee River], is the mission of San Juan of the same name.

A century later, in 1778, when Britain controlled La Florida and occupied St. Augustine, a British surveyor drew a map of the *camino real*. At the time, the surveyor could see the old agricultural fields of many of the Timucua missions, and he noted their locations on the map. One area of "old fields" was recorded in the general location of Baptizing Spring. In a few places he wrote names of former missions, though none was near Baptizing Spring.

With the bishop's narrative and the British map we attempted to identify the Baptizing Spring mission, but without success. The site lay too far east to be the San Juan de Guacara mission on the east bank of the Suwannee River five miles west of Baptizing Spring. Nor did Baptizing Spring's location fit that of Santa Cruz de Tarihica seven leagues east of San Juan. A University of Florida graduate student, L. Jill Loucks, carried out additional excavations at Baptizing Spring. But we never satisfactorily resolved the identification of the mission there, and I went on to other projects unrelated to missions.

In the 1980s I was forced to consider mission geography again when I undertook a study of the Florida portion of the route of the sixteenth-century Spanish conquistador Hernando de Soto. De Soto had landed at Tampa Bay in late May 1539 and marched northward through peninsular Florida on his way to modern Tallahassee. There his army spent the winter of 1539–40. If I could accurately plot the route of the expedition, I could use the narratives penned by members of de Soto's army to better understand the Native Americans encountered in Florida.

One of my graduate students, Kenneth Johnson, was hired to locate de Soto period sites in northern Florida. In the course of his research, Ken determined that old trails connected sixteenth-century villages in the region. One was a predecessor of the mission-period *camino real*. De Soto's army had followed some of those trails in 1539. Not surprisingly, Ken found pre-Columbian villages on the trails, suggesting they had been in use for hundreds of years before de Soto. But we did not expect to find a mission site well north of the *camino real* west of Lake City. Like Baptizing Spring, this Spanish mission's location did not match the bishop's account or the British map. Our

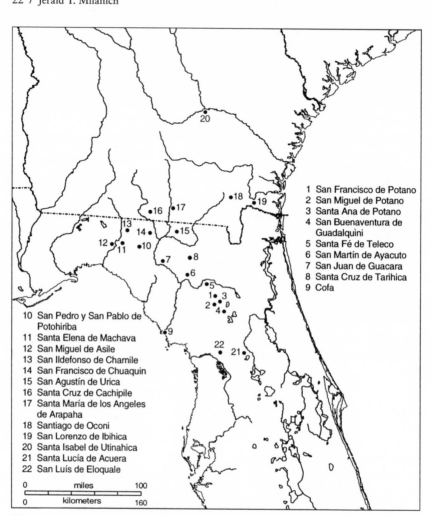

1 San Francisco de Potano
2 San Miguel de Potano
3 Santa Ana de Potano
4 San Buenaventura de Guadalquini
5 Santa Fé de Teleco
6 San Martín de Ayacuto
7 San Juan de Guacara
8 Santa Cruz de Tarihica
9 Cofa

10 San Pedro y San Pablo de Potohiriba
11 Santa Elena de Machava
12 San Miguel de Asile
13 San Ildefonso de Chamile
14 San Francisco de Chuaquin
15 San Agustín de Urica
16 Santa Cruz de Cachipile
17 Santa María de los Angeles de Arapaha
18 Santiago de Oconi
19 San Lorenzo de Ibihica
20 Santa Isabel de Utinahica
21 Santa Lucía de Acuera
22 San Luís de Eloquale

Fig. 1.1. Franciscan missions among the Timucua-speaking Indians of La Florida prior to the 1656 Timucua rebellion. Note the location of number 7, San Juan. (Courtesy of Jerald Milanich.)

knowledge of Timucua mission geography derived from those two sources was not as solid as we had thought. The archaeological evidence and the historical documents were at odds.

Another University of Florida graduate student, John Worth, found the solution to the mystery in the Archivo General de Indias in Seville, Spain. Working in that repository of colonial-period documents, John found legal papers describing the events surrounding a 1656 rebellion by the Timucua living at the North Florida missions. Fed up with their treatment by Spanish officials, the Timucua sought to rid their lands of Spanish soldiers, ranchers, and their servants. They did not threaten the Catholic friars.

The Spanish cruelly suppressed the short-lived rebellion and hanged a dozen Timucua leaders. The governor of Spanish Florida, Diego de Reboledo, seized on the rebellion as an excuse to reorganize the missions in North Florida. In part he did so because diseases introduced from Europe had severely reduced the number of Timucua, curtailing the Spaniards' ability to demand labor from them. Worth's research also showed that prior to the rebellion a network of trails connected the Timucua missions scattered across northern Florida. But after the rebellion the governor abandoned some missions, moved others to what would become the *camino real,* and shifted the location of at least one mission already on the road. The result was a chain of missions on the *camino real,* the pattern noted by the bishop in 1674–75.

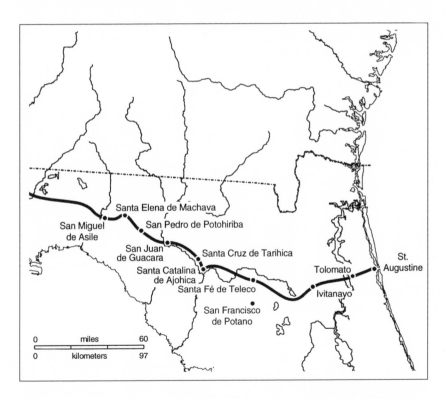

Fig. 1.2. Timucua missions arranged along the *camino real* after the 1656 rebellion. San Juan has been moved west to the east bank of the Suwannee River. (Courtesy of Jerald Milanich.)

That knowledge allowed us to identify our two mystery missions. The site at Baptizing Spring was the first mission of San Juan, moved after the rebellion west to the Suwannee River. There its villagers provided a ferry service for travelers on the *camino real* needing to cross the river. Indeed, the name *San Juan* later became *San-Juanee*, the origin of Suwannee. The mission found by Ken Johnson well north of the *camino real* proved to be Santa Cruz de Tarihica, moved after the rebellion southward to the vicinity of the road.

We still have much to learn about the missions in North Florida, but together archaeological and archival research has provided important clues. We can now plot the pre- and postrebellion missions, and we have found many of them. At these and other missions throughout La Florida, we have uncovered the remains of buildings and meals and tokens of religious belief. We have also excavated with painstaking care the remains of the native peoples who lived and died there. Working with bioarchaeologists like Clark Larsen, we learn much about work, disease, diet, and death from the bones themselves. Together historical archaeology and bioarchaeology are powerful tools. They give voice to people of the past, including the Spanish friars and the Indians who together labored at the missions of Spanish Florida.

2

Bioarchaeology of the Spanish Missions

Clark Spencer Larsen

When most Americans consider what happened when European colonists first encountered Native Americans (believing them to be Indians), two thoughts come to mind. First, that Europeans brought with them all sorts of infectious diseases—measles, smallpox, common cold, influenza, yellow fever, and so forth—resulting in the deaths of millions and the destruction of the Indian "race." Second, that Europeans, and especially the Spanish conquistadores, spent a great deal of time and effort in confronting and killing native peoples. Historians reinforce the former idea, with their accounts framed by what historical documents and other records have to tell. These records speak to the rapid spread of infectious disease throughout the Americas that resulted in widespread death. The second notion—conquest and death by violence—is a perception that has been promulgated as a part of what many call the Black Legend. The legend cast Spain as an evil empire using a ruthless inquisition to pursue its aim of subjugating the world to Catholicism. I have to admit that these notions were the substance of my own perception of the early colonial world of the Americas, especially before I engaged in a research program that has taken the last twenty years of my professional career to develop.

Early in the 1980s I began a collaboration with archaeologist David Hurst Thomas of the American Museum of Natural History on the excavation of Mission Santa Catalina de Guale, established by the Spanish crown in the sixteenth century on St. Catherines Island, Georgia. By the time this collaboration began, Thomas and I had already spent a considerable amount of time working together on the burial complex on St. Catherines that predated the Spanish conquest. He looked at the social, cultural, and archaeological facets, and I studied and interpreted the skeletal remains of Native Americans buried at these sites. My task focused on bioarchaeology, or the study of skeletal remains from archaeological settings, in order to understand the health, biology, and lifestyles of earlier populations living in the region. Bones have a lot to offer in understanding these people, and study of skeletons from prehistoric sites on St. Catherines Island and elsewhere on the Georgia coast taught us a lot about the people living there centuries ago. The Guale, who descended from the prehistoric peoples in this area, were among the first Indians contacted by Europeans north of Mexico. From the beginning I thought that study of the skeletons from the mission site would offer a way of understanding the people themselves.

Little did I know what vast, rich information the skeletons from Santa Catalina and other mission sites would yield in our two decades of work. Early on I realized that, to get a truly comprehensive picture of the native people who lived in the missions, we would first have to study pre-Columbian skeletons from the region colonized by Spain in the 1500s and 1600s. These skeletons would give us a much-needed baseline of information for studying the skeletons from the missions. As the project at Santa Catalina developed, I began collaborations with Jerald Milanich and Rebecca Saunders of the Florida Museum of Natural History on Amelia Island (at Santa Catalina de Santa María and Santa María de los Yamassee), and Bonnie McEwan of the Florida Bureau of Archaeological Research in the panhandle of Florida (at San Luis de Apalachee). I had also realized that I alone could not do all of the specialized kinds of work that had proven so important in studying skeletons from other areas of the world. These involved the analysis of bone chemistry to reconstruct diet, the study of bone structure to reconstruct kinds of activity, and the application of paleopathology to reconstruct individuals' health. For these studies, I persuaded a number of leading authorities to collaborate with me. Just what have we learned and why is this information so important in understanding this complex and fascinating region of the Americas?

The Record of the Bones

Skeletal remains offer a wonderful source of information about who we are as human beings. In particular, our health and quality of life, and our physical activity and lifestyle, leave evidence in our bones. Markers on teeth and bones reveal the consequences of poor diets, physiological stress, and living in impoverished (or wealthy) environments. Physical activity and lifestyle refers to the demands that work and other activity place on the body, including the skeleton. In our study of the mission and premission Indians from Georgia and Florida, we started out by basing our assessment of quality of life on information gained from reconstructing the native diet. Working with Margaret Schoeninger, now of the University of California at San Diego, we analyzed stable isotopes of carbon and nitrogen in order to ascertain what kinds

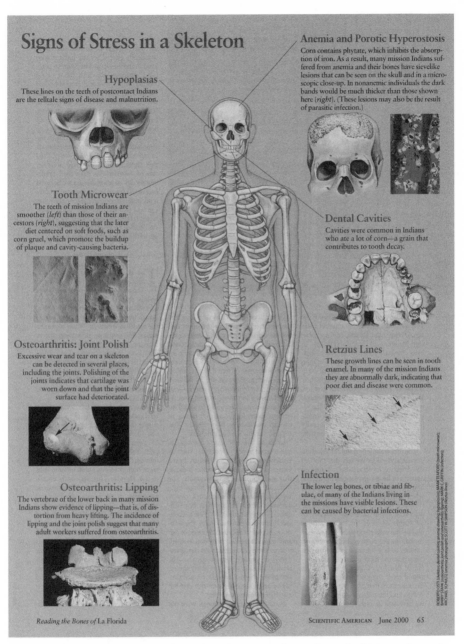

Signs of Stress in a Skeleton

Hypoplasias
These lines on the teeth of postcontact Indians are the telltale signs of disease and malnutrition.

Tooth Microwear
The teeth of mission Indians are smoother (*left*) than those of their ancestors (*right*), suggesting that the later diet centered on soft foods, such as corn gruel, which promote the buildup of plaque and cavity-causing bacteria.

Osteoarthritis: Joint Polish
Excessive wear and tear on a skeleton can be detected in several places, including the joints. Polishing of the joints indicates that cartilage was worn down and that the joint surface had deteriorated.

Osteoarthritis: Lipping
The vertebrae of the lower back in many mission Indians show evidence of lipping—that is, of distortion from heavy lifting. The incidence of lipping and the joint polish suggest that many adult workers suffered from osteoarthritis.

Anemia and Porotic Hyperostosis
Corn contains phytate, which inhibits the absorption of iron. As a result, many mission Indians suffered from anemia and their bones have sievelike lesions that can be seen on the skull and in a microscopic close-up. In nonanemic individuals the dark bands would be much thicker than those shown here (*right*). (These lesions may also be the result of parasitic infection.)

Dental Cavities
Cavities were common in Indians who ate a lot of corn—a grain that contributes to tooth decay.

Retzius Lines
These growth lines can be seen in tooth enamel. In many of the mission Indians they are abnormally dark, indicating that poor diet and disease were common.

Infection
The lower leg bones, or tibiae and fibulae, of many of the Indians living in the missions have visible lesions. These can be caused by bacterial infections.

Fig. 2.1. Diagram showing what bioarchaeologists can learn about the history of population demographics, health, and working conditions from their studies of human remains. (Courtesy of Roberto Osti; originally published in *Scientific American*, June 2000.)

of foods people ate before and after European contact. The amount of carbon-12 and carbon-13 in people's bones depends on the kinds of plants they ate. Our study of carbon in the bones of the late prehistoric people told us that they ate corn, but when the Spanish arrived, the amount of corn eaten increased dramatically, at least for some regions of the province. That is important to know because it tells us that nutritional quality probably declined once the Native Americans had moved to the missions. Corn lacks key essential amino acids necessary for proper growth and development. It has phytate, which prevents the body from using all of the iron in the foods eaten and leads to iron deficiency anemia, and as a carbohydrate it promotes tooth decay. Indeed, our studies of the bones and teeth show evidence of iron deficiency, poor nutrition, arrested growth owing to poor diets, and excessive tooth decay, among other changes.

The health of the mission Indians appeared to be worse than that of their precontact predecessors. But contrary to the popular myth that the Spaniards wiped out the native people in this region (as elsewhere), we have learned that the people persisted for at least two centuries following initial contact in the early sixteenth century. Indeed, they coexisted with Spaniards at these missions. Our study with Christopher Ruff of Johns Hopkins University of the structure of arm and leg bones showed that the people likely worked harder at the missions than they had prior to European contact. Clearly, the finding of change in lifestyle supports the notion that the Spaniards exploited the native people as a labor source. On the other hand, these changes also indicate that Indians in a very real sense adapted to new challenges associated with life in the missions. Overall, there is a kernel of truth to the Black Legend. Life was worse for the native people during the colonial period—but not in the same sense as the legend.

Importantly, we learned that when the Spanish arrived, they didn't come into this region swinging their swords intent on destroying native peoples. Rather, the Spanish wanted to exploit their land and labor and convert them to Christianity. We have drawn this conclusion based in part on our study of violent conflict in the region. Out of the many hundreds of skeletons of mission Indians that we have studied, only one person displays evidence of a violent death. The person, an adult male, had been buried at the altar end of the church at Mission San Luis in a prepared wood coffin, probably during the late seventeenth century. Only a half dozen other people out of the hundreds of burials were laid to rest in coffins. The man's burial in the ritual nucleus of the church and in a specially prepared coffin bespeaks his importance in native society. Found lodged against his spine was a musket projectile, a .44-caliber lead shot. The position of the shot suggests that it entered the man's lower torso from the front, lodging in his spine. The shot presumably killed the man, either through damage to visceral organs, blood loss, or infection. Whichever it was, it was a horrible way to die. Still, the fact remains that this is the only case of violence or violent death that our study of skeletons from Spanish Florida has revealed. At least in this mission setting, other factors led to the decline and ultimate disappearance of native people in the region, including malnutrition, infectious disease, poor health generally, heavy work, and exploitation.

3

African Americans on Southern Plantations

Leland Ferguson, from *Uncommon Ground*, adapted by Lu Ann De Cunzo

Malnutrition, poor health, heavy work, and exploitation: these conditions describe life in North America for many captive Africans as well as Native Americans. But there is more to the story than exploitation. From the slave pens of the African coast to the homes of emancipated black farmers, historical archaeologists have exposed both tragedies and triumphs of African Americans forced into slavery on Southern plantations. Black workers were pioneers who built the wealth of the American South. They hoed tobacco in the uplands of Virginia and piled up hundreds of miles of earthen banks for the watery rice fields of Carolina. Planters enforced this servitude with harsh and often cruel treatment. Some responded by running to freedom, and archaeologists have identified sites of the famous Underground Railroad, as well as the town and fort of Mose in Florida that served as a refuge for runaway slaves from South Carolina. Others resisted their oppressors more subtly by creating a subculture in opposition to the designs of planters.

My introduction to the legacy of these, the black pioneers of America, came long before my training as an archaeologist. I grew up in the South before the civil rights movement and after most southern families had moved from farms to town, at a time when the separation of the so-called races was perhaps more severe than ever before or since. In the summer of my second year in college, 1962, confrontations were sparking change, and the leaders of that resistance commanded respect.

Black leaders were courageous, dignified, and articulate. But where did their strength come from? Most whites like myself could not say. Consciously or unconsciously, the movement forced us to question at least one set of commonly held beliefs. How could Americans of African descent—supposedly primitive at worst and poorly educated at best—gather the strength to fight the establishment and win? The answer, of course, lay beyond the eye and mind of the white majority, where African American culture was vibrantly alive, and had been alive for more than three hundred years. Through that span African Americans combined African legacy with American culture, and along the way they left stories in the ground.

My entrée into the archaeology of African America came via fragments of the hand-built pottery we call Colono Ware. Found on colonial sites throughout the American South, they were especially common in South Carolina, where I worked. Because at least some resembled the ceramics made by Native Americans, archaeologists at first believed industrious native peoples capitalized on the growing colonial market and sold wares to planters for use in kitchens and slave quarters. Planters, we supposed, simply purchased these local wares for less than it cost to import ceramics from Europe. However, we were to learn that the story was much more complicated than this.

One day, as I was sitting in on an introductory folklore class, we began discussing coiled baskets as part of the folk culture of African Americans in the Carolina low country. As I mulled over the idea that a craft like basketry had survived capture in Africa, the dangerous middle passage to the Americas, and the disorientation of slavery, my "archaeologist's mind" wondered about other artifacts as well. If basketry survived, then why not houses, pottery, wood carving, cooking hearths, tools, even pottery? I remembered all that hand-built pottery we were finding, and headed to the library.

Everything I read reinforced the notion that colonial African Americans, as well as Indians, made pots for cooking, eating, storage, and other uses. I soon realized that my history courses neglected many important facts in favor of the political maneuvering of colonial powers, the grand events of the American Revolution, and the birth of the nation. Most archaeologists working in South Carolina, myself included, were ignorant of crucial aspects of African and African American demography, culture, and society. We had not been taught that slaves pioneered in America, carrying from Africa many agricultural and craft skills essential to daily life. Neither had we learned that the first Africans enslaved in the Carolinas came from plantations in the West Indies where they had established a pottery tradition. We were all victims of an education that dismissed the importance of blacks and distorted the role of Indians in American history, and we had carried these distortions into our archaeology.

Forced from their homeland, Africans coming to America were not stripped of their knowledge. Once we opened our minds to this fact, we began to discover that many enslaved Africans in the American South built clay-walled houses, crafted baskets, made dugout canoes, *and* molded ceramic pots in much the same way they had done in their homelands.

Through time Africans and their descendants interwove their ideas with those of Native Americans and Europeans, developing a distinctive African

Fig. 3.1. Servant quarters, Middleburg Plantation, South Carolina. (Courtesy of Leland Ferguson.)

American culture through a process that we have come to call creolization. Conceiving of African American cultures as creolized helps us see the cultural substance behind the buildings, landscapes, and objects we find. It also helps us look at the power relations of slavery from a different perspective. We already know a lot about southern American agriculture and slave labor, as well as the power base of plantation owners. The products of labor we don't know about are those things that slaves made for themselves, with or without their master's knowledge; the power base we have difficulty seeing also belonged to the enslaved.

Following the archaeological trail of pots in two southern colonies, Virginia and Carolina, will show what I mean.

Beginning in 1607, Virginia's English colonists cleared land and farmed tobacco with their own labor and that of servants from the British Isles. As they needed supplies, these settlers and servants bought some of their food, tools, and utensils, including pottery, from Indians. African slaves came slowly into the white world of Virginia tobacco country, and they worked side by side with a mostly white labor force. As blacks became a part of Virginia society, they comprised a minority in a servant class in which low status was as binding as race and ethnicity were divisive. Given this intimacy, there is no question that Virginia creolization, which started with Indian-

European interaction, expanded to include features of African culture. Slavery and African American culture became entrenched in Virginia in the last half of the seventeenth century.

Interestingly, the shape and decoration of much Virginia Colono Ware look British, although the ceramic is definitely the creole product of diverse cultures. At first glance, technology seems to be the major traditional African, and Indian, feature of Virginia Colono Ware, but non-Europeans made a more subtle contribution as well. Responding to their own preferences and the needs of their community, potters determined which forms they would make and how many of each. Archaeology has told us that their choice of shapes differed from that of European Americans. Most striking is that slaves in colonial Virginia did not use hand-built plates. Instead, they used bowls. Even though Virginia slaves adopted the shapes of many European cooking and eating utensils, they maintained aspects of their African culinary culture.

If history and demography assured that white culture would dominate the process of creolization in Virginia, the opposite was true in colonial Carolina. The enslaved population of Carolina was proportionally much larger than that of Virginia, and remained so throughout the eighteenth century. Moreover, settlement patterns differed in Carolina. Many early African immigrants accompanied their captors from Barbados to establish lucrative provisioning plantations on the Carolina coast. Though they experimented with other cash crops, rice proved especially profitable as it thrived in the warm, wet soils of the low country under the expert hands of experienced African producers. While white Carolinians held the balance of political power, enslaved Africans possessed essential practical knowledge of subtropical environments and their products. As a result, they contributed materially to the economic success of the colony.

African Americans in colonial South Carolina not only built miles of earthen banks to support rice agriculture and cultivated, harvested, and processed the crop, they also built their own houses and made many of the objects necessary for daily life. In fact, archaeologists have discovered more Colono Ware in South Carolina than in all the other former colonies combined. Most was made on plantations, in the form of small plain bowls and jars common in West Africa. Attempting to understand their uses and meanings led me back to Africa, and to the culture of food. I learned that the most common rural African meal centers on a starchy main dish, boiled or simmered in an earthenware or iron pot and served in a large ceramic bowl. The serving bowl is placed on the floor or a low table and people sit around the bowl to eat. Relishes of spicy vegetables, meats, and fish are placed in small bowls near the main dish. People eat with their hands and drink from gourds

Fig. 3.2. Colono Ware jar recovered from Cooper River, South Carolina. (Photograph by Emily Short, courtesy of Leland Ferguson.)

and small bowls. Archaeologists excavating at such Carolina home sites have found many fragments of small bowls and cooking pots.

The archaeological trail of these pots didn't end at food, however. As in Spanish America, religion was central to African Americans' lives and culture. In religion archaeologists see, perhaps most clearly, the creativity, diversity, and complexities of African American culture. In South Carolina we began to notice marks on the bases of some Colono Ware bowls. Most were simple crosses or Xs. In some cases a circle or rectangle enclosed the cross. Initially we called these "maker's marks" because they resembled those on European and Chinese pottery. Some marks, however, appeared on the *inside* of the bowls, and many of the bowls were found under water in rivers throughout the Carolina low country. We learned that the marks shared features with Bakongo cosmograms. The Bakongo homeland lies in the area of the Atlantic slave trade, and half of the enslaved Africans who arrived in South Carolina came from the region of Bakongo influence.

Bakongo philosophers understand the earth, the land of the living, as a mountain over a watery barrier separating this world from the land of the dead beneath. Each day the sun rises and then, during earthly nighttime, illuminates the underside of the universe, the land of the dead. The cycle continues eternally, representing the continuity of life: birth, death, and re-birth. The circle of the cosmogram symbolizes this continuity, while the crossed lines represent the watery barrier separating the material and spiritual worlds, and the power of the Bakongo priests to access the spirit world. Sacred medicines or *minkisi* control the spirits connecting the living with the powers of the dead. Clay pots have traditionally held *minkisi,* in Africa and, we now believe, in America, for use in rituals that ended with the pots crossing the watery barrier of low country rivers.

Pots, houses, and other objects of daily life represent a past material world that provided tools and served as symbols reinforcing people's views of themselves as culturally distinct from others. The archaeological record brings us as close to the slave's personal story as we have ever been.

4

Black Seminole Freedom Fighters
on the Florida Frontier

Terrance Weik

The black history that I learned in my youth in the 1970s and 1980s bore the imprint of the civil rights movement of which Leland Ferguson writes. Grade-school classes, movies, and books highlighted the tragic struggles of oppressed people during centuries of enslavement, sharecropping, lynching, and segregation. This story line reached its turning point during a period of protest led by the efforts of such valiant leaders as Dr. Martin Luther King Jr. and Malcolm X. Both of these men were killed in the struggle for civil rights, but segregation in public places was defeated. Then an undergraduate African American history class put a new spin on this story by introducing me to the topic of runaway slaves, otherwise known as Maroons. From archaeological research I have learned that African and African American freedom fighters persistently challenged racism and slavery in the Americas from the beginning. Wherever and whenever slavery occurred, Maroons were there, fighting for a break from their toils or for the freedom to build their own communities. At times, they went on the offensive and helped their enslaved peers escape from plantations. Maroons in places such as Jamaica and Surinam were so successful that thousands of their descendants still own their lands and celebrate their heritage today. Black Seminole Maroons pursued a path to freedom that began and ended deep in Indian territory. While in Florida, Maroons became Black Seminole by joining forces with the Seminole Indians, holding off the advances of slavers, land-hungry settlers, and soldiers from the United States. At a Black Seminole Maroon settlement in Sumter County called Abraham's Old Town, archaeological research has unearthed artifacts and dusted off documents that illustrate the lives of these extraordinary people who share a dual African and Native American heritage.

Some basic questions have driven my research on Abraham's Old Town. First, who were these Maroons? Did they establish new settlements that were independent of enslaved peoples, Native Americans, and colonists? Why did the Black Seminole Maroons succeed, while most enslaved African rebels were quickly suppressed? I sought to explore how this group of people so diverse in languages, cultural beliefs, and political interests managed to reconcile their differences and build a society from scratch.

Various documents provide glimpses of the Black Seminole Maroons' lives. An 1849 surveyor's map bears the name Abraham's Old Town that we use to designate the archaeological site where Black Seminole Maroons lived in central Florida. U.S. military records refer to the town as Pilaklikaha. We are unsure if this name is of African, European, or Native American origin. Because Maroon and Seminole Indian writings were rarely preserved, we do not know what those who inhabited Abraham's Old Town called their home. One visitor's diary explains that a hundred people lived there. Travelers' accounts describe the environment that protected the Maroons from their adversaries. Newspaper advertisements placed by slave owners are one of the most informative sources on the "runaways" who escaped to Abraham's Old Town. The ads relate that Maroons fled from Georgia and South Carolina plantations to the Florida frontier from the 1600s until the nineteenth century. Newspapers suggest that the average Maroon was male, unskilled, in his mid-twenties, and belonged to one of several ethnic groups.

Unfortunately, chroniclers often distorted the Maroons' lives. Many historical documents were written by people—usually white males—who were bent on destroying the Maroons. Statutes prescribed punishments or death for those who fled or resisted their harsh, forced work. The racist perspectives of some led them to think of Maroons only as "fugitive negroes," a category that reduced them to a homogenous group of outlaws. Their unique customs, ethnicities, and worldviews went unnoticed. European traders and politicians who sought profits from Maroons' lands often misrepresented them in order to justify wars and enslavement. For instance, they characterized the Maroons' participation in the frontier economy as "contraband" dealing. Maroons traded the goods from their fields and hunting grounds to colonists in exchange for manufactured items such as the long-necked black-green beverage bottles whose fragments we found at Abraham's Old Town.

The interactions between African, African American, European, and Native American peoples during the colonial period were multidimensional, diverse, and ever changing. Early on during slavery, Africans formed the majority of Maroon populations, but African Americans predominated later. Many found the lands in Florida a welcome refuge because of the lush landscape, distance from plantations, and mild winters. The Spanish colonists encouraged rebelliousness among the enslaved laborers of their British en-

5

Fort Mose, St. Augustine, Florida
Lu Ann De Cunzo

In 1693 King Charles II of Spain issued a royal proclamation granting freedom to all runaway slaves seeking asylum in Florida. Hearing that the Spaniards offered freedom and religious sanctuary to those who would become Catholics, many captives escaped and made their way south to St. Augustine. In 1738 the Spanish colonial government finally established a fortified community, Gracia Real de Santa Teresa de Mose, to house the growing number of fugitives. Fort Mose became the first legally sanctioned free black town in what is now the United States. Two years later, despite the heroic efforts of the African American militia at Mose, English forces destroyed the fort in an attack on St. Augustine. Rebuilt in 1752, the new fort housed mostly African American soldiers and their families until abandoned for the last time when Florida became an English colony in 1763.

Fort Mose, a National Historic Landmark and the only site of its kind in the United States, symbolizes the courage and vision of African Americans who made selfless sacrifices for freedom when no choices seemed possible. Like Colono Ware pots, Fort Mose reminds us that colonial African American history is not just a story of slavery and oppression. Kathleen Deagan led a team of archaeologists, historians, scientists, teachers, and politicians at Fort Mose to unearth the history of African Americans in the Spanish colonies. Their research interweaves evidence from documents, remains of the fort, and fragments of weaponry, Indian pots, Catholic medals, bottles, food bone, and tools into a compelling story of a people's pursuit of freedom.

The Spanish coupled self-interest with altruism in the selection of a setting for Fort Mose, the northernmost frontier outpost built in the eighteenth century to defend St. Augustine. A modest affair of stakes, cactus, and earthworks surrounded by a shallow moat, the original fort enclosed a watchtower, guardhouse, and well. Sited next to a creek for defense, the fort today lies preserved underwater, after a sea-level rise and wetlands development inundated the site. It was the new, much larger but similarly constructed fort built nearby in 1752 that archaeologists rediscovered with the aid of aerial photographs, old maps, and test excavations.

At the site, archaeologists carefully traced soil stains left by wood buildings, palisades, and decayed garbage. They found hundreds of artifacts, most broken into pieces no larger than a thumbnail. Yet often these stains and artifacts offered the only clues we have to daily life at the fort. Who lived at Mose and what kind of a life did they forge at this fortress of freedom?

A mosaic of people with diverse origins in Africa, the Caribbean, Florida, and the Carolinas made Mose their home. Documents tell of intermarriage among Indian, African, and European peoples at Mose, a common practice throughout the Spanish colonies in America. Most people lived with their families, although some resided in all-male households. Soil stains marked the remains of their oval palm-thatch houses. Measuring an average of twelve feet in diameter, they provided living quarters that we would find too cramped to tolerate. Contemporary European observers thought them poorly built and called them "huts" to distinguish them from European-style houses, noting that they looked similar to the huts erected by local Indians. Despite Europeans' discounting of the houses, they met the needs of people who preferred to live and work outdoors.

The Spaniards in St. Augustine wanted people at Mose to farm, to raise food for themselves as well as a surplus for the colony. They grew corn and maybe rice, but documents make it clear that they did not harvest enough to feed their families. Some men hunted and traded with native allies. Other families relied on government rations. The remains of the fish, shellfish, turtles, rabbits, and deer on which they dined survive in the ground. Plant remains did not preserve as well in the soils of Mose, but archaeologists did recover seeds and other remains of oranges, figs, nuts, squashes, gourds, melons, beans, blackberries, blueberries, huckleberries, plums, persimmons, grapes, and maypops. Clearly the residents of Mose came to know their environment well, and invested considerable time and effort in hunting, fishing, and gathering wild plants and animals in nearby woods and streams.

They also came to know each other well, and shared what they knew about everything from cooking to religion. The grinding stones for corn and the clay cooking pots, spoons, and storage jars found by archaeologists show that many households at Mose adopted local Indian ways of preparing and storing food. On the other hand, imported buckles, thimbles, and pins and homemade bone buttons tell us that residents dressed much like other St. Augustine colonists. This sharing of lifeways didn't mean that people no longer showed pride in their own heritage, and people likely still displayed African ornamental features such as scarring and hairstyle to identify themselves with particular social and ethnic groups.

The Fort Mose militia, a community-based free black militia, had primary responsibility for scouting and information gathering on the frontier. They mastered the intricacies of European warfare and integrated elements from their own traditions. At Mose archaeologists found pieces of the flintlock pistols, muskets, and bayonets with which they trained, along with evidence that the soldiers learned to cast lead musket balls and work dense stone into gunflints.

The Spanish shaped African American culture in another crucial way by requiring all runaway slaves given refuge at Mose to convert to Catholicism. Rosary beads and handmade St. Christopher medals symbolized the converts' new faith, although they never completely abandoned their African spiritual heritage. St. Christopher, the patron saint of travelers, had special significance at Mose for those who believed he had guided them along the path to freedom.

Fig. 4.1. Reconstruction of the second Fort Mose, ca. 1752, based on historical research.

emies to the north from 1687 onward by granting Maroons religious sanctuary. By 1740, Maroons who had taken advantage of Spanish protection were persuaded to build and staff Fort Mose. Maroons helped the Spanish survive the British invasions of the century.

Because colonists feared military alliances between Africans and Native Americans, their writings focused on antagonisms between the two peoples and ignored the productive relations they forged. Maroon and Seminole Indian interactions went beyond military alliances, for many intermarried and inhabited the same settlements. Some Africans were slaves or had a client-patron relationship with their Seminole Indian hosts. The Seminole Indians passed on their knowledge of local environment, foodways, and dress to their Maroon neighbors. Enslaved and free Africans reciprocated using their skills in areas such as agriculture, ironworking, and warfare. Because Maroons were familiar with European languages and behaviors, they were valuable translators to the Seminole Indians. During the first half of the nineteenth century, Black Seminole Maroons from Abraham's Old Town allied with

Fig. 4.2. *Burning of Pilaklikaha* by General Eustis. (Courtesy of Library of Congress.)

neighboring Seminole Indians and engaged the United States in wars that cost both sides thousands of lives and millions of dollars.

Black Seminole Maroon cultural practices and beliefs were as much the product of African culture as of Seminole Indian or European colonial culture. Maroon societies were havens where people could more openly express their African cultural background. Naming practices were important ways Maroons preserved their African legacy. A Black Seminole interpreter named Cudjo aided the Seminole Indians and the U.S. government in their negotiations. He served on a delegation that inspected lands that Black Seminoles and Seminole Indians were to inhabit after they were deported to Oklahoma. The name *Cudjo* came from the Twi language of Ghana. Cudjo means "Monday" in Twi, and it was part of a system of day names assigned to people based on their day of birth. In Jamaica another Maroon named Cudjo led his people in an effective campaign against British colonial military forces during the eighteenth century. Cudjo became a popular surname among descendants of Black Seminole Maroons in the western United States, and remains so to this day.

Abraham's Old Town was named after Abraham, one of Cudjo's fellow interpreters. While searching the Library of Congress online, I discovered a painting entitled *Burning of Pilaklikaha by Gen. Eustis,* which may well be

Fig. 4.3. Artifacts at Abraham's Old Town. Top row: fragments of ironstone plate base, pipe stem; bottom row: green bottle rim, brushed pot rim with triangular punctuate, green glass bead; far right: wrought iron nail. (Courtesy of Terrance Weik.)

the only depiction of Abraham's Old Town ever made. Archivists at St. Augustine explained that this painting appeared in a spread of Seminole War paintings published decades ago. However, the publication did not explain the full historical significance of the town. Many readers probably did not know it was a place where Maroons lived for decades, cultivating vast fields of corn, beans, and rice. One of the most powerful Seminole chiefs, Micanopy, lived there with his wives. Abraham advised Micanopy in his dealings with the United States. Black Seminole people revered Abraham even after they left Florida and became "freedmen" in Oklahoma, Texas, and Mexico.

If you visit Abraham's Old Town today, you will see only a cow pasture on a country road. A visitor will see no vestige of the thriving town that was there in the early nineteenth century. The site stands atop an elevated hammock, forming a dominating presence in a state known for its flatness. Nearby is Jumper Creek, named for a Seminole Indian who led his people against the U.S. invasions. At present, cattle drink from the same water holes and graze on the same lands that the Black Seminole Maroons' herds did more than 160 years ago. Apart from the occasional sound of an automobile rumbling by, a bird calling, or a cow bawling, it is very peaceful now, unlike in the turbulent times when Black Seminole Maroons lived there.

Maroons who settled at Abraham's Old Town escaped from plantations in Florida as well as in the northern states. Zephaniah Kingsley, a planter who lived near present-day Jacksonville, Florida, lost forty of his slaves to Black Seminole Maroon and Seminole Indian marauders. Soon after the raids, the Seminole Indians and Maroons were forced to evacuate their North Florida towns with their new recruits. In 1813 they were themselves under attack from Georgia settlers seeking new lands to colonize. Whole families of enslaved people lived in the twelve-by-sixteen-foot tabby cabins standing at Kingsley today. Unlike many European colonists, most enslaved Africans in the Americas did not have a choice where they lived, which home they would inhabit, or when they could come and go.

By contrast, Black Seminole Maroons in Florida did decide where they lived and how their houses were arranged. U.S. military engineer Hugh Young commented that the houses of the Suwannee River Maroon towns in North Florida were large and well constructed. The Maroons' homes at Abraham's Old Town were probably cabins like those depicted in the painting. Maroons constructed them using some of the abundant wrought iron nails that archaeologists have found at the town site. Wooden posts used in house construction, and later burned, have also left round charcoal stains uncovered in the excavations.

The artifacts recovered from Abraham's Old Town offer the most tangible evidence of the inhabitants' activities and belongings. For example, fragments of long clay pipes smoked by former residents were found. Pipe tobacco was one of many scents in the air during the nineteenth century. Fragrant foods simmered in Seminole Indian "brushed" pots whose fragments now lay scattered about the site. Seminole brushed pottery was made with deep abrasions scratched into the brown-gray clay of the globular vessels. The Seminole Indian and Black Seminole Maroon residents used these pots to prepare *soffkee,* a dish resembling pudding made from arrowroot or coontie plant root. Crumbling, rusty fragments of metal suggest the use of kettles and metal tools. People of the time also used baskets and gourds, but these items have eluded our excavations because they disintegrate in the acidic local soils. A nineteenth-century soldier reported seeing ball-sticks, Indian flutes, and tortoiseshell rattles in the charred ruins of Abraham's Old Town. These instruments were probably used in communal ceremonies that we have yet to reconstruct. Pieces of European ironstone platters, pearlware plates, and stoneware mugs and crocks are the most numerous types of artifact at the site. The distribution and qualities of all the artifacts at Abraham's Old Town will provide new clues to the town's layout and size, as well as its connection to other settlements in the region.

Future laboratory analysis of the artifacts will also teach about the spiritual and aesthetic beliefs of the Black Seminole Maroons. The residents at Abraham's Old Town had a definite sense of style. They adorned themselves with fancy metal conical earrings. They made silver into ornate pendants, rings, and bracelets, and they crafted accessories for the men's turbans. Seminole Indians and Abraham were often depicted wearing turbans. On a few occasions, excited volunteers have shown me blue, green, and clear glass beads that they pulled from screens used to sift the excavated earth from Abraham's Old Town. Paintings of Seminole Indians show them wearing bead necklaces, and archaeological research at plantations suggests that enslaved populations also valued them.

Beyond the chains of slavery, people of African descent struggled to bring about their liberation in Maroon societies. Archaeology at Abraham's Old Town illustrates how Black Seminole Maroons created lasting and multicultural societies. By serving as a common ground for Maroon and Seminole Indian inhabitants, Abraham's Old Town shaped the relations between Native Americans and formerly enslaved black people. Abraham's Old Town was no anomaly, for thousands of Maroon towns once existed in the Americas. More than fifteen Maroon and Black Seminole settlements have been discovered in previous studies of colonial Florida, and I expect to add several more to maps by the end of my research. Black Seminoles persevered because they maintained self-sufficient communities, communicated well with different peoples, and created opportunistic trade and military alliances. They also mastered the ability to mobilize quickly, for fight or flight, when threatened by their enemies. Finally, Black Seminole Maroons united people having major cultural differences. These survival strategies are as valuable now as they were then for the people of the African Diaspora, and for all others who seek self-determination.

Creating a new perspective on the history and archaeology of the African Diaspora is an important first step in ending the damaging legacy of racism that still prevents Americans from facing issues rooted in their common, sometimes uncomfortable, past. For centuries, people regularly crossed the lines of race and culture that are used to divide and discriminate against us in modern America. Fortunately, history shows us that we do not have to accept the relations or conditions that alienate us or deny our human rights. Ultimately, the story of Black Seminole Maroons reflects the indomitable human will to be free from all forms of oppression and injustice.

5

The Chinese in the Cities of the West

Roberta S. Greenwood

Over the centuries, America's cities have become home to millions of immigrants. Some, like Africans, did not come of their own accord; many others did, seeking a new life. As we have come to appreciate this diversity represented in our North American heritage, historical archaeologists have learned to do more than simply count, weigh, and measure the artifacts people left behind. As our discipline has evolved, we have learned that much of the past still lies intact below our feet despite all the modern developments, highways, high rises, and parking lots. These remains, even when broken or disturbed, can fill in many of the chapters missing from our history books. In the nineteenth century, California hosted large populations of Chinese immigrants in urban Chinatowns, and smaller concentrations in work camps focused on railroad construction, fishing, or mining. Archaeologists are finding new evidence of their presence in areas that we once thought were hopelessly disturbed, and the sites are speaking to the diversity within the Chinese community. Rather than merely identifying soy sauce jars or attempting to arrange porcelain patterns in chronological sequence, we can now address more substantive issues about what people did, how behavior changed, and why.

In Ventura, a team of archaeologists from my consulting firm, Greenwood and Associates, discovered remains from the earliest Chinatown, occupied between about 1860 and 1900. They had survived beneath the cellar of a historic brick building undergoing rehabilitation in 1998. This first settlement on Figueroa Street and China Alley had been uprooted and relocated onto Main Street when civic pressures developed at the turn of the century to "clean up" and redevelop the property. When the Main Street location in turn became increasingly valuable real estate and the target of urban renewal, we found evidence of the Chinese in the old Hispanic adobes, preserved just under the ground surface. The physical displacement of Ventura's Chinatown had a parallel in Los Angeles, where the earliest settlement of the 1860s took place around the old Pueblo Plaza. As the growing city's core property became more desirable, Los Angeles's Chinatown shifted in the 1880s to the future location of the railroad station, an undesirable property already crossed by railroad tracks, subject to flooding, and beset with fumes from the gas plant. The press reported that the move was encouraged by arson and broadly cheered. While the Chinese community in Los Angeles continued to thrive and grow after the move, Ventura's Chinatown did not long survive the relocation. The population was too small to sustain itself, employment opportunities in the host community were too limited, and new immigrants did not choose Ventura as a destination.

In Los Angeles, the Union Railroad Station built in 1933 displaced the Chinese community that by then numbered in the thousands. Old maps recorded its location, but when planning began for the new Metro Rail subway, some assumed that the station had destroyed all evidence of the earlier community. As consultants to the Metropolitan Transportation Authority, we used an old photograph to show that the station and track bed were actually built on more than ten feet of fill. There was reason to believe that evidence of the old Chinatown dating back to the 1880s survived under the imported soils. As the trains roared overhead and contractors operated their huge earth-moving equipment between the tracks, passenger tunnels, utility lines, and other constraints, our archaeological monitors soon found that the prediction was valid. Although demolition crews had leveled all the buildings to construct the railroad station, they left the rubble. Under it, the surface on which the nineteenth-century Chinese immigrants lived remained virtually

Fig. 5.1. Ventura Chinatown, 1880s. (Courtesy of Ventura County Museum of History and Art.)

Fig. 5.2. Los Angeles Chinatown, Apablaza Street, ca. 1900. (Courtesy of Seaver Center for Western History Research, Los Angeles County Museum of Natural History.)

intact. We uncovered foundations, sidewalks, fence lines, roadways, trash pits, privies, and a broad scatter of discards. The *top* of the site was fourteen feet below the existing modern surface! Our excavation team had to work in concert with the contractor's schedule, below the massive machinery roaring overhead, and often in a restricted area between the tracks. They worked in a space so deep that a crane had to lower a backhoe into the hole to remove the overlying fill and then lower the field equipment, while the crew descended by ladders.

We mapped the community and recovered thousands of artifacts. It was not news that the Chinese had settled this area, but the little written about them appeared in prejudicial newspaper articles biased by fear, hostility, and ignorance. Contemporary histories repeated the typical stereotypes that the residents of Chinatown were single men with no women or children present, that they were all poor laborers, and that their culture was rigid and unchanging. The evidence from the ground together with historical records showed

Fig. 5.3. Excavating California's Chinatowns. (Courtesy of Roberta Greenwood.)

that herbal doctors, teachers, and merchants lived among the laundrymen and produce workers in the Los Angeles Chinatown, and the artifacts included goods reflecting both higher and lower status. The doctors, particularly, interacted with the host community and even learned Spanish to appeal to more patients. The merchants were tied into international trade networks, usually knew at least some English, and related to the local business and political communities. Finding women's jewelry, cosmetics, and clothing, expensive table porcelains, and children's clothing and toys confirmed the presence of families. Women lived greatly sheltered lives by Western standards, and were drastically undercounted in the census rolls. They owned cosmetics, jewelry, and clothing imported from their homeland, while their children were learning American ways, playing with marbles and European dolls.

In smaller towns, too, historical literature and old maps suggest where the historic Chinatowns may lie buried. For example, recent research in Cambria, California, points to the location of a small camp of Chinese seaweed-gatherers who, from the 1880s to 1913, took refuge in Cambria from their dwellings on the open coast during weekends or inclement weather. Historic photos show a small cluster of three to five wood frame buildings, one of them with a false front and a front porch. Oral histories have identified it as a joss house. Historical research suggests that it served as an association hall for the Chee Kung Tong as well as for religious functions. This camp, like those of railroad or agricultural workers, had a short life, impermanent buildings, and predominantly male residents. The archaeological finds, once analyzed, will tell us about the lives of these fishermen and seaweed-gatherers isolated from towns and families. The artifacts will help identify their networks for selling and shipping their product, and the duration and role of the camp in relation to broader patterns in the maritime economy. The joss house and the remains of its furnishings also have much to tell about Chinese ceremonies and ritual in California and the ways these temples helped integrate social life for the immigrant workers.

More frequently than their rural counterparts, immigrants to the urban Chinatowns of the West settled down and prospered, even though isolated by language, crowded within land of low value, and subject to prejudice. They maintained traditional lifeways, especially regarding their foodways and important social and religious organizations. But archaeology has also revealed the presence of distinctive social and economic classes. Remains of the Chinese past in California survive under unlikely circumstances in areas where we thought they had been destroyed. These remains of buildings, landscape features, and artifacts clearly identify distinctions within Chinese immigrant society, and they are forcing us to challenge many traditional assumptions about Chinese life in California, on what the Chinese named Golden Mountain.

Part 2

Challenging and Changing Environments

Exploring New Lands and Exploiting New Environments

Lu Ann De Cunzo

Even before the first Norse sailors debarked at Newfoundland in the eleventh century, people in North America had met and adjusted to new environments as well as new people. Their interactions have not always been friendly. Neither have the environmental consequences of people's actions on the land always been benign. Exploiting and modifying the environment has produced wealth and benefits, but at a cost. And in many places, environmental conditions have determined whether in fact people and their settlements would survive.

In the twenty-first century, managing the environment and its fragile ecosystems in the face of human onslaught has become a full-time pursuit. The results of environmental degradation plague us daily, as mudslides carry homes down overdeveloped and denuded Pacific slopes, birds and other wildlife perish in the toxic, oil-slicked waters of Alaska, and clear-cutting of timber and strip mining leave deep scars across large swaths of our land. The effects of natural disasters on peoples around the globe are equally devastating.

In the early modern era, explorers and settlers traveled to North America seeking both land and its resources. They took timber for ships and buildings, furs and hides for clothing, iron for tools and weapons, plants and animals for food, drink, and medicine, and gold and silver for their precious symbolism of wealth. Archaeology has a long history of studying how peoples use culture to adapt to, make sense of, give value to, and reshape their environments. We bring a unique perspective to environmental history and cultural landscapes because we study the environment and cultural imprints on the land directly. Working with researchers from many disciplines, historical archaeologists have learned much about the constant give and take between people and land inscribed in everything from soils, roads and fences, to buildings, ditches, plants, and animals. In this section we follow past peoples on their expeditions to the Arctic, the coastal plains of the Southeast, the bays of the Gulf of Mexico, and the mountains and deserts of the West.

In each place and at different times, these settlers adapted to hostile environments in numerous ways. In the inhospitable Arctic, both the Norse in the eleventh century and the English mining expedition in the sixteenth century had to weigh the costs versus the gains of exploiting the frozen land. Early in the next century the English found the warm, humid wetlands of Tidewater Virginia barely more welcoming when they planted a colony on Jamestown Island. Still further south, La Salle sailed into the Gulf of Mexico near the century's end, seeking a passage through North America to the Orient and a favorable place for a French settlement. But the mudflats of Texas's Gulf Coast proved hostile to these settlers unfamiliar with its foods and unprepared for its storms, its reptiles, its insects and the diseases they carried. Almost two centuries later, for new immigrants mining the Sierra Nevada to the north and west, the tools of industrialization offered little comfort in the isolation of winter.

The dynamic history of people and the land in North America has many complicated layers. In Jamestown the National Park Service–sponsored team learned to follow the money and the goods, where they came from and how they were used, to unravel the economics of city-building in the early English colony. In the West, the scale of mining and the extent of the environmental consequences have led archaeologists to stories of poisoning and cleanups and, again, of money, this time on an industrial scale. But like the archaeologists excavating La Salle's ship *La Belle,* they also seek to tell stories of people. With their help we can literally see the Irish miners and French colonists and learn how places like target-shooting galleries and objects like ancient Roman coins offered some small comfort against the uncertainties of sea voyages and immigration to an alien land.

For generations many of us learned that the story of the Americas began with Christopher Columbus's "discovery" in 1492. But that is only one place to begin the story. There are other, often less familiar but equally important, stories to tell about encounters between people and the unique and diverse environments of North America.

6

Early Encounters with a "New" Land

Vikings and Englishmen in the North American Arctic

William Fitzhugh

The dramatic effects of the Columbian voyages tend to obscure a different contact history in northern regions of the Americas beginning in Viking times. Here, in the near-mythical lands of the north, Europeans and native peoples of Greenland and North America first encountered each other one thousand years ago.

Navigating without instruments, the Vikings traveled west across the North Atlantic. Sailing little more than two or three days at a time, they voyaged from land to land. As soon as they had set up a colony on one land, they pressed on to other uninhabited lands further west. So it was that Eric the Red, banished from his home in Iceland, sailed west and discovered a land he named Greenland to attract settlers. Within a generation he had established a thriving colony in arctic North America. Norse colonists raised sheep, goats, pigs, cows, and horses, as they had back home. Their livestock provided food, transportation, and raw materials for almost everything they needed, except iron and timber for building and fuel.

Eric's son, Leif, shared his father's wanderlust. Soon he, too, sailed west, and established a new colony in what he called Vinland. The land was rich in game, fish, and berries. But it lay far from Greenland, and natives contested the settlement, so Leif's small band retreated home to Greenland. During the next four centuries, the Norse visited these lands many times to cut wood and to trade for ivory and fur. But by then the era of discovery and colonization had passed. The Greenland colonies, which reached a peak population of some three thousand by about A.D. 1200, faced hard times. Nevertheless, these Norse adventurers and settlers had left an indelible mark on the land and on the native people.

These events were passed down to succeeding Norse generations as oral sagas retold for three hundred years in Iceland. Contact with Greenland ceased in the fourteenth century, but the stories lived on, preserved on sheep-

Fig. 6.1. Longhouse and yard complex reconstructed at Parks Canada's Viking site at L'Anse aux Meadows in northern Newfoundland. (Courtesy of William Fitzhugh, Smithsonian Institution.)

skin parchment that survives to this day. When whalers returned to Greenland in the seventeenth century, they found the old Norse churches and farmsteads abandoned. They also heard Inuit tales of a people they called *kablunat,* or white man, who once lived among them in Greenland but disappeared generations ago.

Three hundred years later, the Norwegian explorer Helge Ingstad found, at L'Anse aux Meadows on the northern tip of Newfoundland, a Viking site that almost certainly was the "gateway" settlement for Leif's Vinland. In the 1960s, Helge's archaeologist wife, Anne Stine Ingstad, led excavations that revealed a settlement conforming closely to the saga descriptions. In the 1970s, Birgitta Wallace and Bengt Schoenbak led a Parks Canada team of archaeologists back to the site on Newfoundland's spectacular northern coast.

Ingstad's and Wallace's teams discovered eight buildings at L'Anse aux Meadows, carefully laid out in three residential complexes around a small cove. At each, one or two small rooms flanked an imposing multiroomed hall. Radiocarbon dating and artifact and building styles confirmed that the

Fig. 6.2. Butternut and husk found at L'Anse aux Meadows. Butternut trees did not grow around L'Anse aux Meadows one thousand years ago, nor do they to-day. Uncovering these pieces suggests the Vikings were traveling further south. (Photo by Peter Harholdt, courtesy of William Fitzhugh, Smithsonian Institution; butternut and husk in collections of Canadian Museum of Civilization.)

settlement dates to early in the eleventh century. The buildings themselves told that the builders meant them for year-round use and that they had housed about seventy to ninety people. With its thick sod walls and roof and paneled walls, each hall required at least eighty-six large trees for support posts and beams, along with more wood to support the sod roof, panel the walls, and build sleeping and work platforms. Each hall had a workshop. Unlike other North Atlantic Norse settlements, L'Anse aux Meadows lacked the barns, stables, and animal pens of a typical Norse farmstead.

Norse chieftains like Leif Ericson kept slaves who cut sod and collected bog iron, while Ericson and his crew explored, experimented with iron-making, and built buildings and boats. Women also had an important place in the community, and they left behind evidence of their handiwork in the form of a spindle whorl for spinning, a bone needle, and a whetstone for sharpening needles and other small sewing tools.

Sometimes the most ordinary things archaeologists find are the most excit-ing. At L'Anse aux Meadows, it was butternuts. A North American walnut tree, sometimes called white walnut, the butternut tree is not native to New-foundland. Its nearest habitat lies in the St. Lawrence River valley, east of Quebec in northeastern New Brunswick. Butternuts grow in the same setting as wild grapes, which the sagas tell us the expedition discovered. Both thrive in New England and farther south as well, but the siting of L'Anse aux Meadows made it convenient to the Gulf of St. Lawrence.

Unlike the Greenland colonies, which lasted nearly five hundred years, Norse settlers remained at L'Anse aux Meadows only for a single season or two. The archaeologists found neither garbage nor cemeteries, but could tell that the residents had planned to abandon the settlement when they left. Unfortunately for us, they took most of their tools and equipment with them, and later Inuit visitors salvaged whatever they could use. Putting all the broken and charred pieces together, Wallace and her team concluded that the Vinland of the Norse sagas encompassed the coast all around the Gulf of St. Lawrence, with the settlement at L'Anse aux Meadows as its gateway. L'Anse aux Meadows served as a short-term base from which to explore the region. Summer expeditions south returned with lumber, butternuts, and probably grapes, which they took back to Greenland the following summer. But why, then, abandon L'Anse aux Meadows? To answer that, we must look at the larger context of Viking exploration in the Arctic.

The Norse sailed the North Atlantic in search of particular resources and settlement locations. In each new territory they evaluated the environment and resources, and pursued only those deemed profitable. In Vinland the desirable resources—prime hardwood, grapes, and walnuts—lay too far from Greenland and required too much time, effort, and expense to exploit. The Norse could import these same goods from Europe at less expense, and choose from a wider selection. Greenland offered sufficient land, pastures, and ivory-hunting opportunities during the early period when the North Atlantic climate was warm, and the Norse assigned a low priority to homesteading among the unfriendly North American natives that they met in their travels west and south. For eleventh-century Norse colonizers, Vinland offered no economic incentive to stay. Its most valuable resource, timber, could be acquired without establishing settlements and was harvested occasionally by the Norse of Greenland and Iceland as late as the mid-fourteenth century, according to Icelandic documents.

Although their history is full of mystery and adventure, the Vikings remain little known, misunderstood, and almost invisible on the American landscape. Few Americans took seriously the idea that Viking explorers had reached the North American mainland five hundred years before Columbus, and that they had a legitimate place in New World history. The finds at L'Anse aux Meadows and the many Norse artifacts and trade materials found in native Dorset and Inuit sites in northern Greenland and the Canadian Arctic have forced us to revise this history, and to give due credit to the Norse and other North European peoples who created and maintained a gateway between Europe and North America for most of the past thousand years.

The English picked up the trail of northern voyaging barely more than one hundred years after the Norse abandoned their churches and farms in Greenland around 1450. Unlike the Spanish and Portuguese, who tried to subdue the native peoples at the missions, the English sought a simpler approach based on trade. Lured by profits from spices, silk, and other treasures, the Cathay Company pinned its hopes on the fabled Northwest Passage and sent out a young captain, Martin Frobisher, who in 1576 was little more than a well-connected brash young pirate, to search for a northern route to China.

The three Frobisher voyages, in 1576, 1577, and 1578, form a worthy sequel to the dramatic Viking tales from Greenland and Vinland. Frobisher missed Greenland but found land on southern Baffin Island, mistaking Frobisher Bay for a northwest passage. While ashore, a group of Frobisher's men were captured by Inuit, forcing Frobisher to abandon his first mission. He returned to England, carrying among his "tokens of possession" a glittering black rock and several Inuit captives. The rock looked like it contained gold, and the natives looked Asian; their copper ornaments, "traded from the west," were all Frobisher needed to fuel speculation fever among Queen Elizabeth and her investors.

Frobisher returned in 1577 with instructions from his Cathay Company investors to mine gold ore. New ore finds easily offset the discovery that "Frobisher's Straits" led into an inhospitable land occupied by people who seemed to the English strange, unpredictable, and dangerous. Frobisher returned for a third voyage in 1578, with four hundred men in fifteen ships. Their mission was to establish a mining colony on Kodlunarn Island, in what is now Frobisher Bay. But the fates did not look kindly on these ill-prepared intruders. Frobisher's fleet was beset and battered by sea ice, and the vessel that carried the building materials and the beer was lost. The others made landfall on the island, where they set up a base camp. There they went to work repairing ships damaged by ice, opening mines, and loading the ships' hulls with hundreds of tons of ore. By summer's end the crews had seriously depleted their provisions. Frobisher called a retreat and the broken, ore-laden, and nearly starving flotilla limped home to England. While they had been overseas, new assays had proven the ore worthless, suggesting that the early results had been fraudulently assayed to promote the expedition.

Frobisher's spectacular failure proved once again what the Norse had already discovered—that while this northern region of the New World promised riches, the costs were too high for their times and technology. The frigid sea and icy arctic lands defied English imagination and survival skills. Worse still, native peoples had already settled the land and were ready to defend it. Despite successes further south, first in Spanish Florida and later at James-town, Virginia, and elsewhere, Europeans would not permanently settle the arctic regions for another two hundred years.

Until quite recently, historians considered the Frobisher expedition a side-bar in the saga of New World exploration. The voyages did not lead to new resources or markets, or to settlement of new lands. In fact, the wealth of written records documenting the expedition actually discouraged further study. With so much already known, what more could be learned?

Frobisher may not have discovered gold, but his voyages are a gold mine of information about the expanding European world at the beginning of the Age of Exploration. We have come to see that the Frobisher story is not only the account of an early English settlement in the Americas; it also documents one of the earliest episodes of contact between Europeans and natives, and it offers a fascinating opportunity for research at the interface of history, ar-chaeology, anthropology, and natural science.

Strangely, though, archaeologists long neglected the physical remains of the settlements. Charles Francis Hall's discovery of the Frobisher mines, workshops, and artifacts in the 1860s failed to excite scholars' interest for more than a hundred years. Pioneer Canadian historical archaeologist Walter Kenyon organized a Royal Ontario Museum excursion to the site in 1974. Shortly after this, our arctic research team at the Smithsonian Institution set out to answer the mystery of an iron "bloom"—a partially processed mass of smelted iron ore—that Hall had found at the Frobisher site. Radiocarbon dating of charcoal embedded in the bloom dated not to the latter 1500s, as expected if Frobisher's men had produced the bloom, but between A.D. 1160 and 1400. This discovery touched off a lively debate. In search of more infor-mation about the bloom and Frobisher's legacy, the Smithsonian teamed with Parks Canada to mount an expedition to Kodlunarn Island in 1981.

We arrived on the island through the broken pack ice of Frobisher Bay in early August and set up a field camp. Amazingly, the remains of Frobisher's mines and activities were still easily detected. Even after four hundred years, their turf-covered wall foundations, trenches, and pits still stand out clearly against the barren gravel surface of the island. We mapped the industrial complex, including two mine trenches, a charcoal-fired assay shop, a char-coal storehouse, a furnace pit, and a blacksmith shop.

The single well still held water (though rather unappetizing), and we even located several cache pits left by Frobisher's men at the end of the 1578 season to store equipment and materials for their projected return the follow-

Fig. 6.3. Researchers inspecting Martin Frobisher's Countess of Warwick Island, known today as Kodlunarn (white man's) Island. (Courtesy of William Fitzhugh, Smithsonian Institution.)

ing year. Like Frobisher, we too returned with samples of ore, slag, blooms, mortar, artifacts, coal, wood, and charcoal, which we analyzed for several years to learn more about this early European attempt to extract resources from the arctic environment.

While research specialists set about analyzing the samples, we planned our return to Frobisher Bay as part of a larger American and Canadian expedition under the aegis of the Canadian government's Meta Incognita Committee. The Canadian team, directed by Reginald Auger of Laval University, would concentrate on excavating portions of the Frobisher sites, while the American group would search for information about the lives of the native Inuit peoples and the impacts of Frobisher's brief visits on them and the environment. We traveled in July 1990 from Newfoundland to our home base at the head of the bay, and spent the next month surveying sites up and down the spectacular Frobisher Bay coastline. We returned again for three more seasons from 1991 to 1993.

Our team located and documented seventy-five archaeological sites. Five are Frobisher mines, each easily identified by their mining trenches, quarry marks, and coal dumps. Frobisher transported great quantities of English coal and charcoal to the Arctic, where his men used them for cooking and heating and for assaying prospective ore samples. Later the Inuit revisited the Frobisher sites, setting up hunting camps and scavenging coal, tile, wood, and other usable items. In fact, more than fifty of the sites we found belonged to Inuit who lived and hunted along the bay after 1500.

These sites hold the key to understanding how Frobisher's visits affected local Inuit culture. They are especially invaluable when you consider that after 1600 the East Baffin Inuit slipped back outside the sphere of European influence for almost 250 years, until English whalers sailed into Baffin Bay in 1830. Future research will help us tell that story.

We also have Frobisher mysteries yet to solve. Ore samples from the mines matched with those collected from Frobisher's storage site at Dartford, England. Contrary to popular belief, the glittering black rocks were not fool's gold (pyrite) but hornblende. The iron blooms still confound us, however. Most of the charcoal embedded in the partially smelted iron came from spruce, which does not grow in England, and the radiocarbon dating indicates the blooms predated the Frobisher expeditions by several hundred years. So who made them? When, how, why, and where were they made? And what function did they serve? The bloom sizes, the manufacturing methods, the lack of other iron smelting evidence, and the large amount of driftwood needed if they had been smelted in Baffin Island all pointed away from Frobisher. But how, then, did they end up in the Frobisher work areas, and why did their archaeological context suggest Frobisher had brought them to Kodlunarn Island as part of his expedition supplies? The fact that all were found in the ship repair areas on Kodlunarn Island suggested they had been most recently used, not as sources of iron for Frobisher's smiths to make new tools, but as hammers, anvils, or ship ballast.

But soon other clues began to emerge. Recording old stories told by Frobisher Bay Inuit in 1861, Charles Francis Hall learned that a group of Frobisher's men had been accidentally left behind when the English departed for England at the end of their last voyage, in 1578. According to the Inuit, these men tried to winter over at the Frobisher site on Kodlunarn Island but began to starve and freeze, not knowing how to hunt seals or make winter clothing. Befriended by Inuit, who showed them how to build snow houses on the bay ice and catch game, they survived the winter and in spring returned to Kodlunarn Island, where they readied a boat and stepped its mast by lowering it down into the boat from the top of a shoreside cliff. Today the cliff is still known in Inuktitut as "the place where a mast was stepped." When the ice began to melt in the spring, the men departed, but their ill-made boat was crushed by the pack ice and they perished.

Metallurgical analysis of a bloom fragment excavated from one of the mining workshops supports this oral history by revealing that the iron bloom contained sulfur, indicating reforging with coal by men who were unaware that this would weaken the iron. Perhaps the abandoned sailors, lacking specialized knowledge of ironmaking, had attempted to forge the blooms into spikes and nails for boat-building, only to have them fail under stress in the ice. Auger's archaeological excavations also provided some corroboration of the Inuit oral history, as they showed stratigraphic evidence that someone had excavated Frobisher's caches containing food, timber, and iron.

A final piece of the puzzle helped resolve the origin of the blooms themselves. The spruce inclusions had seemed mysterious because they indicated production in northern regions rather than in England. The Frobisher inventory lists contain a note about a 1576 Frobisher purchase at Ratcliff on the Thames of "yronstones of Russia . . . for balliste." For Frobisher they offered the advantages of availability, manageability, and metallurgical potential. For us, they emphasize the global context in which we must set our studies of Frobisher and his "fifteen minutes of fame" in the American Arctic.

Although these explorations of early European activities in arctic North America have produced as many questions as answers, they provide new avenues into the past, amplifying and even changing our views of history as known from documentary sources alone. Today these and other sources of evidence have produced a new vision of early European contacts and exploration in a part of North America that produced little of political or economic interest to Europeans until the beginning of modern times. While these contacts never established permanent European settlements or enriched the coffers of Europe, they produced a wealth of geographical and scientific data. Equally important, these contacts familiarized America's northern native peoples with new materials, technologies, and societies that would eventually transform their way of life as no other had before.

7

Jamestown, Virginia

Andrew Edwards

While the environmentally hostile Arctic defied Europeans' repeated attempts at colonization, regions further south posed equally difficult, if different, environmental challenges. Jamestown, the first successful English colony in the New World, served as Virginia's capital and virtually its only town from 1607 to 1699. Now a historical park owned jointly by the National Park Service (NPS) and the Association for the Preservation of Virginia Antiquities (APVA), the island and town site have attracted archaeologists the way any "first" site attracts archaeologists. J. C. Harrington directed excavations for the NPS in the latter 1930s that went a long way toward establishing the field of historical archaeology at a time when both historians and archaeologists questioned whether archaeology could teach us anything about history that we hadn't already learned from documents. John Cotter's appointment by the NPS to direct a major field project at Jamestown in 1954 is a tribute to Harrington's success. Three years later Cotter concluded that further digging at Jamestown should await the development of new techniques to wrest ever more information from the ground.

More than three decades passed before, in 1992, the NPS and the Colonial Williamsburg Foundation (CW) entered into a "cooperative agreement" to conduct further research at Jamestown. The idea behind it was a good one: The Park Service could connect with a not-for-profit educational institution with similar research goals. The NPS would provide financial backing and some facilities, and help cut through red tape. The institution in turn would provide the scholarly framework, educational outreach, fieldwork, and reports. Such was the relationship that developed between Colonial National Historical Park (Jamestown and Yorktown) and Colonial Williamsburg's Research Division. The NPS wanted to assess the archaeology undertaken on Jamestown Island over the last hundred years. We at CW wanted to learn more about Jamestown because it served as the Virginia capital before Williamsburg. Many of Williamsburg's antecedents lay buried in the ground just six miles down the road.

Our challenge was to engineer an effective plan to better understand and manage Jamestown Island, both culturally and environmentally. Colonial Williamsburg's Marley Brown and Cary Carson and NPS archaeologist David Orr designed an integrated multidisciplinary approach. They made sure that diverse scholars would evaluate virtually every aspect of James-town's cultural resources. As a result, our team included geophysicists, histo-rians, marine scientists, architectural historians, archaeologists, and librar-ians, along with a variety of plant and soil specialists.

In June 1993 we began our fieldwork. A year later William Kelso led another team into the field at the other end of Jamestown Island, on APVA land. Our projects have different goals. Jamestown ReDiscovery is a ten-year program to learn as much as archaeology can teach us about James fort, coordinated with the quadricentennial celebration of Jamestown's settle-ment. Our team decided not to conduct any further extensive excavations in an effort to locate buildings and other material remains of the early capital. The NPS repository on Jamestown Island already houses hundreds of thou-sands of artifacts excavated during the 1930s and 1950s excavations. The archaeology that we were to carry out over the next several seasons was designed to answer questions posed by the interdisciplinary team. We carried out most of the excavations in three summer seasons with William and Mary field schools. Each dig consisted of surgical incisions in search of specific answers to specific questions.

We began with geophysical prospecting. Bruce Bevan, a well-known Ches-apeake geophysicist who has worked with archaeologists from Albuquerque to Athens, laid out a sixty-by-forty-meter rectangle in the heart of James-town. He tried ground-penetrating radar, magnetometry, and conductivity and resistivity testing to locate possible archaeological remains without dig-ging. Geophysicists like Bruce interpret their instrument readings by examin-ing the patterns made by measurements higher or lower than what is consid-ered normal. For example, some of Bruce's magnetometer readings may suggest that there is a lump of buried iron or a row of bricks a few centimeters below the surface. He would note these "anomalies" on a map of the area. Our job, as archaeologists, was to place small excavation units where Bruce found the anomalies and see what was actually there. Somehow this process got stuck with the rather awful term *ground truthing*. Sometimes the anoma-lies were modern trash, sometimes they were chunks of metal, and sometimes we found nothing. In those cases, the instruments detected deeper features, probably geological.

A couple of previously undiscovered ground-surface brick kilns signaled strongly on the radar and magnetometer. We uncovered and mapped one of

Fig. 7.1. Aerial view of excavations at Structure 17, Jamestown. (Courtesy of Colonial Williamsburg Foundation.)

these kilns. In doing so, we noticed that John Cotter had described several other similar features in the same vicinity. His photographs showed the same pink and black burned soil in the same configuration, with a few impressions left in the natural subsoil below the later plowed soils. We had a kiln complex. Dating an associated clay-borrowing pit strongly suggested that the kilns were built to burn bricks for the Ambler family house built nearby in the eighteenth century.

Two surgical cuts we made for the architectural historians led to the most interesting results and major changes in the interpretation of Jamestown. The first of these involved a three-section townhouse near the riverbank in the middle of New Town. It had been excavated on several occasions. One archaeologist had drawn the brick foundations with bricks on the southwest corner that suggested a fourth section had been added to the townhouse at some time. We dug up the corner again, then excavated a portion of the area where a fourth building would have stood. We discovered a filled cellar hole, but no brick foundation. It appears that someone had started a fourth section but had halted construction before completing the building. This seemed to jibe with another large rectangular hole found by Cotter just a few yards away, and several other "false starts" around New Town. Many of them seem to be associated with a 1662 building initiative that occurred when the British government tried to make a city out of the capital. Some of these initiatives fell flat, and the speculators ran out of money before they could capitalize on their new properties.

Maybe it is inaccurate to suggest that archaeologists in general get a charge out of dispelling myths or throwing a trowel in the cogs of history—but, then again, maybe not. Our next bit of archaeological surgery was designed to define what the architectural historians hoped was a large U-shaped building located on the highest ground in New Town. Cotter assigned the foundations three structure numbers, but we knew little about its physical components. Was it three buildings or just one? Cotter had uncovered a great deal of decorative plaster, very baroque in style with cherubs and fancy curlicues, in a cellar of a nearby house. We speculated that it might have originated in the U-shaped house. Could it have been the forerunner of Williamsburg's Governor's Palace? The NPS had excavated the area very soon after acquiring Jamestown Island, before it was realized that an archaeologist should be in charge of the building hunt rather than an architectural historian. Only one sketch existed for one of the buildings.

A couple of strategic cuts and trenches later, we discovered that there were three buildings, not one. But the three could not all have existed at the same

Fig. 7.2. Excavating and collecting botanical samples at Jamestown. (Courtesy of Colonial Williamsburg Foundation.)

time and thus could not have been converted into one big building. Secretary Richard Kemp had built the first brick house in Jamestown around 1639. It was long gone before the next "section" of building was erected. Jamestown never did have a governor's palace or mansion or even, based on what we have discovered, a governor's house.

This sleuthing for the historians was very rewarding, but working with the paleobotanical (plant) and micromorphology (soils) people was fun. They actually got into the trenches and got dirty along with us. Part of our study centered on what we believed was an industrial enclave owned by governor and entrepreneur John Harvey in the first and second quarters of the seventeenth century. The enclave consisted of a brewery/apothecary, the brewer/apothecary's house, a kiln/forge, Harvey's house, and a large borrow pit, all of which Cotter had uncovered in the 1950s. In his customary fashion, Cotter had excavated part of the refuse/borrow pit and saved the rest for posterity. We sampled another one percent of the remaining unexcavated portion.

In order to get a good sample for soil and botanical studies, we needed the "clean face" of a trench running through the pit. We removed Cotter's backfill, then recorded the stratigraphy and used the "fresh face" for sampling. Dominic Powlesland, a well-known English archaeologist, wanted to do a peel of the fresh vertical surface (profile) of the pit. "Doing a peel" consists of painting a heavy lacquer on a section of the face, letting it dry, and pulling away the soil that sticks to the lacquer. This produces a very detailed record of the actual stratigraphy that can be preserved—even hung on a wall. Some people, Dominic included, help speed up the drying process by setting the wet lacquer on fire. Not only is the lacquer very flammable, the equally flammable fumes are heavier than air and naturally settle in the bottom of the trench. No big surprise that a wall of fire blazed when the lacquer was ignited—much to the delight of visitors, amusement of Dominic, and terror of anyone near the trench!

A little later in the season, Doug Currie took a somewhat calmer approach to recording the thin soil layers, or microstratigraphy, of the pit. Doug soaked a section of the pit in a form of epoxy that he did *not* set on fire. He let it dry naturally, then cut out the section and took it back to his lab. Microscopic analysis of the thin sections provided a much more detailed sequence of filling than previously recognized, even down to the last layer of *wood smoke* from the adjacent kiln operation before the pit was rapidly filled, probably around the mid-seventeenth century.

Two other experts had their way with the large borrow pit in Governor Harvey's industrial enclave: palynologist Gerald Kelso and macrobotanical specialist Steve Mrozowski. Both took column samples from the fresh face of the pit, Gerald looking for pollen and Steve hoping to find seeds. Gerald's pollen told us about the environmental history of the pit. After the clay mining operation had ceased, opportunistic weeds like goosefoot began to populate the area around the pit. Later, as the sea level rose—a fact demonstrated by the assessment geologists, Gerald Johnson and Carl Hobbs—wetland sedges and cattails crept into the area.

Steve's seeds confirmed the pollen findings and also helped tell a story about another one of Harvey's enterprises. The remains of a building described by Cotter as a brewery lay near the big borrow pit. Sweet woodruff and wax myrtle seeds that Steve found, along with artifacts and historical documents, strongly suggest that an apothecary also used the brewery, perhaps an apothecary who knew how to brew beer. The wax myrtle seeds were used as early as 1610 as a "cure" for dysentery, a very popular malady in early Jamestown's history. Steve had found sweet woodruff seeds at Dominic's excavations in England, and he knew that early uses included dyeing and medicine.

The paleobotanical and microstratigraphic sampling at the borrow pit and the strategic use of archaeology and remote sensing all over Jamestown epitomize the nondestructive approach the team took to achieve the goals of the NPS. But perhaps the best part of the project is that it will never really be finished. Newer and better interpretations will inform public programming, and new research will address Jamestown's role in the seventeenth-century Atlantic world and its impact on the local environment.

8

The Shipwreck of La Salle's *La Belle*

James E. Bruseth

In 1995, while archaeologists in Jamestown were gaining new insight into England's early settlements in North America, underwater archaeologists discovered the wreck of the earliest and most important French ship yet found in the Western Hemisphere—La Salle's *La Belle*. For the next two years, a team of archaeologists and volunteers sponsored by the Texas Historical Commission uncovered the ship's remains. Conservation began immediately and will continue for years as each artifact, from cannon to trade beads, receives careful cleaning and preservation treatments. Our researchers are following the trail of each artifact through documents and comparative studies to piece together their stories, while other team members prepare the hull and artifacts for display in a Texas museum.

In 1684 René-Robert Cavelier, sieur de La Salle, had set sail from France with four ships. He had located the mouth of the Mississippi River in 1682 and was coming back to build a colony there to hold for France what later became the Louisiana Territory. In January 1685 three of his ships, *Le Joly, l'Aimable,* and *La Belle,* sailed into the Gulf of Mexico and entered Matagorda Bay along the Texas coast, nearly five hundred miles from the Mississippi River. He anchored his vessels and set off inland with a team of explorers. They were met by barren plains, mudflats, and reedy marshes, which hosted clouds of mosquitoes, deadly snakes, and unfamiliar diseases. The Karankawa Indians did not take kindly to La Salle's arrival; they showed their displeasure by stealing his supplies and killing his men. When the surviving explorers returned to Matagorda Bay, their misery only deepened. *La Belle* had sunk during a violent winter storm in 1686. With the loss of *La Belle,* La Salle realized that failure for his colony was imminent. His men suffered from hunger and illness, and many refused to leave their settlement at Fort St. Louis. La Salle began an expedition toward New France, today's Canada, seeking aid from French settlers there. Before he could reach his destination, one of his disaffected men shot him dead.

Although La Salle's expedition ended in personal failure, his landing in Texas had broad consequences for Texas and North American history. The French intrusion in Texas reawakened Spanish interest in exploring the northern Gulf of Mexico. This led to Spanish efforts to claim Texas by establishing missions to Christianize the native people and building presidios to guard the new settlements. By doing so, they effectively blocked other foreign powers from future incursions to the west.

The archaeologists working on *La Belle* had an extraordinary experience. A large steel cofferdam was built around the wreck and the water pumped out. This enabled the crew to excavate in relatively dry conditions, much as is done on land archaeological sites. Few archaeologists have had the opportunity to work in a shipwreck with the waters held back by a steel-walled cofferdam. For many of the team, this was undoubtedly the highlight of their careers.

La Salle's loss has been our gain. Each day during the excavation, a joint private-public venture allowed people to boat to the site and watch the team uncover the remains of goods stored in the ship's hold for more than three centuries. One day, visitors saw archaeologists uncover the skeleton of a sailor lying across an anchor rope in the ship's bow. Nearby, another archaeologist uncovered a pewter porringer etched with the name C. Barange.

As the excavation proceeded, *La Belle*'s cargo gave up its secrets. Most of the items were packed in wooden casks and boxes, and these lay in the ship just as the crew had stowed them. A new surprise awaited the excavation team as we uncovered and opened each new cask and box. Some held goods intended for trade with the Indians, others contained the remains of food for feeding the colonists, and still others stored gunpowder and lead shot for defense and hunting. Ultimately we recovered a million artifacts from *La Belle*! They are giving us an unparalleled glimpse into what French immigrants thought they needed to start a colony in the seventeenth-century New World. The wreck itself is also a storehouse of information about seventeenth-century shipbuilding and about how the French provisioned transatlantic voyages.

In the Conservation Research Laboratory at Texas A&M University, conservators are slowly stabilizing and cleaning the artifacts recovered from *La Belle,* including the hull of the ship. While the primary purpose of the conservation is to preserve the artifacts for study and eventual exhibition, the conservators are also making new discoveries in the laboratory. For example, a coin found during excavation was too encrusted to identify in the field, but after cleaning and stabilization we could see that it is a Roman denarius

Fig. 8.1. The hull of *La Belle* exposed by archaeologists. They have removed the contents of the bow and stern areas. (Courtesy of James E. Bruseth)

dating to A.D. 69. Almost certainly, one of *La Belle*'s sailors had carried the coin as a good luck charm, and lost it one day in the hold of the ship.

Perhaps, then, it is not coincidence that a harsh winter storm churning through the Gulf of Mexico brought *La Belle* to rest on the bed of Matagorda Bay and made it a grave for the sailor whose remains we had excavated 310 years later. He captivated us, and we wondered who he was, what he looked like, and how he died. Our efforts to tell this one of *La Belle*'s many stories give you an idea of the task we face in the coming years. Conservators began by cleaning the skeleton. Working carefully and patiently, they found that tendon tissue survives on many of the sailor's bones, and even a large portion of his brain is intact. DNA samples from the brain may help us find the sailor's modern relatives living in France. Technicians at the Scottish Rite Hospital in Dallas created an incredibly detailed three-dimensional image of the sailor's skull. Another team used a new technique called stereolithography to create a model skull from the image. It matches the original in all its details, both interior and exterior. Denis Lee, a professor of medical and biological illustration at the University of Michigan, volunteered to reconstruct the sailor's face. He used the skull architecture and tissue measurements to model the face. In life, it surely bore the marks of pain from a broken nose, arthritis, lower back problems, and bad teeth, afflictions that had left

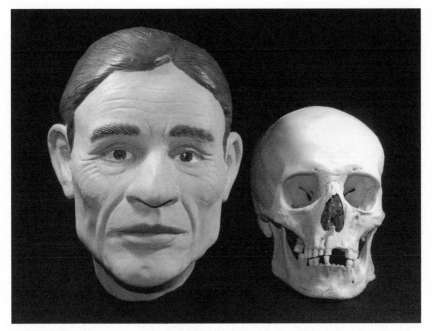

Fig. 8.2. Reconstruction of a sailor's face by Denis Lee. (Courtesy of James E. Bruseth)

their signatures on the sailor's skeleton. Nothing on his skeleton clearly indicates his cause of death, however. Unprepared to survive the Texas winter, he may have died from dehydration or hypothermia, or drowned as the ship went down. We may never know. But DNA testing and the possible clue to his identity scratched on the porringer found near his body may allow us to learn, finally, who he was.

When *La Belle* sank, large quantities of trade goods weighed down its hull, highlighting the great importance La Salle placed on interaction with Native Americans. He planned to trade for food and other goods to help his colony survive, and he also hoped to exchange trade items for furs and hides to send back to France and sell for profit. Other objects are giving great insights into what it took to establish a colony in the New World. Putting together the pieces from an archaeological time capsule like *La Belle* will take many years of patient work, and the expertise of many people.

9

Mining the West

R. Scott Baxter and Rebecca Allen

While some European explorers sailed west in search of a passage to the Orient and its riches, others sought the natural riches of the New World. By the late seventeenth century, mining technology allowed Europeans to exploit the natural resources here on a massive scale. The effects of this mining have permanently altered the American landscape. Nowhere are these changes more dramatic than on the mining frontier of the American West. Here miners adapted their technology and lifestyle to the arid conditions of the Great Basin and Mojave Desert, the mountainous regions of California and Colorado, and the arctic climate of Alaska. The remnants of mining still trail over much of the western landscape, where placer tailings, hydraulic cuts, dredge tailings, glory holes, pocket mining areas, systems of water conveyance with flumes and ditches, dams, ground sluices, machine pads, prospecting pits, tunnels, riffle plates, hydraulic nozzles, and other objects with unfamiliar names abound.

Historical archaeologists study the mines, the evolution of mining technologies, the lives of miners, and their relationship to the environment. Historical accounts document much about mining in the West, but these written accounts were limited to the literate. Much of what they wrote was promotional material, and greatly exaggerated the finds and technology of the time. Government records such as mining claims provided more realistic but brief descriptions of the land and improvements. What was written about the lives of miners is equally biased, seemingly focused on mining activities and alcohol consumption. Contemporaries found some topics, such as diet and health, too mundane to record. They found other activities, such as prostitution and drug use, distasteful, and thus frequently omitted them purposely from their accounts. The lives of some, including Native American, African American, Chinese, Mexican, illiterate European American, and women miners, were never well documented. Removed by time, technology, and culture, archaeologists can now look back at the material remains of this period through different eyes than the writers and historians of the past. We can see the changes in the landscape and the environmental consequences of mining,

Fig. 9.1. Modern view of the Freemont Mine near Amador City, California. (Courtesy of R. Scott Baxter.)

changes in mining technology, and the myriad ways miners adapted to work in the mines.

Studies of the miners can take several paths. At Silver Mountain City in Alpine County, California, archaeologists looked at the ways miners adapted to their isolated setting. A silver mining town established in 1863, Silver Mountain City sat seven thousand feet up the east slope of the Sierra Nevada. During much of the year, snow cut the town off from regular supply shipments. Archaeologists first created a detailed map of the town site with the aid of computerized survey instruments and mapping programs. These tools gave us a graphic display of the landscape features and artifacts left behind at Silver Mountain City. We found that the residents separated metals, primarily tin cans, from other domestic refuse. Analysis of the metal showed that the cans were regularly modified and reused for a variety of purposes, including as sieves and sorters for mining and as siding and shingles for houses and other buildings. Isolated from regular supply lines for much of the year, especially during winter storms, the miners turned to the materials at hand for dealing with day-to-day needs. The dumping of cans into separate dumps provided residents with a ready supply of sheet metal—and gave archaeologists important insights into how the residents of Silver Mountain City adapted to their environment.

Recently a University of Nevada Field School project took a more in-depth look at the miners living on one lot in Virginia City, Nevada. In the 1880s, O'Brien and Costello's Saloon and Shooting Gallery stood on the lot. Virginia City was established in the 1850s by miners in pursuit of gold and silver. It became the heart of the famous Comstock Lode, at its peak boasting a population of twenty thousand people. Situated in Virginia City's infamous Barbary Coast, O'Brien and Costello's primarily served a working-class clientele of Irish descent. The archaeologists sought answers to research questions about Irish ethnicity and consumer practices, including the potentially lethal combination of alcohol and firearms. Using a combination of heavy equipment to define site stratigraphy and careful hand excavation to separate materials from various layers, the archaeological team uncovered a variety of domestic and saloon-related materials.

An unexpected find was the more than three hundred cartridges recovered from the target-shooting gallery in the saloon. Most cartridges were of the same small caliber. Forensic analysis showed that only a handful of guns, probably small "gallery guns," fired the vast majority of the cartridges. Intermixed with these, the archaeologists found a variety of cartridges that had obviously been fired from other firearms. Perhaps some saloon patrons wished to demonstrate their shooting prowess with their own guns. This information, by itself, does not seem of much consequence.

Taken in light of the history of the Irish clientele, however, the cartridges become more important. In Ireland the British government, fearing an armed uprising, had barred the Irish from owning firearms. British landowners consolidating large landholdings forced many Irish off their ancestral land at gunpoint. This dispossession left poor Irish families little choice except starvation or emigration, and many headed to the United States. As Britain's landed elite gained more wealth, they sought new pleasures. One such pleasure was a new form of entertainment, indoor target shooting. In the galleries and salons of their mansions, gentlemen could pass the time shooting small metal silhouettes with what became known as gallery guns. These special pistols and rifles fired small cartridges similar to those found at O'Brien and Costello's.

When the Irish arrived in the United States, they found a country much more open to the possession and use of firearms. As they moved further west, firearms became almost a necessity to put game on the table and for protection against two- and four-legged predators. Ultimately many Irish emigrants settled into the wild mining frontier at Virginia City. Here they found unprec-

1543 Drilling by Compressed Air.

Fig. 9.2. Posed photo of mining equipment, ca. 1900. (Postcard collection of R. Scott Baxter.)

edented wealth, and new ways of spending it. Some devoted their leisure time and money to sipping beer and shooting targets at O'Brien and Costello's. In the wilds of the American West, a firearm was merely a tool. The use of firearms at O'Brien and Costello's represented something much more. Here Irish immigrants could engage in a pastime once reserved for the gentry who forced them from their homes. The cartridges also indicate that at least some patrons owned firearms, which the imperial government had denied them at home. The firearm and target shooting became symbols of status and empowerment.

Some archaeologists, like Donald Hardesty of the University of Nevada at Reno, have focused their studies on the mining technologies developed by miners. Hardesty's work has shown the importance of interpreting archaeological mining remains in three-dimensional space. While a single ditch or pile of tailings conveys little information that cannot be gleaned from written records, examining the relationship of that ditch or tailings pile to other mining features on the landscape increases its research potential. Relationships among these features tell how each component functioned within the overall history of mining. Looking at each as part of a larger system helps us to better understand how mining technology developed over time within a particular mining district. By considering a single feature as part of a larger landscape rather than in isolation, we can learn more about the evolution of mining technology, water use, and transportation systems within western mining districts. Archaeologists and historians can also see how technological innovations affected the miners' lives.

Setting out to record a mining district, and to understand its various components, proves an exciting challenge for archaeologists, but it also fills them with trepidation. Many individual features of the landscape can, in and of themselves, become fascinating, but sometimes they distract us from the larger system. The complexity of the ties can at first glance be overwhelming. Such is the case at the New Almaden Quicksilver Mine in California. This mine produced enough quicksilver (mercury) to make mining for California's gold economically feasible. Prior to its discovery, miners had to import mercury from Europe. Without New Almaden, the Gold Rush would have developed very differently.

New Almaden covers about 2,400 acres. Native Americans and Mexicans first discovered and mined cinnabar there; the mercury mine operated from 1845 until 1972. The site is a National Historic Landmark District, and much has been written about its history. It even served as the backdrop for at least one fictional account. At its height in 1865, New Almaden had more than 700 buildings and 1,800 miners and town residents. Many mines, tunnels, and furnaces, as well as the settlements of Englishtown, Spanishtown, and the Hacienda, where the mining managers resided, spread across the landscape. In 1912 mining came to a halt, only to resurge in 1915, again during the depression of the 1930s, and finally after World War II. Archaeological study of the site promises to reveal much about the evolution of mining technology. But where to begin?

Historical maps, claim records, and newspaper accounts all indicate where we may find specific archaeological features. The town of New Almaden still exists, and many longtime residents have had oral and written traditions handed down to them over the years. They remember active mining at the New Almaden, or have parents, grandparents, and great-grandparents who were miners. Many were miners themselves, and they know the holdings of the local museum. The current task is to study the ground, study the archival record, and identify and interview local people. Our goal is to capture these various pieces of knowledge, order them into a chronology, locate them on a map, and link them with on-the-ground features. Future studies will focus on the miners, their families, and the development of mining technologies.

The larger landscape highlights the dramatic environmental consequences of mining. Early on, California recognized that mining activities could negatively affect the landscape. The Sawyer Decision of 1884 prohibited the dumping of debris into the Sacramento and San Joaquin Rivers and their tributaries. Previously, mud and gravel from hydraulic mining had clogged rivers and streams used for irrigating crops, choked orchards, flooded towns, and buried tilled fields. Other negative consequences, such as the poisonous effect of mercury on the land and the miners, were long understood, but as long as mining was profitable at New Almaden, it continued. After economic factors forced mining operations to cease in the 1970s, the County of Santa Clara and the federal government spent two decades and millions of dollars cleaning up the site. Together, the archaeology and the documents have demonstrated the consequences of a century of mining for mercury.

New Almaden is an extensive Hazardous Materials site. Mercury mining and refining left deposits of free-flowing mercury in the soils. The cleanup led to the study of the area's mining history, as the soils to be scooped up and hauled away contained the archaeological remains of historic mining activity. At many industrial sites, archaeologists encounter toxic substances. In this case it was mercury, but cyanide, lead, asbestos, petroleum products, and hydrogen sulfide gas are also commonly encountered at such sites. As a result, many state and federal agencies require archaeologists to become certified in dealing with hazardous materials in the field, and to develop a safety plan for coping with hazardous materials. The plan may simply call for avoiding certain areas or using the self-contained "space suits" familiar to sci-fi fans.

Other hazards at New Almaden include the many open shafts and adits left behind by the miners, which present a serious danger to anyone entering them today. Most of these openings were systematically sealed in the 1980s to keep the public safe from their many dangers, but some remain.

These examples demonstrate how historical archaeologists' studies of mining in the West offer insight into the development of an industry and a people during periods of great change. These studies also promise glimpses of how miners adapted their lifestyles and technologies to different environments, and how they ultimately shaped those environments. Both of these topics hold relevance as we ponder a world whose resources no longer seem limitless. We must understand the past and future consequences of exploiting our natural resources.

Part 3

Building Cities

Tales of Many Cities

Lu Ann De Cunzo

In the aftermath of the terrorist attacks of September 11, 2001, people around the world have seen both the vulnerability and the resiliency of Americans and our cities. The damage inflicted on these centers of American economic and military power, the World Trade Center and the Pentagon, was both deeply symbolic and horrifyingly real. Images of that day are burned into our memories: the airliners crashing into the Trade Center towers, turning them into balls of fire, the towers' collapse, the dust and smoke clouds, the fleeing people, and the exhausted yet tireless rescuers. In the end, as is always the case in such disasters, we remember the images and stories of people—those who perpetrated the horror, those who did not survive and those who loved them, and all those who reached out to help coworkers, neighbors, and strangers. The urban archaeologists who tell their cities' stories in this section have always known that it is the stories of the people, in the past and in the present, that matter.

Cities across North America have sponsored urban archaeology programs built on partnerships among archaeologists, preservationists, planners, and the public. The programs highlighted here have themselves made history. All thrive on innovation and cooperation among government agencies, museums, universities, corporations, and nonprofit organizations to achieve what any one group never could alone. William Moss directs the city archaeology program in Quebec, Canada. The United Nations has honored the city's distinctive historical character by designating Quebec the only World Heritage City in North America. In New York, archaeologists like Diana Wall and Nan Rothschild have devoted their careers to the archaeology of one of the world's largest, most dynamic, and most complex cities. In the shadow of the United States capital, Alexandrians pioneered the concept of "community archaeology" in Virginia, where Pamela Cressey and her team have created a model citywide program. In South Carolina, the Charleston Museum houses the city archaeology program in this gem of the American South. Martha Zierden writes of their efforts to leaven our image of southern elegance and gracious antebellum life with a heavy dose of the daily realities shaping southern urban living. At the other end of the transcontinental railroad in California, Mary Praetzellis and the team at the Anthropological Studies Center at Sonoma State University met the challenge of a single archaeological project in West Oakland that encompassed forty-three city blocks!

Programs in other North American cities have also helped change the face of historical archaeology, as we realized that the cities' past has survived buried beneath the present. Roberta Greenwood has introduced us to historical archaeology in Los Angeles; Kathleen Deagan has directed the important projects at Fort Mose and many other locations in St. Augustine, Florida; Virginia archaeologists have probed beneath the surfaces of Jamestown and Williamsburg since the 1930s; and John Cotter led field schools to train a host of budding archaeologists in another colonial capital, Philadelphia. The list goes on. In Montreal, Canada, the Pointe-à-Callière history and archaeology museum uses virtual technology, original artifacts, and uncovered landscapes and building remains to bring the city's past to life. For more than two decades, University of Maryland archaeologists working with Historic Annapolis, Inc., have explored another colonial capital city—Annapolis, Maryland. They have used archaeology to expose the powerful economic control and racism that made possible the elegant townhouses and elaborate gardens visitors admire today. The National Park Service has sponsored large-scale excavations in industrial Lowell, Massachusetts, and Harpers Ferry, West Virginia. Both have revealed much about working people's struggles against discriminatory work practices and deteriorating living conditions. They help us see the costs immigrants and natives alike paid as our industrial economy became established, and the ways shared interests supported an emerging consciousness of a working class.

Studying single city lots and entire neighborhoods, archaeologists in all these cities and others are piecing together the stories of individuals and families making their way in the urban environment. They are learning about what survives the continual process of building and rebuilding cities. They are learning about people trying new technologies to *make* land so the city can keep growing. They are learning how and why archaeologists should study landfill. They are learning fascinating things from people's garbage. They are learning about pollution and diseases in cramped urban settings. They are learning about transporting people and goods. They are learning about how people built their economic and social order onto the land. They are learning about the cityscapes and yardscapes people make as they live and work. They are learning how and why people create images of the past that contrast with reality. And they are using what they learn to help create livable places for the present, inspired by that history—the good, the bad, and the ugly.

10

Quebec City, Canada

William Moss

When Samuel de Champlain founded an outpost in 1608 at the narrowing of the St. Lawrence River known to native Algonkians as Kebec, he envisioned the creation of a city to be called Ludovica. Ludovica never came to be, at least not as Champlain imagined it, but Quebec would grow into one of the major cities on the North American continent. Quebec was the capital of New France and, following the independence of England's American colonies, the capital of British North America. The city would become the capital of Lower Canada and finally of the Province of Quebec. Situated at the strategic entrance to the Great Lakes' watershed, Quebec has been fortified since its foundation and, until the beginning of the railroad era, was a major port. Indeed, in 1830 Quebec was the third most important port on the continent, after New York and New Orleans. Champlain recognized the strategic importance of the city he founded, but he would be amazed to see how his frontier post changed over time. The inclusion of the city on UNESCO's list of World Heritage Sites in 1985 would not have been the least of his surprises.

Looking back over the city's past from the vantage point of the twenty-first century is no less a source of wonder. Major geographical features such as the Upper Town plateau, surrounded by steep and sheer cliffs, and the Lower Town plains along the St. Lawrence and its tributary, the St. Charles, still distinguish the city. Yet the urban landscape has undergone many changes. Diverse people, institutions, and events have altered the landscape and inscribed it with history. Archaeologists working in Quebec since the 1970s have helped people understand the physical and cultural processes intertwined throughout the city's history. We archaeologists, particularly the city's research team, have investigated dozens of sites that have come up for development, reconstruction, or landscaping. These sites have opened windows on seventeenth-century urban development, on eighteenth- and nineteenth-century suburbs, on merchants' and military officers' households, on shipbuilding, tanneries, and potteries, on port and fortification works erected during the French and British colonial régimes. Sometimes we have made spectacular discoveries, more often we have pieced together new insights, but always our results speak of the city and its people.

The case of Louis Hébert's farmstead combines both spectacular discoveries and subtle insights in a story that is still unfolding. It also illustrates how the city and its partners incorporate archaeology into the development process.

Champlain founded Quebec with a handful of hired men as the center of French trade on the St. Lawrence River. The population grew slowly in New France, particularly as immigration was restricted until the advent of royal government in 1663. Louis Hébert began the first farmstead in the new colony in 1617 on the Upper Town plateau, in the future heart of the historic district. Traditional histories identify Hébert, an apothecary by trade, as the colony's first farmer. Seventy people inhabited Quebec in 1629 when British pirates captured the town. Hébert had died in 1627, but his survivors—his widow, Marie Rollet, his son Guillaume, his daughters Anne and Guillemette, and Guillemette's husband, Guillaume Couillard—were among the few French settlers to stay in Quebec during the three-year English occupation. By 1663, despite a population of only 750 souls, Quebec had all the features of an urban center at the heart of a colonial empire. In 1666 Guillemette Hébert ceded the farmstead, now a feudal seigneury, to Quebec's first bishop, François de Laval, who began construction of the Séminaire de Québec nine years later. These actions bear witness to the new and urbane status of the town. The Séminaire still exists as a teaching institution, and the complex has matured into one of the city's major architectural treasures.

In the 1990s the Séminaire de Québec and the Musée de la Nouvelle-France, an occupant of the now extensive architectural complex, called in the city's archaeological team in advance of adding underground wings to the buildings. As extensive landscaping and construction had occurred within the complex over the centuries, even as recently as the early 1980s, we doubted that any elements of archaeological importance could remain. The project's promoters and the city's partner, the province's Culture and Communications Department, nonetheless agreed to carry out exploratory excavations in light of the site's rich history. All—even archaeologists—were astounded to discover the vestiges of New France's first farmstead just a few centimeters below the surface of a yard where successive generations of students have contemplated, played handball, skated on winter ice, thrown marbles, or traded cards.

The amazing finds would require the collaboration of historical archaeologists, prehistorians, historians, and specialists in historic objects and past environments, plants, animals, insects, and parasites to unravel their mean-

Fig. 10.1. The Séminaire de Québec, a teaching establishment since 1666, in the middle of the Old Town Historic District, listed as a UNESCO World Heritage Site in 1985. (Courtesy of Pierre Lahoud.)

ing and full significance. The combined work of these specialists tells the story of Quebec City's passage from a trading post to an urban center during the first decades of French rule on the North American continent.

Archaeologists excavated only a part of what we believe to be Louis Hébert's manor house. We knew little about this building apart from its general location and its state of repair in 1639. Historians found a notarized document describing the state of ruin of the building when Couillard had it inspected. According to the contractors who evaluated the building, "the repairs to the house would cost more than constructing a new one." We also know that the house had disappeared from the landscape by the time a city plan was drawn in 1670. As the contemporary landscape suggested that several feet of soil had been removed during previous work, we had little hope that any vestiges would remain.

Following test pitting and core sampling over a large one-meter grid, archaeologist Daniel Simoneau uncovered part of a house wall with several floorboards on the inside and the base of a circular stone structure on the outside. We knew of no other buildings in the area, but how could we identify these features with any certainty? Several courses of investigation provided our answer. The first clue came from the form and the presumed function of the construction. No aboveground circular structures of this type and date have been found in Quebec. Manor houses in the west of France, however, have similar structures serving as pigeon houses, and the prerogative of building one was reserved to seigneurial lords. As Hébert was declared a seigneur in 1623, he could have added one to his manor house, however humble it may have been.

The relative date of the structure lends further support to our preliminary identification. Soil samples from a layer of fine sediments covering the structure contained small snail shells. Their analysis indicated that a pool of stagnant water had formed over the crumbled masonry and that it had stood there long enough for soil to accumulate naturally. We know that this happened before the 1670 plan was drawn. A 1685 map furnishes our last clue, and the only trace of human activity on this part of the Séminaire complex apparent in archival sources. The map shows a rather indistinct form at the spot where archaeologists had unearthed the abandoned masonry. The form has a very intriguing shape in light of the other evidence: it is a rectangle, approximately twelve by twenty-five feet, oriented in the same manner as the archaeological remains. An extension disrupts the rectangular form on the northeast side. The shape on the map and the shape of the building left in ruins in the mid-seventeenth century correspond, suggesting that the ruins were left to decay for at least twenty years.

A stone's throw away from the manor house, archaeologists found traces of an early roadway that crossed the Hébert property heading toward the Récollet monastery along the St. Charles River. The roadway disappeared when a regular town plan was developed beginning in 1636. This discovery helped us to reconstruct the early town landscape, which began changing dramatically in the late 1630s. The roadway linked the manor house to that of Hébert's daughter Guillemette and her husband, Guillaume Couillard, built before 1621.

Archaeologists discovered remains of the Couillards' house, a two-room timber and daub structure with a central fireplace, under levels left by use of the main courtyard after construction of the Séminaire. Coins minted in the late sixteenth and early seventeenth centuries confirm the house's date. One coin was struck between 1574 and 1589, perhaps in Toulouse, whereas two others were minted in 1640 and 1643. According to material culture analyst Céline Cloutier, other artifacts also fit the 1620–60 period, including scissors, pins, thimbles, buttons, combs, and sundry personal effects of the building's residents.

One find was surprising, though. Large numbers of trade beads suggest that Hébert and Couillard drew a part of their income from the very lucrative

Fig. 10.2. Domestic artifacts, coins, and trade beads from the seventeenth-century Couillard house. (Courtesy of Brigitte Ostiguy.)

fur trade. This is all the more surprising as their participation was explicitly forbidden by the royal charter to companies holding the trade monopoly in New France. The picture painted by these finds is also at odds with that presented by traditional histories. Inspired by nineteenth-century ideals, they portray Hébert and Couillard as noble farmers and glorify their agricultural vocation. Though a statue erected in their honor in a nearby city park in 1918 portrays the two as pioneer farmers, the presence of father and son-in-law and their success in the colony may be due in no small part to an illicit stake in black-market fur trading!

Soil samples from the Séminaire complex and neighboring parts of the Old Town show that Hébert didn't settle on the best land for farming: though relatively flat and well drained, the soil is poorly suited to seventeenth-century agriculture. No archaeological evidence yet confirms that they grew crops here, though we know that Hébert did supply the small settlement with fresh vegetables and medicinal plants. Nonetheless, Hébert's choice of this property isn't surprising, as Champlain projected building a city on the St. Charles River's plain. His town plan placed farmsteads on the Upper Town plateau and the Monastère des Récollets at the heart of Lower Town's Ludovica. Following Champlain's death in 1635, exactly the opposite happened! It wasn't until the mid-nineteenth century that the city spread into the area initially identified for Ludovica, whereas the Upper Town became the seat of convents, monasteries, and colleges from 1639 until the end of the seventeenth century. Most of these still exist today. The land grants and subsequent building on these properties eradicated the first town layout done by Champlain. Indeed, virtually no elements exist of the landscape dating before the first plan of the Upper Town, presumably drawn in 1636. The only concrete traces of the early years of the city survive in the archaeological record.

Although original land surfaces and drainage patterns have long since disappeared, core sampling on different parts of the site have allowed us to reconstruct the landscape when Europeans first began exploiting this new environment. The highly organized built environment of today's city core then consisted of a series of natural terraces with a general slope toward the St. Charles River. Early French settlers continued native people's use of the plateau around a spring near Couillard's house. The spring later fed into a cistern holding water reserves for fighting fires.

Using historical maps, archaeologists followed the spring both uphill and downstream as well as through the lives of the area's inhabitants. The spring had its source on the heights where the citadel was built starting in 1831. It flowed past the Monastère des Ursulines, constructed in 1639, and the Collège des Jésuites, built in 1648, before flowing through a cemetery serving the Cathédrale Notre-Dame from 1691 to 1854. The spring filled the cistern in the center of the Séminaire courtyard, then ran into a well in the kitchens. Knowing that drinking water flowed through a cemetery only yards away is astounding in the twenty-first century, but we must remember that the causes of contagious disease were simply unknown at the time. This macabre discovery makes it easier to understand why major epidemics struck the city regularly, almost every ten years, killing hundreds of people at a time.

Stone marbles, tops, bone gaming pieces, buckles, and buttons found in the upper levels of the site tell of the presence of the Séminaire's young students. Three centuries of youths had walked and played over the vestiges of New France's first farmstead without wondering what lay just below their feet. All in all, the surprising quantity of artifacts and the excellent state of conservation of architectural and other remains indicate that this is indeed a rich site.

Fig. 10.3. Students in the Séminaire courtyard in 1890, walking over the site of the Couillard house. (Courtesy of Archives Nationales du Québec à Québec.)

Archaeologists promptly backfilled the structures uncovered in the 1990s with fine sand. We haven't yet fully excavated the site, but we have protected it until we can explore its full potential. Waiting patiently for new research opportunities to occur is also a part of contemporary urban archaeology! More important, this research has shed new light on this most fascinating period. The unexpected discovery of an archaeological jewel beneath an architectural gem is only one example of why UNESCO has recognized Quebec City, the birthplace of French civilization in North America, as a World Heritage treasure.

11

New York City

Diana diZerega Wall and Nan A. Rothschild

Just as historical archaeologists have charted the changing relationships of Québecois to their environment as Quebec grew and people put land to different uses, archaeologists working in other cities have also studied aspects of urban growth. In New York, as in most cities, the gathering of archaeological information has depended greatly on the vagaries of modern development: where the next new office building was going to be built and whether there would be support for archaeological examination prior to construction. What has emerged is a series of snapshots, or windows into different parts of the city over time, which when put together provide insight into the place that became New York.

The city's natural setting played an important role in both its original European settlement and its ultimate transformation into a world-class city. The Dutch claimed New Netherland in the early seventeenth century because of the money they hoped to make in the fur trade there. They traded with Native Americans near today's Albany, about 150 miles up the Hudson River. The Dutch settled New Amsterdam at the mouth of the river both to protect this trade from European competitors and to serve as a port for the oceangoing vessels that would take the furs to the Netherlands. Its site was one of the finest natural ports in North America for ships in use from the seventeenth through the mid-twentieth centuries. Prior to the mid-nineteenth century, the port was located on the East River, which rarely froze over in winter, and the mass of Manhattan Island protected the smaller wooden ships from the harsh westerly winds that threatened them.

With the English conquest in 1664, New Amsterdam became New York. Toward the end of the century, the fur trade waned, but the city continued to serve as an entrepôt. Local agricultural produce was shipped out to the English colonies in the Caribbean to provision plantations there. In 1825 the Erie Canal linked the city by an inexpensive water transport route to the interior of the continent. The completion of the canal allowed the city to seize control of the country's international and domestic trade. New York, with its busy port, became a metropolis, the largest city in the nation, a position it has retained for almost two centuries. In the mid-nineteenth century, the port shifted to the Hudson River on the west side of the island, where water was deep enough for the larger, sturdier ships that had become common.

Archaeologists have looked at several aspects of the city's changing environment—changes both in the infrastructure of its port and in its cultural landscape—that accompanied the transformation from colonial outpost to world metropolis. One characteristic of many modern cities, including Philadelphia, Boston, and New York as well as London and Tokyo, is that they run out of land, and so begin the process of landfilling: claiming land from adjacent bodies of water. Landfilling began in New York in the 1670s and has continued ever since. Archaeologists have excavated both fast land sites and landfill sites in New York.

Modern archaeology in New York City began in 1979 when the authors worked together in directing the city's first large-scale excavation on the block where New York's first city hall—the Dutch Stadt Huys—had stood in the seventeenth century. The block lay on fast land along what had been the East River shore until the addition of three blocks of landfill turned it into an inland site. This excavation became the test case for archaeology in New York. The big question was whether any important archaeological remains could possibly survive at the site after 350 years of development and redevelopment in the Wall Street district, one of the most heavily urbanized parts of the world. Fortunately for the future of archaeology in New York (and much to our relief), we found not only two tons of artifacts dating from the seventeenth through the nineteenth centuries but the foundation walls and artifacts from the King's House Tavern. Francis Lovelace, the second governor of the English province of New York, had ordered the tavern built in 1670, and in the 1690s it had served as a temporary city hall.

Excavations in landfill are different from those on fast land. In New York City landfill sites, archaeologists have discovered clear evidence of what was involved in making land: finding the fill, holding it in place, and building on it. The first large-scale landfill excavations took place at 7 Hanover Square, one of the city's earliest blocks of made land, between today's Pearl and Water Streets. When the authors directed the excavations there in 1981 along with Arnold Pickman, we knew the land makers had to make provisions both to hold the landfill in place so it would not wash away and to support the new buildings as the landfill on the block settled. However, we didn't know how people had done this in seventeenth-century New York. As the crew excavated, they began to uncover old stone walls in unexpected places across the site. Ultimately we realized that these walls formed the foundations of the first set of buildings on the block. The seventeenth-century builders laid these

Fig. 11.1. Seventeenth-century walls exposed at 7 Hanover Square. Robert Livingston built the large house at the bottom of the image, while his Dutch neighbors built the smaller ones toward the top. (Courtesy of Columbia University, Department of Anthropology, William Duncan Strong Museum.)

Fig. 11.2. Backhoe uncovering the bulkhead complex at the Assay site. (Courtesy of South Street Seaport Museum, New York.)

walls on the old beach, using them both to hold the landfill in place and to support the weight of the buildings. One was the home of Robert Livingston, a wealthy Scots merchant who lived on Pearl Street. Livingston built his house on two city lots with its broad side facing the street; he used the grandeur of his home to impress his friends. Next door, seven Dutch families built their more modest houses with their stepped-gable ends facing the street; the Dutch in New Amsterdam were more interested in accumulating movable wealth, and did not invest heavily in their houses. The excavations showed they built their homes cooperatively, with one common rear wall shared by all the houses.

In the eighteenth century, landfilling became a more complex process. The blocks lay further out from the original shore, in deeper water, and required a different technology to hold the fill in place. The row of blocks between Front and South Streets were the last filled on the East River. Roselle Henn and Diana Wall led excavations at one of these blocks in 1984. A 1797 map showed that the block was only three-quarters filled that year. It guided the search for the bulkheads that held the fill in place. We knew that archaeology provided the only way we could discover how the bulkheads were built: there are no plans or how-to books for building in the eighteenth century. We found the log bulkheads and uncovered them with backhoes. Ultimately we uncovered and recorded the construction of more than a hundred linear feet of fill-retaining structures all the way down to the river bottom. We also excavated down inside the bulkheads to document their interior construction.

At the 175 Water Street site, archaeologists directed by Joan Geismar discovered an unusual solution to the problem of holding the landfill in place. Her crew found an entire ship embedded in the landfill on the water side of the block. In the eighteenth century, when the land was being made there, several people on the block got together, found a ship that was no longer functional, stripped it, and scuttled it to form part of the bulkhead chain to hold the new fill in place. Holes left by boreworms native to the Caribbean riddled the ship's hull, showing that the vessel had been active in the West Indian trade that was so important to the economy of eighteenth-century New York. The crew measured and photographed the ship to record how it was built—information not available from any other source. Then, since conserving a wooden object as large as the ship was prohibitively expensive, they removed only the bow for preservation; it now resides in the Mariners' Museum in Newport News, Virginia. The rest of the ship was also removed but, ironically, dumped unceremoniously in the modern-day landfill on Staten Island, the resting place of much of New York City's modern garbage.

During the nineteenth and twentieth centuries, New Yorkers concentrated their land-making efforts on the Hudson River side of Manhattan as well as in the other boroughs. And New Yorkers will continue to make land as long as they need more of it for expansion. In the process, they will remake their city and its environment, as their predecessors have done for more than three centuries.

New Yorkers have also transformed the city's cultural geography over the last four centuries. During the seventeenth and early eighteenth centuries, the city was a tiny "walking city": people walked from place to place and could cross the city in a half an hour. Business proprietors lived with their families in homes that were also workplaces, and those who worked for them—whether domestic help, apprentices, journeymen, or the enslaved—lived with them. People shopped at markets along the East River and attended churches that were never more than a few blocks from their homes. To meet their daily needs, they relied on the products made by carpenters, masons, bakers, and silversmiths, as well as on the labor of enslaved Africans.

The ethnic identity of New York's residents has always influenced the city's social geography. In the seventeenth and early eighteenth centuries, Dutch and English residents tended to cluster in different neighborhoods. Later on, as ethnic identity became less important for members of these

Fig. 11.3. Archaeologists recording the eighteenth-century ship they discovered at the 175 Water Street site. (Courtesy of South Street Seaport Museum, New York.)

groups, they tended to integrate spatially both with each other and with the members of other groups. But this did not mean that the city became ethnically homogeneous. As new immigrants arrived, they formed their own ethnic enclaves, dispersing only when they had become successfully adapted to their new land. Some groups did not follow this pattern, particularly those assigned an inferior status, who were subjected to social and economic discrimination.

During the eighteenth century, enslaved New Yorkers of African descent made up around a fifth of the city's population; in 1703, 40 percent of the city's households included enslaved people. Although these New Yorkers did not live in separate enclaves—they had to live in the garrets or cellars of their owners' homes—when they died, they were buried in a separate cemetery. Their marginal place in the social fabric of the city was expressed in the location of their cemetery, the African Burial Ground, at the edge of the city.

When archaeologists tested the site before construction of an office tower in 1991, they thought that later construction had destroyed the burial ground: there had been nineteenth- and twentieth-century buildings with very deep basements on the site. But once they started digging, they learned that the burial ground lay preserved under about twenty feet of early-nineteenth-century landfill. The archaeologists discovered and excavated more than four hundred bodies there. Members of the local African American community became extremely active in determining the project's direction. Their fight both to stop the excavations and to ensure that an African American perspective would be incorporated into the interpretation of their ancestors' lives was ultimately successful.

Physical anthropologist Michael Blakey, then at Howard University, led the team that studied the African Burial Ground. They have gleaned a lot from the burials about the experience of enslaved Africans in the colonial city. The human remains provide direct evidence of the enormous physical stress in their lives as well as of their roots in west and central Africa. The burial ground has provided palpable testimony of the African presence in early New York, a presence that has been largely ignored.

In the early nineteenth century New York underwent a transformation. There was a general reorganization of the city's space as people from different socioeconomic classes began to move their homes away from their work-places and live in separate residential neighborhoods. Some wealthier families moved to new suburbs in Greenwich Village and Brooklyn. The Robsons, for example, decided to move away from what had become the business district to a house overlooking Washington Square. From there Benjamin Robson and his son-in-law Francis Sage, who lived next door, commuted downtown to work on the omnibuses introduced to meet the needs of these new commuters. Their wives and other middle-class women who had worked in family businesses now stayed at home, defining a set of activities appropriate to women as managers of their homes and families.

Archaeologists led by Bert Salwen and Arnold Pickman found dishes in the privy in the Robsons' backyard. Similar to those used by other suburban families in Greenwich Village and Brooklyn, the dishes attest to these new roles for women. Eliza Robson used plain white dinner plates in the Gothic style, which underlined her role as the guardian of family morals. But she also used a fancy gilt-decorated white porcelain tea set to entertain her friends and proclaim her family's social position to the world; this would be important in finding appropriate spouses for her children and employment for her sons.

Working-class neighborhoods developed closer to the city downtown, so that their residents, who could not afford to commute by omnibus, could walk to work. Not until the 1990s did archaeologists get the opportunity to study the lives of the poor, when the vagaries of modern development led to construction in other parts of the city. One particularly important site was located in New York City's most notorious nineteenth-century slum, the Five Points, the neighborhood memorialized by Martin Scorcese in his film *The Gangs of New York*. Charles Dickens described it vividly in the 1830s: "Poverty, wretchedness, and vice, are rife enough where we are going now. This is the place: these narrow ways, diverging to the right and left, and reeking everywhere with dirt and filth. Debauchery has made the very houses prematurely old." Edward Rutsch and Leonard Bianchi directed the excavation of this site, and Rebecca Yamin directed the analysis of the finds. The archaeology shows that many residents of the block at this time led lives that were in some ways quite similar to middle-class urban dwellers. The people in one tenement used dishes and serving pieces that matched those used in middle-class homes. They also owned a lot of glassware, including an unusual square bowl with a lacy design made in New England, and numerous cut decanters. The tenants ate imported condiments, cured their ailments with patent medicines, and saved their pennies in a redware bank. Unfortunately, the artifacts from the Five Points Site were stored at the World Trade Center when the terrorists struck, and almost the entire collection was lost.

Naturally, it would be ideal if archaeologists working in New York could choose their sites because of the research questions they want to answer. But even though they have to use an opportunistic approach and take advantage of plans for modern development to be able to dig, the study of New York City has provided insight into the lives of many different kinds of people who have contributed to the city's history. We hope that, as time goes by, we can apply new and more sophisticated techniques to these sites, so that we can learn more about the lives of the people here and how they adapted to and modified their urban environment.

12

Community Archaeology in Alexandria, Virginia

Pamela J. Cressey

In 2001 the city of Alexandria celebrated its fortieth archaeological anniversary. Driven by the community's commitment to preserve buildings, trees, sites, landscapes, and buried artifacts, Alexandria has developed a special relationship with archaeology. It has been my good fortune to serve as city archaeologist for twenty-five years in this fourteen-square-mile town along the Potomac River in the Washington, D.C., metro area. My colleagues and I work with the City Council–appointed Alexandria Archaeological Commission, the nonprofit Friends of Alexandria Archaeology, and some one hundred to two hundred volunteers annually. Together we are the brains, brawn, precision, and heart that daily create Alexandria Archaeology.

After the early excavation and reconstruction of Fort Ward Civil War Site in 1961—brought about by one Alexandria woman—others in town perceived the need for archaeology as urban renewal progressed in the National Historic District. The community through its city council adopted a resolution in 1975 for a full-service archaeological program, and the United States' first community archaeology program was born. From the outset our program had multiple goals: To Search, To Study, and To Share. The community members who interviewed me in 1977 outlined these goals, more holistic in many ways than those guiding most archaeological work at the time. Our goal as community archaeologists is to discover the hidden history under our parking lots, wooded terraces, and backyards, and bring it alive to citizens and visitors today.

Since the 1970s our team at Alexandria Archaeology has studied the city's main street and waterfront, explored Quakers' roles as community leaders, and investigated the development of African American neighborhoods. We have learned a stunning amount about topics as diverse as death and burial practices, sugar refining and trade, canal and wharf construction, pottery manufacture, and public works. In the process, our excavations have yielded more than two million artifacts dating as far back as ten thousand years ago.

Volunteers have been the heart and hands of Alexandria Archaeology

Fig. 12.1. Bill Tabor, a member of the Alexandria Archaeological Commission, and son Emmett, pausing to read about the archaeology of the waterfront, one segment of the 23-mile walking and biking Alexandria Heritage Trail. (Courtesy of Alexandria Archaeology)

since its inception. They have contributed more than seven thousand hours of time each year excavating, cataloging, and illustrating artifacts, studying documents, writing papers, giving site tours, and entering data into computers. Adele Dunne, one of our volunteers, has stated:

> I think the community-based archaeology program in Alexandria exists primarily as the result of the exceptionally deep pride that Alexandrians have in their city's unique history and their willingness to become involved in protecting it. Many of our digs have been as a result of private citizens or businesses realizing that they have a "history book" buried in their back yard or under their front parking lots, and wanting to actively participate in reading, interpreting and preserving the pages for future generations. I strongly believe that Alexandria Archaeology has been shaped by a very pro-active public and wouldn't exist without it.

Alexandria Archaeology has enriched our community in many ways. The energy and enthusiasm of the professional-public partnership has rippled throughout the city and generated new museums, school curricula, and neighborhood histories. We have formed a wonderful partnership with the city's art community. The Alexandria Archaeology Museum is situated in the Torpedo Factory Art Center, a living art experience with galleries, an art school for all ages, and 165 working artists in separate studios. Our museum functions as one of these studios—a glass-enclosed living laboratory in which we do our archaeological work.

Let me give another example. Early in Alexandria Archaeology's history, the question arose: "Why not find and register the Alexandria Canal Tide Lock?" Our response was "Okay, let's do it." That simple act of archaeology led to more community questions and responses that spun out beyond our program in many directions. Our team located and registered the canal lock, then excavated and reconstructed it as part of a waterfront legal settlement. Through private developers and civic meetings, the tide lock canal area was designated a park. The process worked because the public demanded access to the waterfront. A new city policy has assured public access to other parts of the Potomac as redevelopment occurred over the last twenty years. Today Alexandria features several waterfront parks with historic themes and markers that help people understand and enjoy the special environment of our port city.

Fig. 12.2. Family Dig Day, when families join Alexandria's city archaeologists and volunteers in discovering artifacts in screens after scientific excavations. Educators discuss with the public the history of the site, the meaning of material culture, and the stewardship of archaeological resources. (Courtesy of Alexandria Archaeology)

Another striking example involved the chair of the Alexandria Archaeo-logical Commission, Ben Brenman, also a member of an ad hoc task force planning an African American memorial. He knew of our archaeological work on an abandoned black cemetery, slated to become the site of a home-less shelter in a large proposed development. Ben's intervention provoked an amazing proposal. By bringing the site to the attention of the task force, he spearheaded a plan to create a commemorative park around this cemetery—all donated to the city at the developer's expense. The archaeology resulted in the Alexandria African American Heritage Park. Designed by landscape ar-chitects to the specifications of the task force, the park blends history and nature, offers a reflective place for personal meditation, and memorializes African American leaders and those buried in the cemetery. I would never in my wildest dreams have imagined such a transformation of this place, from the debris-covered fallen tombstone sitting in the wetlands that I saw on my first visit, to a park that mirrors a people's inner sense of history. The place and the people are protected and now add to our landscape. The community conceived and dedicated this place as theirs.

Most recently, our commission and friends group have worked together on the Alexandria Heritage Trail. The trail links archaeological sites in town and leaves something aboveground, rather than always mining artifacts and putting them in storage. One of our volunteers, Chan Mohney, saw the po-tential for people to ride around town to see archaeological sites, and started to offer an archaeological bike tour. That got us excited, and soon the Tour de Digs was developed and designated in 2000 as a Millennium Trail. People can walk, bike, skate, or drive through nine thousand years of human history using twenty-two miles of city-designated bike trails. The tours broaden archaeology's appeal to those who love to discover history and nature out of doors, and they meet our goal of making historic places—not just the arti-fact—important.

Children have a special place with Alexandria Archaeology, because they will soon hold in their hands the responsibility to preserve our city's heritage. We have worked with teachers to create a program joining classroom archae-ology with experience in the archaeology lab and in the field. Classroom activities like "Trash Can Archaeology" and "Who Am I?" help students explore how archaeologists learn about people and their culture. Adventure Lessons draw on excavations across the city, like those at an early nineteenth-century sugar refinery and in the Hayti neighborhood, settled by free African Americans in the 1830s. They teach archaeological stewardship. They get students thinking and talking about issues important to their future. In the process, young Alexandrians find that issues such as racism, free enterprise, and the impacts of industry on our environment have a long history in the city.

We invite everyone to work and learn with us in the Alexandria Archaeology Adventure so we can touch our pasts as individuals with a collective spirit and truly democratize our history. We "Hold the Past in Trust" for each of us to appreciate and express in our own way. We call this community archaeology.

13

Urban Life in Colonial Charleston, South Carolina

Martha Zierden

"Oh, I see that stuff in my driveway all the time. We don't need to hire anyone to dig it up!" So stated a Charleston preservationist in the early 1980s, in response to a proposal for an archaeological dig prior to construction. Twenty years later, the Historic Charleston Foundation requires archaeological research prior to any construction or renovation on the hundreds of properties it protects through easements. What has changed? And how has archaeology changed the story of Charleston's past, for residents as well as visitors? In Charleston, community archaeology has taken on its own unique form.

Charleston began in 1670 as a frontier city and quickly rose to prominence as the economic and social center of a wildly successful plantation system. Beginning about 1750, some white residents and investors made fortunes from rice and cotton grown by black bondsmen. They spent this money on material goods and social events that proclaimed their status. Then the city's fortunes declined with the Civil War and emancipation, and Charleston spent most of the last 150 years in economic stagnation. Today the city is once again booming, driven by a successful tourism industry and the desirability of coastal living to new residents and visitors alike. Both new development and renovation of historic buildings have prompted archaeological work.

Urban archaeology arrived in Charleston in the early 1970s, about ten years before I did, at a time when the discipline was beginning to make inroads into other American cities like Alexandria. Urban planners, preservation administrators, and field archaeologists alike came to realize that archaeological remains could lie hidden beneath pavement and buildings as well as beneath cornfields. This, plus federal grants for urban renewal and infrastructure, brought archaeologists, with their field and analytical tools, to the city. In Charleston we expected archaeology to give us a view into the rigors of daily life for colonial and antebellum urban dwellers. How did these people feed, clothe, and maintain themselves when confronted with the issues

Fig. 13.1. Excavations on the north side of Charleston's Powder Magazine, which was constructed in 1712. (Collections of the Charleston Museum.)

particular to the city: population density, the close proximity of residences, commercial buildings, and even industries, and the increased availability of consumer goods? We also believed archaeology is a fruitful avenue to study *all* urban dwellers, not just those wealthy and powerful enough to leave a legacy of documents, houses, gardens, and heirlooms.

A decade of small projects at construction sites in Charleston culminated in 1980 with construction of Charleston Place, a hotel/convention center covering an entire city block. Salvage excavations by the Charleston Museum followed research by Nick Honerkamp of the University of Tennessee–Chattanooga. We found the artifact deposits and soil layers of the city overwhelming. Here were ceramics, glass, tobacco pipes, toys, and animal bones from nearly three centuries of life on the block. Some lay discarded in broad soil layers we call zones, but residents had shoved other refuse into large pits such as abandoned wells, privies, and building foundations, collectively called features. Some of the refuse was concentrated in layers that we could relate to a single household on the block, but other soil layers were clearly moved about, used to fill and level the block. The trash in these layers belonged not to a single documented family but to a large, anonymous group of urban residents. Recovery of such deposits, particularly in deeply filled waterfront areas or other city dumps, prompted a debate with archaeologists in New York City, Alexandria, and all across the continent over just what we could learn from them. It would take the advantage of hindsight to see that both types of deposits were part of the archaeological record of urban life. And we had to learn that such voluminous, complex deposits required not a quick backhoe trench but carefully controlled hand excavation and analysis of individual soil layers to reveal details of the city's past.

The excavations at Charleston Place, located in the heart of the nine-teenth-century city's commercial core, revealed the pressures of urban life. Wells to gather groundwater, privies to discard human waste, and drains to remove storm water and waste water all appeared in ever-increasing proxim-ity as the nineteenth century wore on. After 1850 Charlestonians also built cisterns in increasing numbers to collect rainwater channeled through gut-ters, in an effort to avoid the by-now-toxic urban groundwater.

But the refuse from this supposedly commercial block told us principally about the domestic side of life here. And we were frustrated in our attempts to study the trash of individual families and tenants. Each yard was full of trash, but we began to learn that urban dwellers, when faced with crowded conditions, put their trash in *any* convenient place, often not in their own yard. A vacant lot, an open marsh, or even over a neighbor's fence would do. Artifacts specific to a particular Charleston Place resident, such as clay to-bacco pipes from the Masonic Lodge, were found several lots from their expected place of origin. So how to study the daily lives of colonial city dwellers?

Armed with a broad research plan developed in 1984, we moved our research focus, and our excavations, to domestic townhouse compounds. These sites, both privately and publicly owned, contained intact historic buildings *and* intact property lines, complete with walls and fences. This allowed us to study household life in the colonial and antebellum city. At the same time, our work helped change the way that others interpreted and stud-ied such sites. Excavations in the work yards, for example, led to a focus on the whole property, not just the large house that faced the main street.

Behind or beside these large houses had stood service buildings and a busy, dirty work yard crammed with resident slaves, who lived in crowded quarters above the kitchens. These African bondspeople took care of most chores of daily life, including tending the livestock and gardening, along with cooking, cleaning, and refuse disposal. Though white and black people lived in sepa-rate social spheres, the refuse of all townhouse residents is combined in the ground, making it nearly impossible to isolate the possessions and activities of the materially poor. Bringing the black residents to life through archaeol-ogy, then, has been somewhat frustrating. The archaeological materials clearly attributable to an African cultural origin are few. African residents

Fig. 13.2. Heyward-Washington House, Charleston. (Collections of the Charleston Museum.)

may also have owned and used a variety of European manufactured items and cooked their own meals in a manner different from white residents, but such things are more difficult to isolate and define.

And what about the urban livestock? The presence of horses would not surprise tourists, for they ride in horse-drawn carriages, but the urban homesites also housed cows, assorted fowl, and, in the eighteenth century at least, pigs. Two decades of dietary and environmental research by zooarchaeologist Elizabeth Reitz have revealed that these animals more commonly appeared on the properties of the elite. Moreover, these same elite households butchered cows and discarded the butchering remains in their yards. The presence of bones from the entire carcass and a low percentage of sawed

6

Archaeology of African Americans
Martha Zierden

Long famous for its "gracious heritage," Charleston has become equally well known as a cradle of African American culture. The city was the port of entry for the majority of Africans forced from their homes to a life of bondage on American plantations. Sheer numbers and relative isolation on plantation tracts combined to create a dynamic African American culture that evolved through the centuries and remains a defining social force in the lowcountry. Archaeological artifacts attributable to people of African descent are few, despite the claim of archaeology that all people are equally reflected in the ground. Urban sites have revealed quantities of Colono Ware, pottery made locally in African style first recovered in quantity on plantation slave sites and studied by Leland Ferguson and others (see chapter 3). Such ceramics comprise about 5 percent of those recovered on Charleston sites, attesting to the presence of African people and African practices. Other items that were likely the cultural and physical possessions of enslaved Africans include quartz crystals, silver Spanish coins pierced for wearing as charms, and possibly carnelian and glass beads in a variety of colors. While archaeologists have always focused on these unique artifacts, most scholars now recognize that they were only a small part of the possessions of black residents.

---

bones indicated on-site butchery. Behind the elegant 1808 Nathaniel Russell House stood a neat brick kitchen, its basement filled with three feet of soil, ceramic and glass fragments, and the bones of butchered cows. At the 1769 Miles Brewton house, the remains of cleaning large fish filled an eighteenth-century drain in the work yard. Its kitchen basement, too, contained butchering remains from cows. The presence of animals and the processing of them for food in the work yard are known only through archaeology, yet the cumulative evidence is compelling enough to be a certainty.

Thirty years after urban archaeology began in Charleston, I have excavated on nearly thirty sites. Other historical archaeologists have excavated nearly a dozen more. We have been hired by private developers and city officials, but also by preservation groups, museums, and private property owners. Some are motivated only by permitting requirements, but most have hired archaeologists to "learn more" about their properties. Archaeology has proven itself an important source of site information, and in many cases the only source.

Like the team at Alexandria Archaeology, we always ask ourselves how to share these new ideas with the visiting public. Visitors to Charleston travel

7

The Nathaniel Russell House Project
Martha Zierden

Built in 1808, Nathaniel Russell's stylish mansion loudly proclaimed his social and economic status to guests and passersby, right down to the wrought iron balcony embellished with his initials. In 1994, Historic Charleston Foundation embarked on an ambitious program of restoration, renovation, and reinterpretation of this historic house museum. The archaeological team was charged with exposing and recovering evidence of architectural changes to the house, the nineteenth-century formal garden, and the work yard. Based on previous work and revelations, we hoped to retrieve artifacts relating to the daily lives of the Russell family and of their servants. We were not disappointed.

The formal garden that now covers the entire yard was installed in the 1980s. Though beautiful and inviting, it does not convey the realities of nineteenth-century life. Excavations in the front yard revealed rectangular beds and paths likely from the antebellum pleasure garden, while a layer of imported red clay remains from a mid-nineteenth-century rose garden. The area of the work yard, in contrast, is filled with a good bit of the debris of daily living. But the biggest surprise came beneath the neat brick kitchen building itself. Here, three feet of soil and coal dust contained fragments of elaborate Chinese porcelain from Mrs. Russell's dining room and the bones of butchered cows, deposited layer after layer from about 1820 until 1850. The three sets of Chinese porcelain, as well as the gentleman's buckles and buttons and the pieces of elaborate furniture hardware, were somewhat expected, but the butchering remains were not.

The dig also uncovered artifacts from those who likely did the butchering. The resident slaves most likely owned the annular ware bowls and glass beads recovered across the site, as well as the Colono Ware bowls. Most tantalizing was a cleanly cut strip of a slave tag, a local license for slaves hired out to others. While late-nineteenth-century family memoirs recall many of the "servants" with fondness, the implication of Mrs. Russell's slave Tom Russell in the 1822 Denmark Vesey insurrection suggests that master and slave lived in the same compound but worlds apart.

The layers of earth at the Nathaniel Russell House produced material culture that reflects the purchasing power of Charleston's elite, which was the greatest of all late colonial or antebellum cities. It simultaneously presented the muffled voices of the city's middling and poor, free and enslaved residents who understood this language of artifacts, even if they did not share its rewards.

Fig. 13.3. Ronald Anthony of the Charleston Museum excavating the work yard of the Miles Brewton house. The brick drain, yard paving, and various refuse layers reveal the complexities of urban life. (Collections of the Charleston Museum.)

the historic neighborhoods in horse-drawn carriages and air-conditioned buses. House after house is perfectly restored or sympathetically reused, surrounded by attractive fences and walls, and embellished with scrupulously maintained gardens. They range from multistory mansions to demure tenements to former kitchens and slave quarters, their interiors converted to apartments or condominiums. Large or small, colonial or Victorian, all are expensive. Only on the northern edges of the historic district, just off the carriage routes, can one find properties still seemingly the home of working-class people, many owned by black families whose ancestors were once residents in the back buildings of Charleston's big houses.

But do visitors see the "real" eighteenth-century city or a modern version? The renovations and redevelopment bring with them amenities that never before graced the property. Even historic house museums feature closed windows and the hum of heating and cooling systems, a bow to the preservation of the material culture displayed in the buildings. At the same time, these house museums are abuzz with scholars from a variety of fields, each uncovering new aspects of the daily lives of colonial and antebellum residents. We regularly work with architects, paint analysts, furniture conservators, paper and print specialists, and garden historians, as well as archaeology's own retinue of specialists—zooarchaeologists, pollen specialists, phytolith (plant cell) experts, and ethnobotanists. Restoration architects and carpenters, museum curators and interpreters are adding their data to museums. Just as Charleston blazed a trail in the founding of the historic preservation movement in the 1920s, local institutions now lead research efforts to broaden, and complicate, our understanding of past peoples and events. Archaeology is part of this team effort.

Still, it is difficult to "see" the archaeological resources of a historic property. The underground complexities of the urban landscape—the drains, privies, wells, and cisterns so integral to daily life—are invisible. Visitors may hear about a refuse-strewn work yard, but maintaining one creates the very public health hazards that nineteenth-century urban residents worked to offset. There are as yet no live, or recently slaughtered, cows at the Nathaniel Russell house—or chickens, turkeys, ducks, or doves either, for that matter. Still, the information retrieved from the ground is shared through photos, text, and guided tours. Archaeology has served to make the physical and social accomplishments of Charlestonians all the more remarkable by focusing on the rigors of daily life in the city.

"A Place to Start From"

West Oakland, California

Lu Ann De Cunzo and Mary Praetzellis

Now that you have read about archaeology in Quebec, New York, Alexandria, and Charleston, can you imagine directing the archaeology of forty-three city blocks? Archaeologists at Sonoma State University's Anthropological Studies Center (ASC) got the chance after the great Loma Prieta earthquake of 1989 devastated West Oakland, and their uniquely California story is fascinating. California's Department of Transportation has rebuilt several miles of collapsed and crumbled freeway. Archaeologists are making sure that construction doesn't destroy important remains that have already survived both the original highway construction and the earthquake. It is an immense undertaking mandated by federal law. Where would you start? ASC archaeologists and historians mined the libraries and archives first, gathering maps, photographs, and other hints of the city's land-use history. They discovered that some areas remained under water for much of West Oakland's history, until they received a capping of fill in recent years. Modern construction destroyed early remains in other areas, and land use in yet others left toxic soils unsafe to excavate. In the end, archaeologists determined that fragments of West Oakland's history might still lie buried on twenty-two of the city blocks.

Even that made for a project of enormous proportions. The scale of the excavations seems astounding, yet it is not atypical of urban transportation projects. Excavation took seventy-eight field weeks with a crew of about a dozen archaeologists. They uncovered 227 house lots and excavated 521 trash pits, 23 wells, and 183 outdoor toilets, or privies. Study of the hundreds of thousands of artifacts they recovered, and of the people who used them, will continue for years. The archaeologists estimate that lab work, research, report writing, and other interpretation projects take at least three to five times as long to complete as the fieldwork.

Fig. 14.1. Archaeologists working adjacent to the elevated BART tracks, excavating trenches, wells, and privies in West Oakland. (Courtesy of Jack McIlroy and Anthropological Studies Center, Sonoma State University.)

The project has generated an enormous amount of community interest in West Oakland archaeology and history. Together archaeologists and residents have revived forgotten memories and retrieved a part of Oakland history that would have been lost forever. Archaeologists gave tours of the excavations and produced a video on historical archaeology. Working with community members, they created a series of mobile exhibits like "Holding the Fort," a tribute to the African American labor movement in West Oakland.

What makes West Oakland's history, and its archaeological and oral history legacy, so important? The answer is transportation. West Oakland is the gateway to the East Bay, the link to San Francisco, and a crucial node in a rail and water transport network extending far beyond California. The economics of transportation defined the city's growth from its beginnings in the 1850s. Oakland began as a peninsula bounded by San Francisco Bay and a broad tidal estuary with a long sandbar silting in its entrance. Since Californians relied entirely on shipping for communication, the timing of landing a vessel became a significant problem. Then in 1862 the Central Pacific Railroad chose Oakland as the terminus for the transcontinental railroad and

West Oakland as the locus of its immense shops and yards. Over the next few decades, workers transformed the peninsula environment.

The construction of the railroads created a demand for labor that lasted through the early twentieth century and drew successive waves of immigrants. Many found a specific niche in the industry. For example, Americans of European descent often worked as engineers, while British immigrants labored in the railroad shops, Portuguese and Italians on the track gangs, and African Americans as porters. The workers also found niches in the urban environment, creating a social landscape at once unique and typical of America's later nineteenth-century cities. Snow and Roos's *Bird's-eye View of Oakland* in 1870–71 captures an important moment in the building of the city, when some envisioned it as an elite suburb of San Francisco while others imagined getting rich developing their land into a grid of city row houses. More than a dozen genteel suburban estates gave the city a distinctive form, with widely spaced large houses set in extensive grounds and orchards. Nearer the railroad, at Oakland Point, an urban streetscape appears half complete in the 1870 view. Long, narrow houses and shops crowd together along the streets, the beginnings of West Oakland's worker housing community.

As overland and water transportation came together in West Oakland, and as the population grew, the marsh and estuary that surrounded the city provided outlets for raw sewage. By the 1880s an area admired for fishing and hunting three decades before had become the object of serious concern for public health. Railroad piers, breakwaters, the sewer system, and all the wastes of humans, animals, and industry dramatically transformed the West Oakland shoreline by the late nineteenth century. The rapid rate at which the city and its population grew had simply outpaced investment in public improvements.

By 1900, rats were the least of the city's problems. Typhoid, cholera, dysentery, and other epidemics took their toll each year. Blamed first on "miasmas" from the mudflats and marshes and later on bad water and poor sewerage, these diseases and the generally dismal conditions in the marshy lowlands drove the middle class onto higher, healthier ground. The railroad, other industries, and the working class crowded the mudflats. It was, as West Oakland native Jack London wrote in *Valley of the Moon,* just "a place to start from."

How, the archaeologists asked, did working-class immigrants to West Oakland deal with these challenges of urban life? Mostly, they worked hard, joined unions and ladies' auxiliaries for solidarity and socializing, joined churches, and sent their children to church schools. They drank, fought, and generally raised a racket in the saloons along Seventh Street, and at the end of the day they went home, to the places where the archaeologists came face to face with what they left behind.

While archaeologists uncovered history underground, other researchers encouraged community members to share their memories of West Oakland's history. People of Greek, Italian, Slovenian, Chinese, Mexican, and German descent told their stories and shared family photos. Dozens of African American railroad workers shared "laborlore"—stories about how they did their jobs and what the jobs meant to them.

The archaeology in West Oakland is teaching us about people to whom the railroad gave everything they wanted, and about those who were not so fortunate. Many of West Oakland's early residences were comfortable in size; some were architecturally fashionable. Many families who lived here in the 1870s enjoyed comfortable existences in homes that were not cramped, either on the lots or in floor plan. They ate well, entertained in style, and in some instances had servants to do the housework. Over time, living conditions became more crowded, as owners built additional rentals, families shared living space and took in boarders, and women had greater numbers of children. Eventually this situation became formalized, with residences replaced by or divided into flats.

Although some landowners preferred to rent to individuals of their own nativity, West Oakland was not racially segregated. African Americans with well-paid jobs owned and rented various houses in the area. Their material goods were indistinguishable from those of their affluent neighbors, such as the Mann family.

The Mann household, headed by two "capitalist" brothers from New Hampshire, lived in one of the houses studied by the ASC. Archaeologists excavated the backfilled privy in their yard, remarkable for its large quantity of porcelain dishes, parlor trimmings, and other indicators of affluence. The brothers speculated in various risky endeavors until the early 1880s. Mrs. Eunice Mann, two decades younger than her once-wealthy husband, spent her married life managing the household, caring for her children, and nursing the brothers and her mother through their final illnesses. She had been nursing her brother-in-law for two years when he finally died of a stroke on New Year's Eve 1884. It is not surprising, then, that Eunice discarded their household goods into the privy when she remarried and moved away. These were the items carefully excavated by archaeologists more than one hundred years later.

Unlike some neighbors, Mrs. Mann apparently did not have live-in domestic help. Aside from cleaning and cooking for four adults and three chil-

Fig. 14.2. Artifacts from the Mann household, West Oakland. (Courtesy of Anthropological Studies Center, Sonoma State University.)

dren, she also appears to have canned fruits and vegetables, sewed new clothes on a sewing machine, and darned old ones. She owned a corset, jewelry, and fancy women's clothing. Two empty bottles from a French *injection brou* were found in the privy; such concoctions were commonly used in the nineteenth century to prevent both conception and venereal disease.

Finds in the privy tell us that the Mann family ate and drank well in their early days. One can imagine the fancy china cabinet in the dining room, fresh flowers in the parlor, and wine bottles stored in the cellar. By the time Mrs. Mann nursed her ailing brother-in-law, however, times were not so flush, as indicated by the bones of cheap cuts of meat they now ate, and by the lack of any substantial assets when he died. After years working as housekeeper for her relations, it is not surprising that Mrs. Mann wanted new things when she started over with her new husband. Neither brother had been successful over the long term in his business dealings. Even their residence, which had once been the most fashionable on the block with its bay window and Victorian bric-a-brac, stood in need of repairs and housed a disparate group of work-ingmen by 1890.

About twenty years later and two doors down the street, we find the home of Nellie Carter, whose husband, James, was a Pullman porter. Along with the railroad came the Pullman Palace Car Company, whose sumptuous sleeping and dining cars catered to the well-heeled traveler. A Victorian home on wheels, the Pullman car was the context for genteel social activities. By company policy, only blacks were hired as Pullman porters. In keeping with the practice of the time, the Carter household contained several boarders, including an insurance agent, a pharmacist and his family, two railroad porters, and Nellie's brother, who worked as a railroad mechanic. The collection from the Carter household's backfilled well is remarkable for the quantity, quality, and variety of artifacts. The shoes, clothing, and toys suggest a household of several workingmen and women, plus children. The adults, all of whom were literate, held relatively high-status jobs with the railroad or as professionals within the community. Their refuse consisted of unique teacarts, dolls, parlor display items, and other memorabilia that had accumulated over the years. They ate well, sometimes in a formal setting, and served tea and alcohol in a variety of styles from plain to festive. In keeping with their high status within their community, African American porter households seem to have replicated in their homes the Victorian formality and opulence found in the Pullman cars in which they worked.

Not everyone was welcome in West Oakland, however. The local boys made tormenting the Chinese laundrymen a favorite pastime, throwing stones from the passing steam train until the laundry doors and windows were battered and barricaded. Remains from an archaeological feature excavated behind a West Oakland laundry tell another story. The materials used by these hardworking men show them in their daily life. They discarded bluing balls for whitening dingy laundry, buttons lost during washing, wood abacus beads for tallying bills, and a Chinese inkstand for writing. The men ate foods both local and imported from China on a mixture of white English plates and colorful Chinese bowls. They drank Hostetter's Bitters from Pittsburgh and rice wine from China, and smoked American tobacco and Chinese opium.

Archaeologists also found remains of another Chinese immigrant who never made it home. Sometime around 1900 a well-dressed man was buried under the floor of a rental cottage in a backyard on Filbert Street, on top of a privy that residents had abandoned and filled. Study of the young man's skeleton told us that he was Asian, and on the day he died he wore size-seven boots with rubber heels, a twenty-nine-inch leather belt with a copper buckle, a union-suit undergarment, and wool flannel trousers. He carried a silver pocket watch and an expensive black silk handkerchief. The clothing and dates on other artifacts found in the privy below tell that the burial occurred between 1895 and 1910. Who was the young man, and was he the victim of foul play? We will probably never know, because the burial cannot be precisely dated and the cottage's tenants changed frequently. Archaeologists may never solve this mystery, but they are helping to tell the stories of this city the railroad built, and of the people who got a start there.

Part 4

Making a Living in Rural America

The Archaeology of Work

Lu Ann De Cunzo

In industrial nations around the world, workers spend at least one-third of the day performing a service or producing a commodity to sell. In preindustrial societies, workers often devote even more time to production. Our jobs frequently define who we are and how we live. Thus the world of work offers historical archaeologists innumerable opportunities to study how past people made their living and how they thought about their lives.

Have you ever traveled down the highway and seen abandoned farmhouses, mills, fences, or fields? Have you wondered who lived there and worked there, and what happened to them? Archaeologists view every agricultural and industrial site as unique: we want to discover what these past builders and producers learned and whether this technology still has value. By piecing together the fragments of artifacts we dig up with information from historical documents, building and landscape remains, and oral histories, we can open a window into the everyday lives of rural Americans.

Over the years, we have learned to apply archaeological methods to study industrial features as large as canals and as small as the privy pits in the canal diggers' backyards. We can understand the "big picture" only by linking workers and their daily lives to the technological and engineering developments that guided their work, and to the things they made. Working with historians of technology and social historians, we are learning about the Industrial Revolution as a *process* of change. The process followed different courses in different places at different times, influenced by a complex array of environmental, political, and economic forces, and by the cultural experiences and practices of the local people.

In 1959 and 1960 Bernard Fontana directed a team of Arizona Archaeological and Historical Society members in an excavation of "Johnny Ward's ranch." What was so special about the ranch project? In Arizona—one of the bastions of prehistoric archaeology in North America, where older was definitely better—Fontana's team excavated a ranch occupied by Anglo-American settlers from 1859 to 1903. Although farms and ranches once formed the foundation of American life, they had attracted little attention from archaeologists. Fontana's study has served as a model for a generation of archaeologists, with its detailed studies of the ranch architecture, landscape, and artifacts of everyday life on an industrial, Victorian-era ranch.

Today we bring new skills and interests to our studies of rural Americans. Our list of questions is constantly growing. Women, children, and minorities have become the foci of much research because their stories remain incomplete when told only with the sparse information contained in historical documents. As archaeologists we want to learn about family life, work roles, and children's schooling. We consider people's economic means and how these affected what and how they ate, what they chose to purchase from the store, and the products they raised or grew or manufactured. We look at building practices and how people arranged their work areas on the landscape. We ask about their ethnic heritage and religion and how these shaped people's everyday lives. We have analyzed everything from milk pans and canning jars to plows and waterwheels. Pieced together, these tiny fragments of glass, ceramics, and bone, and large and small rusty tool parts, tell of men and women at work in fields, farmyards, shops, factories, and homes. They highlight the choices people made when first colonial expansion and later industrialization challenged the rhythms of rural life and work.

15

The Archaeology of Agricultural Life

Sara Mascia

A few years ago I was reading my local paper when I came across an article about the vanishing American farm. The headline read: "Suburban growth threatens a family tradition with extinction." Although the United States has its roots as an agrarian nation, the future of small farms is uncertain. As more people move to rural areas, family farms are slowly disappearing from the landscape.

When we have had the opportunity, archaeologists *have* studied American farms, plantations, homesteads, tenant homes, and ranches in the last quarter century. We usually know them by the name of one or more of their past occupants, such as the Sherwood Farm, the Spencer-Pierce-Little Farm, and the Jethro Coffin site, a practice that reflects the traditional association of the farm with a specific individual or family. Each farm is unique and produced different goods for sale. Archaeologists have excavated at dairy farms, tobacco, corn, wheat, and other single-crop farms, market gardens, and fruit farms, as well as cattle and sheep ranches.

Historically, some Native American peoples had raised crops and domesticated animals for centuries before European exploration. Colonial settlers traveled to America for the promise of available land, promoting an agrarian ethos in this country that became deeply ingrained. America was truly a nation of farmers. Leaders such as Thomas Jefferson extolled the virtues of agrarian life, where free and independent farmers provided the foundation for the economy and lived good and healthy lives. During the nineteenth century, farming began to undergo changes due to technological innovations, the establishment of agricultural newspapers and journals, a huge influx of immigrants, and the opening of the American West. As immigration increased at a fast pace, freedom for many meant the chance to secure land on the frontier. But for many Native American groups, the westward expansion of the United States meant displacement and disruption of a way of life inextricably tied to the land. For example, the Homestead Act of 1862 divided and redistributed the land, offering parcels of land up to 160 acres to European American settlers for a small fee.

8

Farmstead Archaeology in the Arkansas Ozarks
Leslie C. "Skip" Stewart-Abernathy

I knew I wanted to be an archaeologist when I was six years old, but somehow Egypt and Greece seemed too far off, and I really wasn't interested in arrowheads. Nonetheless, I had a misspent youth because when I got my driver's license, I spent weekends exploring the many abandoned farmsteads on Crowley's Ridge north of my home in Jonesboro in northeast Arkansas. I was intrigued by all the effort of so many families who ended up leaving their marks behind in the form of farmhouses, outbuildings, and fields that were disappearing under scrubby vegetation. I came to understand how many North Americans had lived and worked on farmsteads such as these. The house I had grown up in, a "ranch house" in the suburbs, was actually the odd case. What seemed normal to me was a recent occurrence, the end result of people abandoning their farms and moving to towns. Eventually they or their children moved to the suburbs where I grew up.

By the late 1960s archaeologists were doing historical archaeology, and though they often focused on military sites or the homes of the rich and famous, they also recognized that the powerful integration of documents, archaeology, and other data sources such as old photos and old memories could be brought to bear on understanding "ordinary" farmsteads in North America. These farmsteads were created by English and Germans and French and Hispanics and Africans and others who built the North America we know through farming. Historical archaeologists also recognized that they couldn't really find out everything they wanted to know about all those farm families just from finds at flea markets, or even in memoirs or contemporary descriptions by visitors to the countryside. What is the value, after all, of someone claiming to describe a "typical farmstead" in New England or the South or the Midwest, when in fact we don't know precisely what all those farmsteads looked like because so many had been abandoned and transformed into archaeological sites? At those sites we can find evidence of what those many farm families thought and desired and needed and used, but not if we dismiss that evidence, and their lives, as irrelevant.

At the Arkansas Archeological Survey, we have discovered just how much we can learn by doing archaeology at Ozark farmsteads. In 1983 we excavated the Moser Farmstead Site for the Arkansas Highway and Transportation Department and the Federal Highway Administration prior to construction of a new interstate through northwestern Arkansas. We discovered rich deposits of late-nineteenth- and early-twentieth-century artifacts in a number of farmstead features including a cellar under what had been a log smokehouse, a cellar under what had been a kitchen ell, a cistern that had been under the kitchen porch, and a storm cellar out in the backyard. Extensive oral history from people who knew the farmstead well helped us to reconstruct the farmstead plan in detail, including where the house, barn, privy, chicken houses, smokehouse, and wagon shed had stood. They also gave us

Fig. 15.1. Dallas Moser (left) explaining details of the Moser Farmstead, remembered from his childhood, to archaeologist Skip Stewart-Abernathy on the farmstead site (3BE11) in July 1982. (Courtesy of Arkansas Archeological Survey.)

a more thorough understanding of how the artifacts we found fitted into the lifeways of the Moser inhabitants.

Consider, for example, the smokehouse. Say that "everybody had a smokehouse" and this is true, but what does this say about the place of smoked meat on the family farm in the centuries before refrigeration? At the Moser site, we found that the log smokehouse had the only door on the entire place that had a lock, and that lock also protected the contents of a storage cellar underneath the smokehouse. And into that cellar, when the farmstead was abandoned and demolished and the place cleaned up about 1920, were thrown fragments of glass canning jars, British and United States–made ceramic dishes for the dining table, and even a crosscut saw that the Moser occupants had used in the previous four decades. What was that? Imported tablewares and glass canning jars and other products of the Industrial World being used by isolated Ozark hill people? Yes, people who were independent, but not isolated, who used the goods generated in the increasingly alienating world of cities and factories to construct a way of life that celebrated family and community sufficiency and strength. A useful thing to learn today, for a boy who grew up in suburbia wanting to be an archaeologist.

The concept of an "agricultural ladder" has been used to describe the levels of advancement toward land ownership. Common farm laborers clung to the bottom of the ladder, tenant farmers perched on the middle rungs, and independent farmers balanced at the top. Landless people struggled to climb until they could buy a farm. Reaching the top of the ladder was one way to achieve the American dream in the nineteenth century. Industrialization, however, was changing the economic foundation of the Americas, as factories

9

Archaeology on Western Ranches
Margaret Purser

The first thing you notice about working ranch sites in the arid West is their visibility, at a variety of levels. The sheer openness of western space can be daunting to an easterner's eye: weather you can see coming for an hour before it arrives, lines of sight that stretch to the horizon. What this means for archaeologists is a constant, pervasive stretching of the relevant scale of analysis. Even if you weren't inclined toward landscape approaches to begin with, you would be inexorably drawn that way, just to make sense of what you were seeing and digging. For example, you can be excavating a trash pit at one ranch, and raise your eyes to see not just the neighboring house site a mile away but the entire settlement system of a twelve-by-twenty-mile valley floor, all at a glance.

Visibility in western ranching sites is also an archaeological visibility: preservation here is dramatic, and it pushes excavators to radically expand what counts as material data. For instance, you can see the entire valley settlement system because, in the arid environment, the presence of trees means the presence of people, at least at some point in the past. So the cottonwoods and imported Italian poplars that ring old homestead sites are artifacts, as are the relic fence posts, the trampled bare ground of abandoned corrals, the rutted scars of old wagon roads, and the myriad ditches, gates, dams, and flumes that channeled the western rancher's most prized possession: water. Trash from a camp tossed into the brush more than a hundred years ago looks as if it could have come from last week's meal. Even in the fire-prone areas, standing structures of a wide variety of functions can still be present, at least as scattered spars of lumber, crumbling stone walls, or dusty mounds of old adobe melting slowly into the sagebrush. So although the archaeological record of ranch-

Fig. 15.2. Cultivator, Stewart Ranch, Paradise Valley, Nevada. (Courtesy of Margaret Purser.)

ing can often be sparse, it is just as often marked by radically wide ranges of artifact types, and equally broad spatial scales.

While this plethora of artifact types and spatial scales can challenge our analytical approaches, it can also beguile us into a sense that the material record here is self-evident: that it is all visible, and what you see is what you get. But reality is far different, and it can take much longer to read from this wealth of data the complex systems of environmental manipulation, economic demand, and social networks that created this peculiarly diverse but attenuated material record. Perhaps the most useful strategy is to keep reminding yourself that what appear as fragmentary patches scattered ephemerally across this landscape were really articulated elements in an elaborate system.

Western ranching, for all its evocative romanticism in today's world, was as much a feature of nineteenth-century expanding industrial capitalism as its eastern, urban counterparts. In much the same way that Don Hardesty has defined western mining sites in terms of "feature systems," the ranching complex worked to sustain high levels of production in places that were often both environmentally marginal and economically isolated. The key to the system is in its grand spatial scale, and the key to archaeological analysis is to keep looking ever farther away from the initial test pit. The ranch's water may have come from four miles away through a series of ditches, with the house sited where it was because that location was optimal for the gravity flow. The property around a given ranch house may be relatively small, but the "ranch," as a productive unit, included summer grazing lands miles away in the mountains, and hay lands for winter feed leased on the other side of the valley where the water was better. Linking all these elements was a crazy quilt of property relations, from squatting to tenancy to leasing to homesteading, and ultimately to large-scale corporate industrial cattle and sheep ranching, financed by speculation out of places like New York and London.

In much the same manner, consumption patterns on ranches have to be seen in terms of economic supply and individual choice that were structured more like what one might find at a lunar colony: sophisticated technology, fashionable but oddly assorted goods, and sporadic access to the market. Ever since William Adam's work at Silcott, Washington, in the 1970s, this mosaic of choice and availability of goods has been the source of curiosity. Brand-name bottles, labels on empty tin cans, and ceramics makers' marks testify to access to markets by western ranchers in the nineteenth century, but the real connections to distant manufacturing centers ran through complex and ever-changing networks. Small towns and commercial outposts brokered the availability of mass-produced goods through an economy that was highly seasonal and chronically cash-poor. The differences between family- and corporate-owned ranches in this regard can mirror the differences between individual and other corporate living contexts of the industrializing nineteenth century: corporate ranch bunkhouses can look a lot like the tenement residences of their eastern cousins, or the company-run camps of their western neighbors in the mining and timber industries. Understanding how these complex economic and inherently social networks defined western communities, and tied them into broader national networks, is an aspect of western sites study that is still largely in its infancy.

and businesses displaced farms. Since World War II the burgeoning financial and technological worlds have further reduced our reliance on agriculture as a source of economic security.

Archaeologists have explored different aspects of the agrarian world in different ways. We study life on farms and compare urban and rural life. We examine changes in rural consumer choice, labor, and farming methods. In the early years of historical archaeology, archaeologists concentrated on excavating and restoring "famous" sites. The earliest archaeological studies focused on the farms of famous people such as George Washington. Although most of these sites were once working farms, initially only the house and portions of the formal landscape were excavated, and the end result was a brief description of what was found, a discussion of family genealogy, and an attached artifact catalog. The majority of early research in the South also concentrated on the area around the farmhouse or, on a plantation, the great house. Some archaeologists tried to identify and explain the patterns of behavior that produced particular patterns of artifacts in the archaeological record. This led us to develop models that characterized plantations, farms, and urban homesteads. We also used models to compare urban and rural sites. The discovery that buildings and spaces on urban lots were set up in much the same manner as their rural counterparts led Leslie Stewart-Abernathy to designate these sites as "urban farmsteads."

With the help of historical documents, archaeologists have also conducted consumer choice studies, measuring the wealth and status of farmers by the objects they purchased and discarded. Studies of animal bones excavated on agricultural sites have taught us more about rural people's diet and livestock farming. We are now beginning to explore the choice of crops and the methods employed to increase production on farms. This important new avenue promises to help us better understand the history of farm production in particular places, and how and why farmers made the decisions they did.

Early archaeological studies of plantations in the American South focused on the labor system before and after the Civil War, especially the institution of slavery and the emergence of African American cultural identities (see chapter 3). More recent studies compare farmsteads owned or rented by Americans of European descent with those owned or rented by African Americans. In contrast, archaeologists have not yet looked in depth at the labor force on farms and ranches in other parts of North America.

We have begun to study farm sites as the sum of all of their parts—in other words, as rural landscapes. We first started studying aspects of the farm complex like farm fences and outbuildings, and how they were used for specific agricultural purposes. This led to studies of farms as functioning entities in the rural environment. Understanding the purpose of a farm as a place of

Fig. 15.3. Spencer-Pierce-Little house (right) and attached tenant house. One of the farm's work areas was the domestic farmyard, which contained a variety of "feature systems" including an underground cistern, a woodshed, and fences protecting the yard from farm animals. (Courtesy of the Society for the Preservation of New England Antiquities.)

food production is the first step in understanding people's motivations behind altering the landscape. The National Park Service defines rural historic landscapes as places featuring continuity of "areas of land use, buildings, vegetation, roads and waterways, and natural features." The definition also emphasizes rural landscapes as "reflect[ing] day-to-day . . . activities of people engaged in traditional work," and that landscapes have "developed and evolved in response to both the forces of nature and the pragmatic need to make a living." Research by Old Sturbridge Village archaeologists on the changing rural landscape in New England builds on this view of rural sites as "single complex artifacts."

Other archaeologists, such as Patricia Rubertone, who also works in New England, have encouraged us to look beyond individual farms and investigate clusters of farms within a region. Richard Waldbauer has looked at farm communities in the White Mountains of New Hampshire, focusing on how these communities interacted. The results enabled him to interpret the effects of regional agricultural strategies pursued in the past. The Delaware Department of Transportation has published a series of archaeological and architectural reports on historical sites throughout the state. The majority are studies of rural sites, including a number of farms. Many of these researchers have compared finds among farm sites. Synthesizing these data steers archaeologists toward understanding agricultural land use within a wider context.

10

Feminist Archaeology at a Dakota Village
Sarah McDowell

What comes to mind when you think about rural life? The family farm or a western ranch? Long rolling fields? Animals grazing in a pasture? Men plowing, women churning butter, and children with milk pails? What if the images were somehow different? Rather than that big farmhouse, picture hide-covered lodges. Instead of churning butter, perhaps a woman harvests corn. Possibly a young girl works on a new hide. While these images may challenge our traditional Eurocentric view, they too represent rural life. They remind archaeologists, as well as a host of others, that different cultures and ways of subsisting also need recognition and research.

Archaeologist Janet Spector applied the perspectives of feminist archaeology in her pioneering study of the rural lifeways of the Wahpeton Dakota. This approach, she believes, grants us a more balanced understanding of both this minority popu-lation and the roles that women played within the community. Because the Dakota pass on their history through oral tradition, written accounts provide an outsider's view of their world. Challenging the dominance in the Western world of the written word as the ultimate historical truth, Spector involved the Dakota community in her work. Together they created a more complete and relevant history of the Dakota village of Little Rapids, Minnesota.

Spector and her team conducted summer field schools in the 1980s at the nine-teenth-century site of a summer planting village. She admits that the first field schools were difficult. The team dug up not just artifacts but also strong feelings concerning the past. Burial mounds at the site had intrigued amateur archaeologists and looters for generations, and many had dug into them without a second thought. This invasiveness, demeaning to the Dakota people, was one of Spector's early hurdles. After learning their language and getting to know members of the community, Spector slowly gained their acceptance. They contributed much to Spector's multidisciplinary and multicultural team and ensured the preservation of the sacred burial mounds.

In the first half of the nineteenth century, the Wahpeton village and an adjacent fur-trading post reflected the growing tensions and challenges that two different cultures face living side by side. This struggle continued over time, and in some ways continues today. One of Spector's goals was to bridge the distance between the outsiders' written history of the Dakota and their own oral tradition. Chris Cav-ender, one of the team members, is descended from the Dakota living at Little Rapids in the 1800s. With his help a more complete history of the site unfolded. For Spector this meant putting names with artifacts, rather than letting the artifacts take precedence over the individuals who used them.

One object that caught her attention was a small awl, a handheld tool used for hide work. When archaeologists discovered the awl in a dump, they knew little about it. With help from the Dakota community, Spector learned the significance of her find. In Dakota tradition, a young woman who had just officially entered womanhood would receive such an awl, and use it to master the work of transforming animal hides into objects of use and beauty. But this awl differed from others archaeologists had excavated, with its red circles and inscriptions on the handle. What did they mean? Chris Cavender's great-grandmother Mazaokiyewin had lived at Little Rapids. Known as an accomplished hide worker, she may even have owned this discarded, fragmentary awl. Descendants taught Spector how a young woman carved circles into the handle of her awl to keep track of how many hides she worked. Each object she made represented a gift to her community, and each year the woman making the most contributions was honored.

The awl shows how significant hide work was to a Dakota woman's daily life. Archaeologists found other traces of rural life as well. During the field schools, they excavated a community dump, possible lodges in which the Dakota lived, and many storage pits. These different features, together with Dakota traditions and the documents and drawings of missionaries and traders, allowed Spector to understand how the Dakota moved throughout the year. Unlike family farmers in the European-American tradition, the Dakota moved with the seasons to hunt, gather, and farm.

The summer planting village at Little Rapids revealed the importance of raising corn. In late spring the Dakota set up their lodges near the fields. Here, from June through August, they grew corn. Excavated storage pits contained remains of century-old corn stored after harvest until needed to survive the deadly Minnesota winter. Dakota women were largely responsible for planting, hoeing, and harvesting the corn. With the corn harvested and safely stored at the end of summer, the Dakota moved on to their fall rice harvests and hunting grounds.

For many Americans, our history is the story of European settlers and their descendants marching across the continent. These pioneering men cleared the forests and broke the sod on the Great Plains, taming—or, some argue, violating—the wilderness with their farms and ranches. Spector's feminist archaeology challenges this male-centered view. A feminist perspective is sensitive to the contributions of groups we define as minorities, such as, but not limited to, women. Bringing a feminist perspective to Little Rapids helped provide a new voice to the Dakota. Recognizing the importance of farming to the Dakota, and the role of women in farming, reminds us that many more important stories remain buried in the rural landscape across the nation.

11

Tenant Farmers in Delaware
Lu Ann De Cunzo

What, after all, is agriculture but the "culture of the fields," the "science and art of cultivating the soil"? It is living between nature and culture. In Delaware, farming shaped the economy and everyday life beginning in the early colonial period, and the mixed farming of grain and livestock that developed in Delaware and neighboring Middle Atlantic colonies set the pattern for later American agriculture. The lives of these farming people beat a rhythm of work, sociability, rest, and worship punctuated by moments and events that exploded the surface of daily routine. Someone's sister had a baby. Another got married. Many brothers never returned from war. The first shipment from the Orient arrived at the local store. The sons went in search of work and didn't come back.

These folks produced and exchanged what they could wrest from the land. Certain soils on certain slopes could grow wheat or only hay or, worse, could only support a few pigs after the trees were cut down. Do your children want to be farmers? They have a lot to learn, and a lot to worry about. The farm isn't large enough to divide among them. Maybe you will be able to buy more land next year. Your son wants to know how that new corn sheller works. Your daughter is learning how long it takes the cream to rise and the butter to come in the churn. Should you trade the team of oxen for mules? The manure is piling up. The fox got in the chicken coop again. Will it ever rain? Will it never stop?

These farming folks were also builders, on small lots at the edge of town and on large farms sprawling across the state. Those closest to the coast and the broad, meandering rivers built dikes and drained the marshes. Everyone built fences. They required regular maintenance, fit in between all the other chores. So did all the buildings. The corner posts holding up the corncrib have rotted. The barn hasn't been painted in years. The last farm journal featured plans for laying out your farm to run as efficiently as a factory. A place for everything and everything in its place.

Folks also thought about a place for every*body* and every*body* in that place. Who are you—mother or father, daughter or son, single or married, black or white, Presbyterian or African Methodist Episcopalian, rich or poor? Sometimes there are opportunities. The politician promises to make the world a better place for your children, the newspaper says, if you vote for him. The neighbors agree, though, that he doesn't know very much about your world or your children. Your daughters help feed the family. They are learning to can meats and vegetables, they care for the strawberry patch, and they help their grandparents at the market every week. On rainy days in their bedroom, they imagine another world playing with their china dolls and teapots.

In the later eighteenth and early nineteenth centuries, capitalism transformed life in the Middle Atlantic region, in ways I hint at above. Archaeology at a tenant farm in Delaware helps tell the stories of this transformation.

In the 1760s William White built a store on his farm. After his son-in-law moved the business to Smyrna about 1800, the old store was renovated for tenants. A frame addition was built along one side of the old store, and a yard out back was fenced for work, storage, gardens, livestock, and trash.

Stewart Redman and his household may have moved into the old store soon after the renovation. Period written sources tell us little about Redman or his family, except his name and a few purchases he made at local stores. The archaeological record tells more about their lives. Discarded bones and shells, for example, show that the family relied on meats and shellfish available through a local network of production, harvest, and exchange. The small number of cow bones, especially butchering waste, argues against the tenants having raised many cows. They likely kept one or two cows for milk, butter, and cheese as well as meat. Fragments of butter pots and milk pans attest to the tenant women's dairying. Other excavated bones identify pigs raised and butchered in the yard. Still other bones and butchering marks also document that the household ate chicken, goose, and waterfowl frequenting the local marshes, as well as muskrat, opossum, squirrel, and turtle. Oysters harvested near the old store also provided an important source of protein.

The Redmans entered local stores to acquire other things they needed and wanted for their work and home. When they did, they faced shelves and counters and barrels crammed with everything from pots of their neighbors' butter to silks and teas from the Orient. Broken ceramics tell of purposeful choices the family made from among wares arrayed along the store's shelves. They were either not concerned with or could not afford to invest much in the expensive imported pieces that the merchants brokered as tokens of success and a refined lifestyle. Instead, locally and regionally made wares predominated in their kitchen and on their dining table. Many multipurpose forms were used to prepare, cook, serve, eat, and store food. Later tenant families selected increasing numbers of imported ceramics.

Hunting, trapping, oystering, fishing, farmwork, hauling goods, and perhaps sailing the boats that plied local goods to Philadelphia engaged many landless men like Stewart Redman. Their labor made the crops grow, brought them in at harvest, and transported them to mills for processing, to the landing for shipping, and aboard ship to market. But these tasks that they repeated each year also contributed to soil exhaustion and erosion. Eventually they brought on a crisis in the region's agricultural economy that deeply affected all their lives. The example of these tenant families suggests that, at least through the 1820s, they retained a culture and vision that valued goods produced and exchanged within the community. Yet they purchased more and more of the imported goods that merchants proffered. As they did, they became more deeply enmeshed in a world market.

The buried remains of Delaware's farms still have much to teach us about pigs and dairy cows, wheat, corn, fences, drained marshes, plows, barns, work, and much more. Through studies of these things, these people, and the thousands of farms across the state in which their histories reside, historical archaeologists will learn more about Delawareans and the "culture of agriculture."

When I was a child, my family would climb into our Country Squire station wagon and travel the eastern seaboard during the summer months. On these trips, the highway seemed to be surrounded by farms as far as the eye could see. Growing up in suburban New York, I felt that working farms were as exotic as a tropical island. I soon became fascinated with farming and the families who worked with the cows and horses I viewed along the highway.

My first experience with archaeology was in high school. One of my closest friends dragged me to a local excavation at the Requa farm site in Tarrytown, New York. Under the direction of Louis Brennan, volunteers were excavating a tenant farm that had stood from 1720 to 1783 on part of Philipsburg Manor. The discovery of household items mixed in with farming tools piqued my curiosity and lingered with me through four years of college.

In graduate school I had the good fortune to work with Mary Beaudry at Boston University. In the fall of 1986 I began to work with her at the Spencer-Pierce-Little Farm in Newbury, Massachusetts. A working farm since 1680, this site provided me with the opportunity to closely examine farm life beyond the backyard. Beaudry has long been a proponent of examining the farm as a functioning agricultural entity. For my dissertation I focused on the mid-nineteenth-century resident of the farm, long-term tenant farmer Edward Little, who purchased the farm and rose up the agricultural ladder to become a landowner.

At the Spencer-Pierce-Little Farm we applied Donald Hardesty's concept of "feature systems," which he developed to study mining landscapes (see chapter 9). These feature systems may be widely dispersed geographically. Agricultural activities such as collecting salt hay in marsh areas, building fences around fields, and constructing pens around a barn leave traces, or "features," over a large geographic area. Together these features form systems that enabled farm production. A trash dump may contain household refuse and perhaps materials such as milk pans used for specific farm activities. By determining how all farm components work together, archaeologists gain a clearer understanding of the larger, more complex agricultural system.

During my eight years of research at the Spencer-Pierce-Little Farm, the belief that land ownership was a primary goal of farming people also influenced my thinking. It followed that the land, and its quality for agricultural production, would provide the means for farmers to measure their status. Studies of rural consumer behavior by archaeologists in New Jersey and Virginia suggested that farmers expressed their wealth not by buying material goods but by improving the farm, a practice dubbed "conspicuous production." At the Spencer-Pierce-Little Farm we found that once the mid-nineteenth-century tenant farmer became the property owner, he made numerous

Fig. 15.4. Tree-lined drive. When the mid-nineteenth-century tenant became the owner of the Spencer-Pierce-Little Farm, one of his many changes to the landscape was the introduction of this formal drive. (Courtesy of the Society for the Preservation of New England Antiquities.)

improvements to the farm. After these changes were completed, the owner began to purchase various consumer items that represented his upward change in status. For such farmers, an investment in the future of the farm came first. Not only do archaeologists need to study the influences on the farmer, such as progressive farm movements and new tools and inventions, they must have an understanding of the agrarian nature of farming itself. This will help everyone learn about the culture of agriculture in North America and how it came to be.

Perhaps America's historical agricultural places belong on the "endangered places" list, and not only because of development threats. New technologies of cultivation threaten them. The scale of agribusiness threatens them. In some cases, even archaeologists threaten them, especially those farms established between the middle of the nineteenth and the middle of the twentieth century. In fact, some archaeologists have expressed a casual attitude toward the preservation of agricultural places, saying that we have got thousands of these sites and perhaps not all farms are important. Even after

Fig. 15.5. Cover of May 1884 *American Agriculturist.* One of the greatest influences on nineteenth-century America was the establishment of the agricultural press. Beginning in 1819, agricultural publications provided information on crops, results of experiments, accounts of farm practices, farmhouse architectural plans, new inventions, and, most important, timely market prices and stock reports. Many of these journals also had sections devoted to political events, county and state agricultural societies, agricultural fairs, rural poetry, humor, farm women (often called the "Ladies Department"), cures and medicines, and accounts of travel. Advertisements for machinery, tools, employment, medicines, and household products were also standard fare. (Courtesy of Sara Mascia.)

all the federally funded highway, sewer line, and airport projects have paved over or trenched through those in the path of progress, we might still have thousands of these sites. Of course we cannot and should not try to save, or even study, every one of these historical agricultural places. But we have given up too many without trying to preserve or at least record the archaeological remains left in the ground by those who lived in the houses, worked in the fields, and trapped in the woodlots. To counteract this, the SHA played an important role in a successful lobbying effort to include a clause in the most recent farm bill that will promote preservation of historic farm complexes and archaeological sites on farms across the United States.

Today, or tomorrow, as we drive down the highway or along rural roads, we will see fewer and fewer family farms along the route. While we might lose many of those in the paths of new developments, there are still thousands left to preserve, as well as documents, maps, photographs, farm collectibles, and memories in which are inscribed the stories of those places and their people. The challenge for archaeologists is to study these sites before they vanish under new suburbs and to help preserve as many of these "endangered places" as possible. Through our excavations, public participation, and political activism, archaeologists will ensure that rural agricultural sites don't become a lost American resource.

16

The Archaeology of Rural Industry

David R. Starbuck

I grew up on a family farm, and I know from experience that industry is just as important a source of revenue as crops, orchards, or dairy products for people living in rural areas. Americans had industrialized the countryside long ago, and rural industries help generate the extra income that makes country life more comfortable. Over the past several centuries, nearly every town or hamlet and many farms and plantations in the United States, Canada, and the Caribbean had mills for processing natural resources and grain, blacksmith shops for maintaining tools and making nails, and oftentimes potters' shops and kilns for manufacturing storage vessels. Other industries had more local bases in available natural resources. Extractive industries grew up where furnaces processed iron ore, smelted copper, made glass from sand and lime; sawmills shaped wood products; woolen mills created blankets and clothing. Historical archaeologists have conducted research projects at these and many other kinds of sites, frequently discovering that history has left behind very few records with which to explain just how these industries operated or exactly where they stood. Still, most of us have seen old mill foundations while walking alongside streams in the woods, or gazed up at an old smokestack that has fallen into disuse, or walked along the bed of a canal that has not held water since the mid-nineteenth century.

Many historical archaeologists also do industrial archaeology, but most industrial archaeologists record aboveground remains, whereas historical archaeologists more often conduct excavations. Also, we historical archaeologists devote greater attention to pre-1800 industrial sites, while industrial archaeologists may spend more time studying later (and larger) industries, especially those that postdate the Industrial Revolution. Still, both of these fields rely heavily upon the written record; we both conduct interviews with informants who have worked at these industries; we both conduct regional surveys as well as site-specific projects; we both prepare detailed measured drawings, site plans, and photographs; we both create rich written descriptions of the architecture, artifacts, and by-products of past industry. And

12

Shaker Industry
David R. Starbuck

The Shakers, or the United Society of Believers in Christ's First and Second Appearing, provide the best example of the pervasiveness of rural industries throughout America. This utopian movement of Christian believers arose in Manchester, England, in 1747. In 1774 the first Shakers journeyed to the American colonies, where they subsequently established nineteen small communities that are often portrayed as an agrarian reaction against nineteenth-century urban life and its reputed vices. The Shakers' efforts to escape the lifestyle of the mainstream culture, while devoting themselves wholly to the service of God, resulted in their developing dozens of industries at every community. In doing so, they ultimately achieved a very high level of economic independence and self-sufficiency.

In 1977 I commenced a long-term project at one of these Shaker villages, in Canterbury, New Hampshire, where three Shakers were still very much alive. One aspect of this work involved documenting all of the archaeological sites that dot the three thousand acres of Shaker-modified landscape. Because this rural society had produced so much maple sugar, seeds, field crops, honey, beef, pork, dairy products, apples, and more, I did not immediately realize the importance of the industrial sites to the Shaker experience. However, after twenty-five years of recording headraces, dams, mill foundations, wheelpits, spillways, trash racks, ditches, and dumps, I have to acknowledge that the Canterbury Shakers were intrepid industrialists who operated no fewer than four blacksmith shops, eighteen mills, and a host of craft shops. They did woodworking, wheelmaking, shoemaking, spinning, weaving, sewing, and printing, and typically each Shaker learned more than one trade to ensure that no industry would come to an end with the passing of a member.

Shaker industry was highly respected and innovative, as the members made products of considerable quality. The Shakers researched business decisions well, accumulating equipment catalogs and magazines like *Scientific American* to ensure that their purchases of turbines and related supplies would meet their needs. The desire to power many industries simultaneously resulted in the creation of a mill system that snaked for several miles across a landscape that sloped gently downhill, with water continuously reused as it collected in millponds, then flowed through headraces and into wheelpits where it powered waterwheels and turbines. The students exposing and mapping these remains discovered that the ground surface was littered with machine parts, abandoned equipment, spent fuel, and unfinished products, and the Shakers helped me to realize more clearly than ever just how integral industry is to every rural setting.

Fig. 16.1. Factory Pond dam and trash rack at Canterbury Shaker Village, Canterbury, New Hampshire. (Courtesy of David R. Starbuck.)

13

Lessons from Two Shaker Smoking Pipe Fragments
Kim A. McBride

Shaker landscapes certainly have taught us much about Shaker rural industries, but so have two small fragments of unglazed clay smoking pipes excavated at the Shaker village of Pleasant Hill, Kentucky. As David Starbuck notes, the Shakers were one of the most successful Christian utopian societies in nineteenth-century America, and are today known mostly for their craftsmanship and their dancing, which led the outside world to call them Shakers. Their song "Simple Gifts" was made famous by composer Aaron Copland's inclusion of it in his *Appalachian Spring*. This, along with an appreciation of their straight-lined furniture design, has encouraged us to focus on the Shakers as seeking, and representing, simplicity. While simplicity was a part of the Shaker lifestyle, too much emphasis on it takes us away from other concepts important to the Shakers, especially order and union.

These two smoking pipe fragments excavated at Pleasant Hill are a perfect example. We knew the Shakers used tobacco, even incorporating it into their religious worship in special Smoking Meetings. But I found many pipe fragments at the Shaker washhouses, where the Sisters (Shakers often referred to women within the Society as Sisters, and men as Brothers) washed the clothing for each communal Shaker family. This suggests that smoking was also common among the women doing hard, tedious laundry work. Our popular image isn't of Shaker women smoking tobacco pipes!

One of the first things I noticed about the Pleasant Hill pipes was that they were less decorated than those I excavated on non-Shaker sites—ah, there is that simplicity! But as I researched the pipes further, I realized that the matter was more complex. Two specimens included stamped letters that spelled "Pleasant Hill, Ky." In the late 1970s archaeologist James Murphy had written about pipes called Shakers made by a private company in Akron, Ohio. He hypothesized that these pipes were named Shakers because their form was similar to those the Shakers had made. He contacted the Pleasant Hill village seeking information on pipe production, but little was available. Pipes with "Pleasant Hill" stamped on them had yet to be excavated.

The desire to understand these Pleasant Hill smoking pipes led to two avenues of research common in historical archaeology: more documentary research and comparisons with other collections. I had learned that, because the Shakers were innovative and lived lives not typical of the outside world, the best explanations of the things they built and made were often found in their own journals or letters rather than in outside history sources.

Turning to the rich documentary record left by the Shakers, I found an 1810 Pleasant Hill letter that mentioned going "beyond Salt River to get some Pipe Clay." This helped confirm that pipe manufacture was one industry established at Pleasant Hill. Then we found two entries in the Pleasant Hill journals recording the sale of pipes, one in March 1814 for two dozen pipes for forty cents, and one in September 1814 for six thousand pipes at two cents each. Numerous entries in the Pleasant Hill journals recorded the purchase of tobacco, usually in pounds or kegs. These entries helped us understand why we excavated so many smoking pipes at Pleasant Hill— more than 124 to date—and why some were lettered. Many were intended for sale and carried their own form of advertising right on the bowl.

Even with this greater understanding, the contrast to non-Shaker pipes still intrigued us. Not only are non-Shaker pipes often glazed, and decorated with a variety of borders or molded figures, but they are typically shorter and more angular than the Pleasant Hill pipes. Was there a broader Shaker style, as perhaps suggested by the Ohio company's use of the name Shaker for its smoking pipes? We contacted colleagues working at other Shaker villages and visited several Shaker sites and museums in New England. We learned that this same style of pipe, with some variation in exact dimensions, was made and used at most of the Shaker villages. Archaeologist Kurt Fiegel has documented similar pipes at South Union, Kentucky, and David Starbuck has found similar ones at several New England villages. Archaeologist Leon Cranmer sent me pictures of smoking pipe fragments excavated from Sabbathday Lake, Maine; they look almost identical to those found at Pleasant Hill. We saw more when we visited the Shaker museum and library at Old Chatham, New York. And perhaps most instructive is that brass molds for these pipes have been located at Canterbury Village, New Hampshire, and at Sabbathday Lake. All in all, these pipes speak of the importance of unity and conformity within the Shaker villages—something the Shakers referred to as Union—as much as they do about simplicity within Shaker lives.

Yet there is a tension within this unity. Interestingly, I know of no lettered pipes from the other Shaker villages. Perhaps Pleasant Hill was unusually interested in the commercial potential of pipe manufacture. This would not be out of keeping with the documented history of Pleasant Hill within the larger Shaker community, as it was sometimes characterized as overly independent and worldly. And so these two little fragments continue to instruct us!

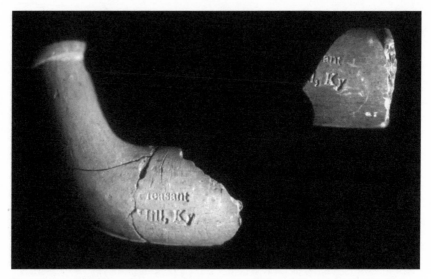

Fig. 16.2. Marked pipe fragments from Shaker Village of Pleasant Hill, Kentucky. (Courtesy of Kentucky Archaeological Survey.)

both fields would no doubt point out that industrial historians frequently ignore rural industries in favor of the larger commercial operations located in cities. Perhaps this is because many rural industries were small-scale and family-run. Given their low visibility on the landscape, rural industrial sites and technologies are constantly in danger of destruction. This is especially true of the mills and factories located along waterways where modern industries seek to locate on top of earlier mill foundations, raceways, and spillways. The future of these sites' archaeological remains thus appears rather bleak, unless archaeologists first discover and document them. Fortunately many federal, some state, and occasionally even local laws require that archaeologists explore the sites before construction begins, and dedicate public monies to this endeavor. In other cases archaeologists work with museums, universities, and community groups to uncover the remains of past industries.

Perhaps the greatest problem for archaeologists like me is deciding which industrial sites are important, because I am inclined to say "all of them!" So many mills, mines, and potteries left archaeological remains that it is hard to establish which ones feature examples of rare, older technology worth preserving, and which are no different from thousands of other industrial ruins. And is it only the rare, older examples that we should study and preserve? Some industrialists patterned their mills after a standardized guidebook, such as Oliver Evans's *The Young Mill-Wright and Miller's Guide,* whereas other rural craftsmen showed a remarkable amount of ingenuity and creativity. That is why we need to view every industrial site as unique, a potential source of useful knowledge. In studying industrial processes, we want to rediscover what the millers learned through trial and error and to find out whether their old technology still has value and applicability in the world today.

The first rural industrial sites excavated were on the East Coast, and interested nonprofessional archaeologists often directed the work. Roland Wells Robbins, popularly known as the "pick and shovel archaeologist," directed

---

14

Eli Whitney's Gun Factory
David R. Starbuck

Between 1972 and 1975 I directed a series of excavations for Yale University at the site of Eli Whitney's Gun Factory in Hamden, Connecticut, just north of New Haven. Beginning in 1798, this early and outstanding example of an industrial complex had contained a workers' village and even a company farm, and the factory produced thousands of firearms for the United States government and for state militias. The armory continued to operate until 1888, after which nearly all of the buildings were removed, along with any evidence for Whitney's manufacturing processes.

Perhaps more than any other site in the history of American industry, Whitney's gun factory gave archaeologists a chance to examine one of the "big" questions of American technology: Had interchangeable parts been invented there at the side of the Mill River? Before his death in 1825, Whitney claimed that his water- powered machinery was so well designed that even unskilled laborers could turn out parts that were highly uniform, rendering obsolete the older practice of fabricating muskets entirely by hand. Under my direction, a team of Yale students excavated the massive 1804 forge building, along with part of the 1860 main armory building and the 1798 filing and machine shop.

As we excavated the foundations and dumps of the factory complex, we found many files and grindstones but no pre-1825 evidence for the milling machines that would have ground down gun parts to really close tolerances, or for molds suggesting that some parts had been cast. In this way we helped debunk the myth of two centuries—first propagated by Whitney but perpetuated by many others—that the American System of Manufactures had begun at this very site. Edwin Battison's analysis of filing marks on curated artifacts from the site provided the first evidence challenging Whitney's claims. Whitney knew that self-promotion was good for business, but the use of archaeology at his factory site helped us all to realize that Whitney's manufacturing processes were no more innovative than those of the other manufacturers of his day.

15

The New England Glassworks
David R. Starbuck

In 1608 Jamestown, Virginia, became the first site of glassmaking in the New World, and thus the manufacture of glass became England's first industry in the American colonies. This prompted a National Park Service team led by J. C. Harrington to excavate the Jamestown glasshouse in 1948. Others later excavated several other glassmaking sites. However, one of the most precocious, and short-lived, of the early glass factories clung to the side of a mountain in Temple, New Hampshire, far from good roads and markets. This was the New England Glassworks, in production only from 1780 to 1782, during which time it became the first glass factory in the newly formed United States. This isolated but forward-looking manufactory made the first crown window glass in America, as well as multipurpose bottles and vessels for use in chemistry. To make crown glass, the worker blew and whirled the molten glass on his rod into a disk, from which the panes were then cut.

In 1975 Boston University hired me to lead four years of excavations at the New England Glassworks, together with codirectors James Wiseman and Frederick Gorman. In one of the largest industrial excavations at a rural factory, we exposed most of the main glasshouse, several workers' cabins, dumps, and specialized industrial features such as ovens and kilns. The factory's remoteness had helped to ensure its lack of contamination from later activity at the site, and its very brief period of use helped give us a very exact look at just two years in the life of a significant early American industry.

Thousands of fragments of glass, clay crucibles, and the waste from glassmaking known as cullet provided samples that we analyzed to determine the precise chemical formulas for the factory's products. Our excavations into the remains of the rough workers' cabins also gave us everyday artifacts that suggest the glassblowers and their apprentices lived rather spartan lives. While glassmaking efforts here met with some success, and the large quantities of glass waste reveal much product experimentation, the distance from markets and the difficulty in obtaining a skilled workforce no doubt doomed the enterprise from the beginning. In a way, that was most fortunate, because two hundred years later we archaeologists were delighted to discover what an amazingly pristine industrial site this is.

many of the earliest projects. He excavated at least thirty-two industrial sites, including the Saugus Iron Works in Massachusetts, Philipsburg Manor in New York, the John Winthrop Jr. Blast Furnace in Massachusetts, and a host of other ironworking sites. Robbins geared his work chiefly toward restoration and public interpretation, and he made intensive use of large mechanical equipment. Early industrial archaeologists commonly excavated with bulldozers. In 1977 I watched Robbins deliver a slide lecture that began with

Fig. 16.3. Furnace inside the glasshouse at the New England Glassworks, Temple, New Hampshire. (Courtesy of David R. Starbuck.)

views of a ruinous, overgrown site; the power equipment then rolled in and the buildings were reconstructed, and by the end of his presentation, everything had been rebuilt and the sun was setting in the background. Unfortunately, this made it hard to tell what Robbins had actually found at these industrial sites, and a healthy imagination often appeared to be central to each reconstruction effort. A lack of careful techniques was just as common among many professionals. I can remember the day in 1974 when an historian of technology told me that I should dig industrial sites with bulldozers—that you need industrial-strength equipment to dig industrial ruins. At the time I was directing excavations at Eli Whitney's Gun Factory. Subsequent industrial archaeology efforts have shown this sort of attitude is nonsense, and today archaeologists use the same meticulous excavation techniques at both industrial and nonindustrial sites.

As the field evolved in the 1970s, the Whitney Gun Factory and the extensive work conducted by Edward Rutsch at the Rogers Locomotive Company and other mill and canal sites in Paterson, New Jersey, helped to bring visibility and growing precision to industrial digs. Then, between 1975 and 1978, Boston University conducted a large-scale excavation at the site of the New England Glassworks that operated in Temple, New Hampshire, from 1780 to 1782. Mary Beaudry of Boston University and Stephen Mrozowski of the University of Massachusetts–Boston later directed a long-term study of do-

16

Musseling in the Mississippi Watershed
David R. Starbuck

Up and down the Mississippi River watershed, mussels have supported important industries and produced millions of dollars in income to men and women since the 1860s. Until the turn of the twentieth century, pearl rushes created boom-town atmospheres, and in many areas the revenue from pearl sales exceeded that of almost every other natural-resource industry except timber. In the twentieth century, shell buttons eclipsed pearls as the mainstay of the mussel industry. Remains of musseling vessels and of processing and transport facilities line riverbanks in sixteen states. Together with the written records of these industries and the recollections of musseling families, they tell the important history of "washboards, pigtoes, and muckets."

In a most fascinating study, Cheryl Claassen of Appalachian State University has visited many sites of the mussel industry, ridden on the brail boats, interviewed the musseling families and fisheries officers, and examined the production of shell and pearl buttons between 1891 and about 1950. While freshwater bivalves from the Mississippi watershed may seem an unusual basis for a high-profile industry, some individuals became instantly wealthy from the discovery of freshwater pearls, and many others made a satisfactory living for generations through the production of buttons. Over a period of years, inventors designed the machinery needed to process buttons from hard freshwater shells. Dozens of manufacturing plants and blank-cutting shops opened, and this natural-resource industry spread out along dozens of rivers. Unfortunately, as Claassen has documented, the shell button industry had died by 1950, and now the cultured pearl is rapidly replacing the natural pearls that commercial musselers used to harvest in the Mississippi watershed.

mestic life in the Boott Mills boardinghouses in the city of Lowell, Massachusetts, for the National Park Service, which became a model for another NPS project at the industrial community of Harpers Ferry, West Virginia.

These large East Coast projects have been increasingly complemented by studies of such diverse industries as copper mining in Michigan, musseling on the Mississippi River, gold mining by Chinese laborers on the Oregon frontier, sugar processing in the Caribbean and Florida, and salmon canning on the Pacific Coast. One of the best-researched examples of this last industry comes from British Columbia, where many remote, seasonal cannery operations stood close to the main salmon fishing grounds where salmon came upriver to spawn. Nearly all of these canneries have now been abandoned, and archaeologists and historians like Dianne Newell of the University of British Columbia have documented the extensive ruins.

17

Yulee Sugar Mills
Robin Denson

The Gulf Archaeology Research Institute (GARI) has a simple mandate: connecting the past with our future. To this end, the staff of archaeologists and scientists involves teachers, students, and the public in all of their research projects in central and Gulf Coast Florida. At the 1851 Yulee Sugar Mill Ruins State Historic Site in Homosassa, for example, GARI archaeologists and volunteers documented the mill's boiler, wells, grinding machinery, and cane-processing kettles. They prepared a floor plan of the mill and pieced together the process by which cane became sugar at the innovative steam-powered mill that employed one thousand people at its height. On the basis of GARI's research, park staff better interpret and manage the site visited by more than 35,000 tourists each year. Thousands of schoolchildren are also benefiting from a new Florida Heritage Education lesson plan on Historic Mills. They are learning about the technology, social issues, and traditions that shaped agri-industry in Florida. By exploring the impacts of farming and milling on the environment, they begin to see how the past has left its imprint on the present, and to think about what they will do about that legacy in the future.

Oftentimes open-air museum villages have re-created the buildings and processes of rural industries to give visitors a firsthand experience of just how each industry functioned. One of the early leaders in combining public education with archaeology is Old Sturbridge Village, which conducted many successful archaeological projects at industrial buildings or sites before moving or re-creating them at their mid-nineteenth-century community in Sturbridge, Massachusetts. These included the Nichols-Colby Sawmill, originally sited in Bow, New Hampshire; the Emerson Bixby Blacksmith Shop; and Hervey Brooks's Pottery Shop and Kiln, formerly located in Goshen, Connecticut. Every time I have visited Old Sturbridge Village, I have been thrilled to watch and listen to the operation of the old saw blades, grindstones, and waterwheels, for they are noisy, dirty, inefficient, and absolutely reeking with nostalgia! In most cases, though, it required archaeological discoveries to get this equipment up and running again.

Of the many categories of industrial sites, perhaps none has seen as much work as the blast furnaces and forges that sprang up throughout North America wherever there were natural deposits of iron. It is an unforgettable experience to climb to the top of an abandoned furnace stack and peer down into the "bosh" where workers dumped loads of iron ore, lime, and fuel when the furnace was "in blast," or to crawl inside and discover a great "sala-

Fig. 16.4. Grist mill at Old Sturbridge Village, Sturbridge, Massachusetts.
(Courtesy of David R. Starbuck.)

mander" of hardened iron left in the base of an abandoned furnace. I have crawled through the remains of furnaces in New York, Vermont, Massachusetts, and New Hampshire, and it never becomes boring—every site has piles of by-products, the foundations of outbuildings, traces of the bellows apparatus, and slag and charcoal scattered underfoot for hundreds of feet in all directions. Excavated blast furnace sites include Hopewell Furnace (now Hopewell Village National Historic Site) in Pennsylvania; Charlotteburg Middle Forge and the Long Pond Ironworks in northern New Jersey; the Upper Forge at Valley Forge in Pennsylvania; Catoctin Furnace in Maryland; the Eaton (Hopewell) Furnace near Youngstown, Ohio; Bluff Furnace in Chattanooga, Tennessee; and most recently the Bloomery Forge at Clintonville, New York, where Gordon Pollard of SUNY-Plattsburgh is exposing the forge building and associated bellows houses. At many of these sites, the blast furnace stacks and architectural remains are imposing even today.

Every rural community had blacksmith shops, and archaeologists have stories to tell about how black we became while digging through the charcoal, ashes, and cinders. I have excavated the dumps from three forges—always a filthy job!—but it is most rewarding to study the tools used by the blacksmith and to find examples of the wrought iron objects that smiths repaired. John Light and Henry Unglik undertook one of the best studies at

18

Bluff Furnace
David R. Starbuck

Bluff Furnace was a traditional charcoal-fired blast furnace built in Chattanooga, Tennessee. In 1859 workers converted it into a cupola-type furnace fueled by coke. At the same time, they modified it from a square stone structure into a cylindrical boiler-plate stack. The conversion from charcoal to coke, which led to increased impurities, proved troublesome, and in late 1860 the furnace was allowed to cool and was then abandoned. This short-lived furnace never went back into blast, and it lay abandoned until 1977 when the late Jeffrey Brown of the University of Tennessee at Chattanooga commenced excavations there that Nicholas Honerkamp and R. Bruce Council later continued.

During their fieldwork, under the auspices of the Jeffrey L. Brown Institute of Archaeology, Honerkamp and Council exposed a circular hearth surrounded by a six-sided base for the large cast-iron pillars that supported the stack of the furnace. Honerkamp and Council, like most archaeologists, have described their finds and the furnace operation in great detail. But they also viewed the site as representative of much broader trends. They saw the changes at Bluff Furnace as a response to some of the larger economic and technological forces faced by southern industry on the eve of the Civil War. In effect, the changeover from charcoal to coke had been risky. The costs of modernizing had been too high, the coke was high in impurities, and the owners just could not obtain enough of the coke. Bluff Furnace faced insurmountable odds, and it ended in failure all too quickly. Still, Honerkamp and Council successfully related events and processes at Bluff Furnace to a much larger world.

---

the shop at Fort St. Joseph (1796–1814) on St. Joseph Island, Ontario. This shop was in use sometime before 1810, and it consisted of a wood building on a stone foundation, with a dirt floor on a base of rounded boulders. The archaeologists discovered a forge against one wall of the structure and a base for the anvil in the center. But most important, by studying the distribution of tools, iron fragments, and slag, they determined the shop layout and demonstrated that the smith shod horses and mended household equipment along with his more general blacksmithing.

An equally widespread rural industry was pottery making, and archaeologists have dug literally hundreds of pottery shops and kilns throughout North America. We have found tons of "wasters," the pottery vessels ruined during firing in the kiln, and "kiln furniture," the wedges, tripods, and setting bars that separated and leveled the pots inside the kiln. Waste products help us understand the range of vessel forms and decorations rural potters used, and

Fig. 16.5. Blast furnace, East Dorset, Vermont. (Courtesy of David R. Starbuck.)

wasters reveal the technological problems that the potters encountered and how they met these challenges. Regional pottery studies often began when ceramicists such as Lura Woodside Watkins, the leading expert in New England, conducted small-scale digging at dozens of abandoned pot shops and kiln sites. The goal was typically to determine the kinds of products made and the techniques used at each shop, and over the past century, archaeologists have discovered and excavated pottery-making sites in nearly every community that had good sources of clay and customers that needed inexpensive, utilitarian vessels. In the 1980s I excavated the remains of a nineteenth-century shop and two kilns in Concord, New Hampshire. Virtually every depression, ditch, and cellar in the vicinity was crammed with thousands of wasters and pottery fragments, the ubiquitous by-products of many years of pottery making by Joseph Hazeltine, one of the most prolific local potters.

Practical concerns determined the siting of many rural industries. Generally they had to be where fuel and raw materials could be obtained cheaply, where the labor supply was adequate, and where transportation could carry products to market. Unfortunately, we are now losing many of these sites of rural industry to development or "progress," and so we must decide how to preserve and study these former ways of life before they are lost forever. We historical archaeologists have a tremendous opportunity to rediscover the lost beliefs, values, and technologies of rural America by studying the many

Fig. 16.6. Inside the blacksmith shop at Sanborn Farm, Loudon, New Hampshire. (Courtesy of David R. Starbuck.)

abandoned or soon-to-be-demolished industrial sites. Mills, furnaces, mines, craft shops, canals, fisheries, railroads, and many other industrial places have potential to provide technological knowledge that is no longer used in today's workplaces. Too often industrial processes are forgotten in the rush to innovate and modernize. The remains and lessons we discover at industrial sites are helping to reconstruct a recent but poorly known past.

Part 5

Cultures in Conflict

Contests on Land and at Sea

Lu Ann De Cunzo

The clashing of cultures, at times violently, has punctuated the history of North America. Indian wars. Revolution. Civil war. World wars. Global terrorism. To understand these "cultures in conflict," historical archaeologists probe their technology, economics, and battle strategies. Our experience with the conflicts of our own time reminds us to also look closely at the personal side of human conflict. We struggle to make sense of these conflicts, studying the memorials honoring our fallen heroes and the scenes of their battles along with the causes and effects of war.

The European conquest of North America provoked contests of cultures that continue to this day. In the 1930s archaeologists like George I. Quimby first developed a deep interest in the ways Native American and European colonial peoples affected each other's cultures. Quimby told the stories of native and European—especially French—colonial contact from the perspective of the people. He wanted to know what motivated the people behind the trading posts, forts, and goods that formed the archaeological evidence of their encounters. He began by following the trail of that evidence, and established a subfield within archaeological material culture studies on Indian trade goods. What goods, he asked, did the French produce to trade with northern native peoples? Where, when, and how were they produced, transported, and shipped? What was their value to the French and native traders? How were they used, and what does their disposal or loss tell us about their owners' lives and important events in the history of native-French colonial interaction? Like other pioneers of his generation, he chose not to highlight the violent conflicts that erupted between native peoples and

European Americans. Yet his work still stands as a vivid reminder that we must seek a holistic understanding of colonialism and its consequences. David Starbuck's studies of colonial forts and battlefields across New England and the innovative work of Richard Fox and others at Little Bighorn battlefield carry on that legacy.

When Quimby began his studies in 1935, the "early years" of underwater archaeology in North America still lay more than a quarter century in the future. John Broadwater began his career in underwater archaeology in the 1960s. He later formed a group of avocational divers who pioneered the use of archaeological techniques to explore North American shipwrecks, many of which sank during violent encounters. Since underwater explorations began in 1978 on the USS *Monitor,* Broadwater has worked to preserve and explore the first shipwreck designated a National Historic Landmark. The ironclad *Monitor* became an American myth after its much-publicized battle with the CSS *Virginia* (ex-*Merrimack*) during the Civil War. The second National Historic Landmark shipwreck, the USS *Arizona,* lies on the seabed in Pearl Harbor, one of the most emotion-laden war sites in the world for two generations of Americans and Japanese. For the past two decades, archaeologists, conservators, and divers have labored to preserve the remains of that day of infamy, "lest we forget."

The Archaeology of America's Colonial Wars

David R. Starbuck

In school, we are exposed to mind-numbing lists of dates for battles, victories, and treaties, along with the names of forts, generals, and patriotic heroes, all of which seem very remote from us. Nevertheless, because of the drama and emotions connected to warfare, every child fantasizes occasionally about becoming a soldier and accomplishing great deeds in battle. Or at least I did. After all, armies and the fortifications they occupy have helped to determine the destiny of nations, and the modern cultures, languages, and worldviews of the North American continent were shaped during the colonial wars of the seventeenth and eighteenth centuries. But as adults we come to realize the significance of those distant events in shaping our modern regional, national, and ethnic identities, and then we discover that the sites of long-ago battles can still be visited. Hundreds of forts and battlefields have been excavated, interpreted, and oftentimes reconstructed, and millions of visitors each year are able to appreciate how very near to them the past can be.

Most of these military reconstructions and open-air interpretations required archaeologists to put in years of archival research, excavation, and artifact analysis. Many of the early engineers' drawings of forts and battlefields are highly schematicized or incomplete, with ordinary soldiers' huts, lookout posts, and latrines rarely depicted, and with many details not drawn to scale. The surviving construction plans for forts were typically drawn before laborers began to build the walls, and thus French, British, and Spanish forts that have been reconstructed without the use of archaeology tend to be woefully inaccurate.

Archival research may uncover the daily diaries of soldiers and officers, the letters "from the field" that soldiers sent to their loved ones back home, lists of provisions and ordnance, and copies of the orders issued by officers to their men. Still, it requires archaeological fieldwork to locate sites on the ground, to determine the building techniques whereby structures were hastily erected, and to learn the consumption patterns of large camps of men—and camp followers—who were far from home and standardized types of provisioning. The ability of historical archaeology to go beyond the behavior prescribed in regimental manuals and orderly books, to describe what actually took place under rugged field conditions, is certainly one of the great strengths of our discipline. It also is fortunate that recent technological advances in geophysical information systems and in remote sensing techniques, especially in ground-penetrating radar, have made it easier to locate and plot features scattered across the large areas covered by battlefields.

Each European power that colonized the Americas created its own distinctive fortifications, from the Spanish settlements of the 1500s where forts were constructed to protect them from French attack, to Dutch trading posts in New York that were protected by forts during the early 1600s, to the more permanent French and English settlements that clashed with each other in the 1600s and 1700s, to the forts that the United States and Canada built over the past two centuries, reflecting the War of 1812, the American Civil War, and various so-called Indian Wars during the opening of the West. The most important of these to archaeologists are those that tell stories about the lives of ordinary soldiers who were marking time while waiting to fight, and where archaeological projects have successfully gone beyond the confines of the documentary record.

Military-sites archaeology began with the systematic collection of regimental buttons, belt plates, and ordnance by enthusiastic amateurs. But it did not take long before the public interest in military sites caused government agencies, most notably the U.S. National Park Service and Parks Canada, to make it a very high priority to excavate and re-create various types of fortifications for mass audiences. For example, in the United States one of the earlier National Park Service projects was conducted at Fort Necessity, Pennsylvania, where J. C. "Pinky" Harrington dug during 1952 and 1953. While modest in its reconstructed form, Fort Necessity is generally remembered as the site where a youthful Colonel George Washington and his Virginia militia surrendered on July 3, 1754, to a seasoned force of French and Indians from Fort Duquesne, where Pittsburgh is today. But archaeologists are more likely to think of Fort Necessity as a site where early-twentieth-century excavations repeatedly misinterpreted the shape of the fort as quadrangular or triangular, and where it required improved field methods in the 1950s to establish that the stockade was, in fact, circular. Such refinements in methods have been critical in helping archaeology to go beyond the written record.

Forts have been excavated in North America that date back even to the sixteenth century. One of the earliest Spanish forts excavated was the 1566 site of Santa Elena, on Parris Island in South Carolina. To the north, near

19

Fortress of Louisbourg, Nova Scotia
Lu Ann De Cunzo

Parks Canada holds hundreds of historical and archaeological sites in trust for the Canadian people. One of the brightest stars is the Fortress of Louisbourg National Historic Site on Cape Breton Island in Nova Scotia. By the time the French first settled Louisbourg, Cape Breton Island (then Isle Royale) had served for years as the base of the colonial cod fishery operating on the Grand Banks. The town soon became a commercial hub, trading dried cod for goods imported from Europe and the Caribbean. In 1758 the English besieged the fortress for the second time. Without a strong navy to patrol the surrounding waters, the fortress fell to a British army force supported by 150 ships. The British made sure Louisbourg would never again serve the French empire by destroying the fortress.

Two centuries later, the government of Canada began a massive project to reconstruct one-quarter of Louisbourg so Canadians and visitors from around the world could experience life in a French colonial outpost of the 1740s. Years of research buttress the creative living history program at Louisbourg. Archaeology began in 1961 as a prelude to reconstruction, with former coal miners providing much of the labor. By the time digging ended in 1979, the archaeologists had recovered roughly 4,500,000 artifacts, totaling about one-fifth of all the artifacts owned by Parks Canada. They have also uncovered and recorded traces of many eighteenth-century buildings, gardens, streets, and fortifications. Historians have collected and studied 750,000 pages of documents and more than 500 historical maps and plans. The research at Louisbourg has opened an unrivaled window into the past.

Today the fortress comes to life each spring, and costumed actors "take up residence" in sixty-five reconstructed buildings along commercial avenues and the busy waterfront. Visitors walk among Louisbourg's soldiers, merchants, fishermen, musicians, servants, and mothers with their children, and experience life in the colonial town and fort *almost* firsthand. More than thirty-five years of archaeological research have made possible this world-class heritage experience. At Louisbourg visitors see the artifacts, discover the ways that historical archaeologists pieced together their stories, and experience the stories acted out before them. The stories lead the visitors through time, revealing a history of Anglo-French colonial rivalry and the vagaries of a northern maritime economy built on the cod fisheries and trade.

20

Colonial Michilimackinac, Michigan
Lu Ann De Cunzo

A "sister city" to Louisbourg, Michilimackinac was also built by French colonists and soldiers in the early 1700s. The French strategically located the fortified settlement on the Straits of Mackinac separating what we now know as Michigan's Upper and Lower Peninsulas. From this prominent location, Michilimackinac promoted and protected the French fur trade in the region for nearly fifty years (ca. 1714–61). At the conclusion of the French and Indian War, the French transferred the post to the British. When they in turn moved their garrison to a new fort on Mackinac Island, they destroyed all aboveground evidence of the old fort. Today the reconstructed settlement is a National Historic Landmark, a status granted by the United States government only to those sites significant to the history of the nation as a whole. It also boasts the longest ongoing archaeological program in the country.

Over the course of more than four decades, archaeologists have painstakingly uncovered the traces of the palisade, the remains of more than a dozen buildings, and fragments of the furnishings, clothing, tools, and food and other trash discarded by the residents. From the thousands of wooden post stains, stone hearths, remnant garden soils, and artifacts, Michilimackinac has risen again from the sands along Lake Michigan. Visitors can explore the life of the village's military contingent and their families, fur traders, tradespeople, and Native Americans with the aid of costumed interpreters. A wonderful exhibit, "Treasures from the Sand, Archaeology at Michilimackinac," presents the techniques and results of decades of archaeology at the site, and displays hundreds of carefully conserved and researched artifacts. Remains of the underground powder magazine and several root cellars have been preserved in place for viewing. Each summer an archaeological team returns to Michilimackinac to uncover the past before the visitors' eyes.

Lynn Evans directs the current program, as curator of archaeology for the Mackinac State Historic Parks. She writes, "Michilimackinac is a wonderful place to do archaeology. The site is incredibly rich, due to excellent preservation and because it was set aside as a park in 1857. Because of the long-term nature of both the archaeological and historical research at the site, we have been able to learn detailed information about the daily lives of the inhabitants of the fort. This helps make the past come alive for our visitors. This is the first time many of them have seen an archaeological dig and they are fascinated to see pieces of history unearthed. It is rewarding to be able to share our results with the public through conversations, interpretive programming, and exhibits, in addition to more traditional reports."

Fig. 17.1. Digging in the heart of the reconstructed post of Michilimackinac. The excavation of the east end of the South Southwest Row House, shown here, began in 1998. (Courtesy of Mackinac State Historic Parks.)

Jamestown, Virginia, the Colonial Williamsburg Foundation dug a 1619–22 English fort at Martin's Hundred in the 1970s.

The Dutch also had a very early presence in the Americas, and in upstate New York the ruins of Fort Orange were discovered underneath the streets of modern Albany. This half-acre, wooden-walled earthwork was occupied first by Dutch and later by British garrisons between 1624 and 1676. The richness of the finds, including decorative delft wall tiles, fine glassware, glass beads, fine German stoneware, and more, suggests that the employees of the Dutch West India Company were importing large quantities of European goods, which they traded to the Mohawks and Mohicans.

The French occupation of the New World included the construction of impressive fortifications in Quebec City and Montreal, as well as coastal forts like Pentagoet (1635–74) on the Acadian frontier, but their largest fort in North America was Fortress Louisbourg on Cape Breton Island. Far into the interior of America, in what is now Mackinaw City, Michigan, the French began work on Fort Michilimackinac around 1715, after which the British and then the Americans occupied the site.

Military-sites archaeologists tend to specialize in a single century, or a single culture, or even a single conflict, and my own specialty is British military sites of the eighteenth century. I have excavated at several of the forts and battlefields that date to the French and Indian War (the Seven Years' War) and, twenty years later, to the American Revolution. These engagements decided the fate of the North American continent and determined that the United States and much of Canada would be English-speaking, with a foundation in English law and tradition, even as Quebec would retain its French language and culture.

The English initially lagged behind the French, building very insubstantial fortifications that were often little more than log stockades. In the 1750s, though, they began to imitate French defenses when they built two bastioned forts in northern New York State. The first of these "improved" English forts, Fort William Henry, was raised at the southern end of Lake George in 1755. The second and larger fort, Fort Edward, was constructed fifteen miles to the south, on the Hudson River where it could easily receive supplies from Albany. It stood adjacent to the vast site of Rogers Island, where fifteen thousand British soldiers, colonial militia, and rangers camped during the late 1750s in between attacks upon the French forts in the north. Fort William Henry proved short-lived, falling in 1757, prompting James Fenimore Cooper to write his famous novel *The Last of the Mohicans* in 1826. The Fort Edward/Rogers Island complex lasted through the American Revolution.

The excavations at Fort Edward and Fort William Henry have revealed the remains of British barracks, huts, hospitals, storehouses, dumps, and military artifacts from the mid-eighteenth century. Each, in its own way, demonstrates how military-sites archaeology does not simply duplicate what is known from history but instead tells some very new stories. At Fort William Henry, the cellar of the West Barracks has been dug, exposing charred wood timbers and the base of a massive fireplace, along with many exploded fragments of mortar bombs that probably date to the destruction of the fort. Part of the fort's main cemetery was excavated, and forensic studies have revealed that soldiers lived an extremely stressful life on the northern frontier. The skeletons at Fort William Henry are literally covered with evidence for chronic stress, herniated discs, infections, tuberculosis, amputations, and even scalping.

The archaeological evidence at Fort Edward is rather different, because it never experienced a serious attack. On Rogers Island the excavation of huts and barracks was accompanied by the discovery of the island's smallpox hospital, the first such hospital excavated in the United States.

Fig. 17.2. Excavating a barracks fireplace on Rogers Island in Fort Edward, New York. (Courtesy of David R. Starbuck.)

It is often the less-known military sites that are the most intact, because they are less likely to have been subjected to the constant looting and metal detecting experienced by more famous forts and battlefields. One of the most notable fortifications of the French and Indian War was Fort Stanwix in Rome, New York, which was dug by the National Park Service beginning in 1970 and was then completely reconstructed as part of a downtown urban renewal project. Remote sensing and hut excavation has uncovered the 1777–78 camp at Valley Forge near Philadelphia; extensive rows of winter huts from 1777–80 have been excavated at Morristown, New Jersey; barracks, artisans' quarters, and an armorer's shop were excavated at the site of the Continental Artillery Cantonment of 1778–79 in Pluckemin; and all of

Fig. 17.3. Butchering pit at the Revolutionary War fortress of Mount Independence on Lake Champlain, containing leg bones from at least seventeen cows consumed in the General Hospital there. (Courtesy of David R. Starbuck.)

the Saratoga Battlefield was mapped in the 1970s, including redoubts, the American and British lines, field hospitals, and more.

However, of the many surviving sites of the American Revolution, easily the most intact site that I have ever witnessed and studied is Mount Independence in Orwell, Vermont, overlooking the narrowest point on Lake Champlain. From this three-hundred-acre mountaintop, American forces effectively blocked the passage of British ships as they attempted to venture south from Canada in 1776–77. I directed excavations there for the Vermont Division for Historic Preservation, uncovering a blockhouse, lookout posts, many soldiers' and officers' huts, barracks buildings, storehouses, battery areas, and the general hospital. Evidence for the daily lives of the soldiers included the bones from many fish caught in Lake Champlain and thousands of fragments of wine bottles, including one on which a soldier had scratched his name: "James Hill 1777."

Military sites of all time periods and national origins share many of the same characteristics. They were largely male enclaves, usually occupied for short periods, often with difficulties in obtaining adequate provisions or up-to-date goods, and they were generally located in contested frontier settings. These conditions are well suited to archaeological analysis, and many of the research questions examined by military-sites archaeologists involve aspects of provisioning (especially diet), modernity, gender, differences in living standards (between officers and enlisted men), adaptation of construction techniques and camp layout to frontier landscapes, and willingness to adhere to prescribed behavior as defined by military manuals.

Military-sites archaeology is unquestionably one of the most popular and dynamic subfields of historical archaeology, attracting millions of annual visitors to reconstructed sites. No doubt this level of interest is due to the dramatic, even catastrophic, events that occurred at many military sites, and these were certainly seminal in shaping the direction of the nations that formed in North America. But past glories or disasters on the battlefield or ramparts are not the greatest thrill for the archaeologist: rather, the real excitement comes from examining the lives of soldiers and officers who have not had a voice until now, yet who left us with a rich record of hut outlines and fireplaces, latrines, garbage-filled wells, wine bottles, exploded mortar shells, armament, and more. These are the pieces from which we can reconstruct a bit of their humanity, and perhaps our research will help to honor the early soldiers who made sacrifices under extremely harsh frontier conditions.

The Civil War Under Water

Sarah McDowell, with contributions by Mark Wilde-Ramsing

When I was growing up, my family spent a week every summer on the Outer Banks of North Carolina. Here I fell in love with the ocean. For me, the ocean was a source of mystery—and never more so than the year Robert Ballard discovered the RMS *Titanic*. Our video collection offers testimony that I watched every *Titanic*-related National Geographic, Discovery Channel, and PBS special ever made. The footage of the *Titanic* was gloomy, dark, and mysterious. I remember watching Ballard's robotic sub gracefully weaving in and out of the rusted bow. Images of people walking on the now corroded decks or lounging in their opulent staterooms immediately came to mind. A child's doll still waiting for its "mother" . . . a porcelain shaving basin without a razor . . . blackness, now the only view from the portholes.

For me, and for many others, these images sparked an interest in the underwater exploration of shipwrecks. Since Ballard's initial discovery, various groups have asserted their interest in the *Titanic* as well. Their efforts to reexplore the vessel and retrieve artifacts stirs an ongoing debate over the best way to preserve and study the mighty ocean liner. Some feel that recovering artifacts is valid, but that they should not be sold; others believe that the artifacts should remain in public collections, while still others feel the gravesite should be left alone. For many underwater archaeologists, preservation of the *Titanic* has become a battle cry. Their approach to the *Titanic* reflects the basic ideals of underwater archaeology: strive to maintain the integrity of historic shipwrecks, preserve them, and share archaeological findings with the public.

Wrecks closer to home in American waters, while often less fiercely debated, are equally important. Recently Civil War–era wrecks like the *H. L. Hunley* and the *Monitor* have attracted public interest. Before these ships became hot topics, wrecks like the *Maple Leaf* proved that their archaeological remnants are crucial to understanding the history of these ships. But what do all of these ships have in common? Why are they so important to archaeologists, social scientists, and the public? What do they say about the past and

Fig. 18.1. Mustard bottle from the *Monitor,* mute witness to the men who once served aboard the vessel. (Courtesy of Mariners' Museum, Newport News, Virginia.)

the Civil War? No document or photograph could match the value of wrecks such as these. They are time capsules, some still carrying the armament, cargoes, even crew from the day they sank. They were the technological forerunners of the modern navy, and they were the graves of thousands of men.

We begin our survey of Civil War wrecks off the coast of North Carolina, where archaeologists are struggling to preserve one of these technological marvels, the USS *Monitor.* Even though the *Monitor* rests in the "graveyard of the Atlantic," it does not rest peacefully. It is constantly threatened by its own structural failings, as well as unforgiving storms and thoughtless boating accidents. In efforts to protect the *Monitor* from these menaces, in 1975 the nation founded its first marine sanctuary. Here scientists debate and plan the future of the famous ironclad. Although avoiding full recovery because of the *Monitor*'s fragility, they did recover some salvageable parts, ones that are critical to understanding the *Monitor*'s technological significance.

These parts are helping archaeologists concentrate their studies on the *Monitor*'s revolutionary design and construction. In a ship with more than one hundred patented innovations, such information is extremely valuable.

Built in only three months, the "cheesebox on a raft" was the first vessel designed to hold all machinery and personnel below the waterline. The one key innovation that was not below deck was the *Monitor's* famous revolving gun turret. In August 2002, the last season of a five-year recovery expedition, underwater archaeologists successfully raised the 235-ton turret, along with its two guns. These recovery efforts took years of planning and work. Given the *Monitor's* fragile state, precautionary rigging was set in place, sometimes years before excavation. For fear of the hull collapsing, scientists prepared arduously for each recovery attempt. So archaeologists were excited when, in the 1990s, they successfully recovered sections of the hull. They became eager to excavate the *Monitor's* famous steam engine, which was accomplished in 2001. Without this dedication, many of the *Monitor's* technological innovations would still be at the mercy of the Atlantic. Now, however, they are displayed at the Mariners' Museum in Newport News, Virginia, for the public to once again appreciate.

Like the *Monitor,* the Confederate submarine *H. L. Hunley* is a brilliant example of Civil War technology brought to light by underwater archaeology. Only forty feet long, the *Hunley* was a curious-looking vessel with its porpoiselike shape and long metal spar extending from the prow. The *Hunley's* unsuccessful missions cost the lives of many eager volunteers. Though revolutionary, the technology still needed improving. Inside the small cavity, a crowded eight-man crew literally cranked the sub into motion. For the crew, every mission was a test of endurance and a race against the clock. Oxygen and manpower were at a premium.

The *Hunley* gained global fame when it sunk the USS *Housatonic* off Charleston, South Carolina, on February 17, 1864. Before the *Housatonic's* crew could react to the approaching vessel, the *Hunley* rammed the hull of the *Housatonic* with its long metal spar and succeeded in planting a torpedo inside her as well. As the *Housatonic* quickly sank, the *Hunley's* crew signaled a success to shore. But they would not celebrate for long. Mysteriously the *Hunley* sank in Charleston harbor only minutes after the battle. For the next 131 years people wondered about its tragic fate.

With the help of a magnetometer, archaeologists located and planned to raise the *Hunley* in 2000. Since 1996 they knew that the hull was intact and in relatively good condition, but they did not know the strength of the original riveting. If they lifted the *Hunley,* would it split apart? Fearing this scenario, archaeologists took into account the weight of the vessel both in the water and upon arriving at the surface. Before they could even begin to use their scientific plan to raise it, divers went to the site to vacuum away mud and silt. After the ship was successfully freed, a large crane lifted it out of the

Fig. 18.2. Detyens Shipyard crane lifting the *Hunley* to the conservation lab. (Courtesy of Friends of the *Hunley*.)

murky water and into the twenty-first century. Only after it was raised could the excavations begin.

Archaeologists anxiously waited for a glimpse into the body of the *Hunley* as work began in January 2001. At the Warren Lasch Conservation Center the vessel, in a large tank of water, first underwent a desalination process. While it acclimated to its new home, computer imagery carefully mapped the inside so that archaeologists could begin to excavate the ship. The imagery was important, as the body of the vessel was filled with fine sediment. The hours of painstakingly scraping away the mud proved worthwhile. The artifacts on board were amazingly well preserved. The boards that the crew sat on looked just as they had in the 1860s. In close proximity to them, bones of the same men lay awaiting identification.

Using recovered artifacts, archaeologists are identifying remains and learning about the material life of the *Hunley*'s men as well as exploring theories concerning its mysterious fate. One major finding is that the crew did not in fact drown. Stalactites found in the submarine, resulting from a slow, steady drip of water, suggest that the ship did not immediately fill with water and sink. More likely, the crew died from a lack of oxygen. Perhaps this

Fig. 18.3. Archaeologist Shea McLean drawing a sketch in the submarine. By this point, most of the sub's contents had already been removed from the center crew compartment. (Courtesy of Friends of the *Hunley*.)

supports the finding of the bones so close to the boards that the crew sat on. To scientists, the men did not seem panicked; rather they died dutifully at their posts.

But what about a more complete picture of life as a sailor on that day? Recovered artifacts such as buttons, ID tags, personal trinkets, lanterns, and combs provide insight into this question. The material culture from the *Hunley* reveals the human dimension of the ship. Trinkets remind us of men separated from loved ones, the lanterns and combs about working on the ship, the buttons and ID tags about the pride of being a sailor.

Like the *Hunley*, the discovery of the federal transport ship *Maple Leaf* has also contributed to understanding the material life of the Civil War sailor. In the St. Johns River near Jacksonville, Florida, the *Maple Leaf* now rests, like so many wrecks, in an underwater environment that is not conducive to archaeological excavation. The ship is not structurally intact and is severely damaged. Rather than attempting to raise the ship, as they did the *Hunley*, archaeologists rely on diving to the site. Here their goals are to carefully retrieve artifacts and to map the ship.

During the war, the *Maple Leaf* was an important ship in President Lincoln's naval blockade against the Confederacy. It was originally built in Ontario and used as a merchant ship. In 1862 a group of New England investors sold it to the Union, which then used it as a blockader. In transit on the St. Johns River on April 1, 1864, the *Maple Leaf* was steaming along routinely when a Confederate mine exploded nearby. Suddenly the ship began filling with water and quickly sank, taking with it equipment and personal belongings from three Union regiments. Like the *Hunley*, the *Maple Leaf* is a Civil War time capsule. Its hull still contains the cargo that it carried the day it sank.

Since one photograph and a few sketches are all the historical documentation that exists concerning the *Maple Leaf*, archaeologists must rely on information from the *Maple Leaf* itself to record its history. Their first goal was to map what remained of the ship. Unfortunately, in the late 1880s the Army Corps of Engineers destroyed much of the ship's structure. Resting at the bottom of a vital waterway, the vessel was a navigational hazard, prompting the engineers to scrap anything above the riverbed. Mapping is critical to work on the *Maple Leaf*, as divers in 1992 found the deck severely damaged, partially by the engineers' work. They realized that the ship, plagued by more than one hundred years of human activity, would only continue to deteriorate and that mapping was the best way to preserve what survived of the *Maple Leaf*.

Inside the broken ship, archaeologists found well-preserved Civil War goods in the cargo holds. Boxes of military supplies, medical supplies, weaponry, and camp and mess equipment were stenciled with regiment names. As in the *Hunley*, archaeologists also found personal effects, which gave them a glimpse into the life of a Civil War sailor. They found everything from wallets, writing utensils, and gaming pieces to legible pieces of paper! In many ways, the artifacts are like those of the *Titanic*. They now lie lifeless, but they allow us to imagine the people who used them. Looking at the gaming pieces and the writing materials, one can imagine a soldier passing the time with friends or writing to a loved one.

At these shipwrecks, archaeologists do a different type of archaeology. Though they are diving and not digging, they are still challenging the human mind to think about the past. These sites, hidden beneath the waves, still have stories to tell. Even sites that appear too damaged, like the *Maple Leaf*, can offer insights otherwise unfound. The artifacts that are recovered, like those from the *Hunley* or the technological marvels from the *Monitor*, all remind us of the human side to the Civil War—great minds making stunning innovations, sailors sacrificing their lives, all stories waiting beneath the waves.

Native and "Newcomer"

Battle of Little Bighorn

Richard A. Fox

Archaeologists can also learn how land battles played out and, by incorporating the voices of minorities, we begin to understand better the clashes between cultures. One of the most prominent clashes between cultures in North American history—Custer's battle—took place on June 25, 1876, in what is now Montana. There, along Little Bighorn River, troops of the Seventh U.S. Cavalry led by Lt. Col. George Custer met defeat at the hands of the Sioux and Northern Cheyenne. Much has been said and written about the battle of Little Bighorn River, but our histories of this conflict largely exclude perspectives of the native victors. Now historical archaeology has challenged that bias and revised our understanding of what happened there.

More than a century after the battle, we began digging at the site, now the Little Bighorn Battlefield National Monument, a U.S. National Park Service property. Our team investigated the entire battlefield. Dedicated volunteers systematically surveyed the terrain using state-of-the-art metal detectors, while others carefully excavated test units. As we planned the project, we weren't sure if much remained. Then came our first day in the field, the day that our uncertainty vanished, the day we knew our efforts would be rewarded. That day we wound up with over a hundred artifacts. And our excitement did not end there. Day after day the artifacts of battle flowed in, until we had unearthed thousands.

Our team recovered many artifacts indicative of military life, things like buttons from military tunics, parts of a pocket watch, a Civil War–vintage picket pin for tethering a horse, a spur, a carbine strap snap hook, and more poignant reminders of the pathos of battle such as cavalry boots. The Sioux and Northern Cheyenne did not leave much behind, except such basic reminders of war as iron arrowheads.

While all of these and more were useful in our analysis, the hundreds of lead bullets and spent cartridges proved especially crucial in helping us under-

Fig. 19.1. Metal detector operators in action at the battlefield site.
(Sketch courtesy of Ed Smyth.)

stand how the battle was fought. Bullets from Sioux and Cheyenne warriors' guns helped us identify where troopers fought; those from soldiers' firearms signaled Native American positions. Spent cartridges proved especially valuable. They not only marked locations of the adversaries but also showed us how combatants moved about as the fight unfolded. To track the combatants across the field, natives and soldiers alike, we relied on firearms analysis techniques used at crime labs. Because each gun has a unique firing pin, forensic specialists can match a cartridge case with the gun that fired it. Although we found no guns at the battlefield, we did find casings with firing pin marks. Microscopic analysis of the marks allowed us to group spent cartridges according to the gun that fired them.

Fig. 19.2. Excavated unit at the battlefield. (Courtesy of National Park Service.)

Because we had routinely recorded the precise location of each artifact during fieldwork, we could see how spent casings from each gun were distributed across the battlefield landscape. Our analyses strongly indicated that the tactical stability of Custer's cavalry fell apart as the battle progressed. We learned that fighting began with soldiers in skirmish order just as prescribed by cavalry tactics—shown in the spent cartridges between A and B in figure 19.6. But at some point, pressure from warriors caused skirmishers to shift into position C-D. The line connecting casings found at A-B and C-D represents the movement of one soldier, and shows how the skirmish line that he helped to man had shifted. As tactical stability began to erode, soldiers bunched together at point E, the location of numerous casings with unique firing pin marks. Marks identical to two at E appeared on casings found further north, suggesting flight represented by lines G and H.

Patterns in cavalry casings on the battlefield mirror what military strategists know about combat behavior. Soldiers facing the intense pressure of battle tend to seek safety by bunching together. Left unchecked, bunching can lead to panic and flight, even among determined, courageous soldiers. And that is what the archaeology told us. Tactical unity in Custer's battalion collapsed or, more technically, disintegrated. With this information in hand, we wondered if we could find the story of disintegration in the historical record.

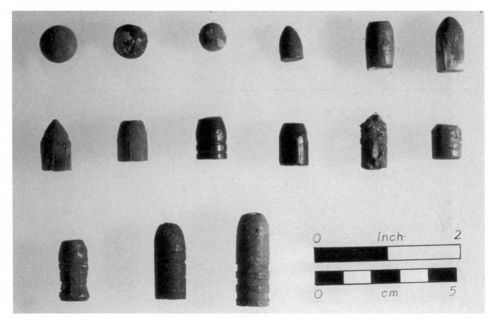

Fig. 19.3. Array of bullets from the battlefield. (Courtesy of National Park Service.)

Fig. 19.4. Cartridge case from the battlefield. (Courtesy of Nebraska State Patrol.)

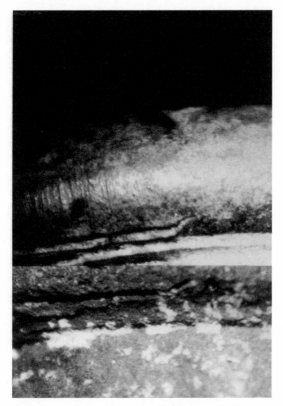

Fig. 19.5. Firing pin marks on cartridge case base. (Microphoto courtesy of National Park Service.)

And after weeks and months of digging in libraries and archives, we found that story.

Sioux and Cheyenne warriors who were there that day spoke of these very kinds of combat behavior reflected in our interpretation of the archaeological record. Some warriors recalled that the troopers entered the fray bravely and in good order, but they remembered too that stability ultimately disintegrated. They spoke of flight and of seemingly odd behaviors such as abandoning guns or firing aimlessly, even playing dead. Others metaphorically described the soldiers as intoxicated. Even today, one Sioux oral tradition recalls that the soldiers were so confused that they were brought down like ducks in the hail.

Our analyses—putting the artifacts and documents together—are like those of detectives, who consider not only the physical remains of a crime but also eyewitness accounts. We learned that for the five companies in Custer's

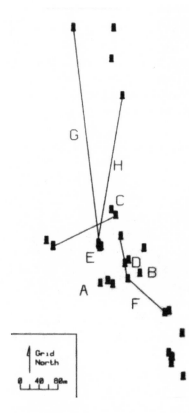

Fig. 19.6. Cartridge case distribution. (Line drawing courtesy of Richard Fox.)

command the end came swiftly—a half hour is a reasonable estimate. First one company collapsed, then the panic spread to two more, both of which rapidly disintegrated. The few survivors fled north to Custer's remaining two companies. Huddled on a knoll inaptly called Last Stand Hill, what was left of the command faced a desperate situation. Nearly surrounded, one company broke toward the river, but it too was quickly routed and driven into a rugged, deep ravine. Meanwhile, warriors overran the soldiers remaining on Last Stand Hill. Then they spilled into the ravine to finish their work, fighting there with the last troopers to die. So not only was there no gallant "last stand," but the last fighting did not take place on Last Stand Hill.

None of this fits popular images of Custer's Last Stand—a resolute but doomed band of soldiers all of whom fought to the last man and last bullet. Yet it is what we now know. While traditional history is dominated by the last-stand legend, our historical archaeology work at the Little Bighorn battlefield has replaced legend and myth with a shared history. By listening to the voices of the battle's only survivors, the Sioux and Cheyenne warriors, and to the artifacts of battle—that is, by turning not just pages but also the ground—historical archaeology has painted a clearer, more accurate picture of the Battle of Little Bighorn.

Indeed, our work has given voice at Little Bighorn Battlefield National Monument to the Sioux and Northern Cheyenne. Now you will hear their stories through our historical archaeology interpretations in ranger programs, which before had largely ignored native accounts in favor of traditional white American viewpoints. And more and more people hear that story than ever, as annual visitation has skyrocketed since we began our investigations. Visit the national monument today and you can watch a special video that details how we went about our investigations, and view many of the artifacts our team recovered.

Prior to our work at Little Bighorn the general consensus was that battlefields held little interpretive value. That has now changed, as David Starbuck says in chapter 17. Historical archaeologists are at work at many battlefields, often incorporating strategies and methods pioneered at the Little Bighorn. Doug Scott, my NPS counterpart on the Little Bighorn project, has worked with Southern Cheyenne, Southern Arapaho, Northern Cheyenne, and Northern Arapaho to relocate the site of the 1864 Sand Creek Massacre in Colorado, in which 150 Cheyenne and Arapaho elders, women, and children died at the hands of American soldiers. As far away as South Africa, our work serves as a model for ongoing investigations at Isandlwana, where Zulu natives fought British colonialists just three years after the Little Bighorn. Interest in American battlefields has also risen. One project focuses on the Fallen Timbers battlefield where, in an early U.S. conflict with Native Americans,

> **"Custer's men in the beginning shot straight, but later they shot like drunken men, firing into the ground, into the air, wildly in every way."**
>
> **Iron Hawk**
> **ca. 1906**

Fig. 19.7. Quote from Lakota Sioux warrior Iron Hawk. (Courtesy of Richard Fox.)

> **"The soldiers in running away . . . would fire their guns in the air, making them easy victims."**
>
> **Runs after the Clouds**
> **1909**
>
> **". . . some fired in the air and acted as if intoxicated. . . ."**
>
> **Bear Lying Down**
> **(date unknown)**

Fig. 19.8. Quotes from Lakota Sioux warriors Runs After the Clouds and Bear Lying Down. (Courtesy of Richard Fox.)

Shawnee, and allied warriors were defeated by General Anthony Wayne in 1794. Historical archaeologists have also illuminated our understanding of the U.S.-Mexican War battle at Palo Alto, Texas (1846). And the same can be said for projects at Civil War battlefields, including Antietam (1862) in Maryland.

Battlefield historical archaeology is here to stay. The stir in interest is perhaps no better exemplified than in the National Park Service's American Battlefield Protection Program, which recognizes the importance of battlefields in American history—and the major role archaeology has in interpreting them.

20

A Global Contest

World War II

*Daniel Lenihan, Gary Cummins, James Delgado, David Clark,
and Lu Ann De Cunzo*

All the survivors of the Battle of Little Bighorn have died, but thousands upon thousands of Americans alive today saw military action in World War II. Millions more did not serve in the military, but lived through the second "war to end all wars" from 1941 to 1945, and will never forget the experience. Governments around the world committed military personnel and huge quantities of supplies and equipment to this conflict. World War II sites dot the landscape. Incredibly, more than 77,000 American military personnel who participated in this global conflict are still "missing in action."

Growing cities, accidental discoveries, and a refusal to forget have led archaeologists to many of the sites of this global contest. One such discovery occurred in October 1992. A B-17 bomber crash site was accidentally uncovered in a dense mountain forest in the highlands of Papua New Guinea, more than 8,300 feet above sea level. Inspection revealed extensive plane wreckage, remains of the flight crew, and personal flight gear. A pilot's name bracelet matched a crew member from a B-17F, number 41-24552. This plane, while returning on September 15, 1943, from a successful bombing mission over Lae, Papua New Guinea, disappeared without a trace. In 1993 the U.S. Army Central Identification Laboratory at Hickam Air Force Base in Hawaii planned an archaeological survey and excavation of the wreck site. Ironically, archaeologists completed the project almost exactly fifty years after the plane was declared "missing in action."

High, thick mountain forest with a carpet of soft moss blanketed the crash area. The wreckage lay scattered across a narrow, steep-sided gully with a dangerous 36° slope. Seasonal stream gullies cut down through the forested hillside, creating a difficult working surface. Cold weather, high winds, thick fog, and occasional minor earthquakes turned work in the area into a real challenge.

Initial survey located the boundaries of the wreckage, scattered across an area measuring 76 by 72 meters (249 by 236 feet). Archaeologists set up a grid of 8-meter (26-foot) squares to excavate the site. As they excavated, they drew a detailed map showing the wreckage and crew members' remains in relation to specific sections of the plane. The team recovered the human remains and personal gear, carefully cleaned them, and returned them to the Central Identification Laboratory for final analysis.

The archaeology offered considerable insight into the final minutes of the B-17F's flight. An unknown problem or malfunction caused the plane to leave formation, and the pilot became disoriented or lost. Trying to fly out of trouble, the plane headed at full speed up a deep, narrow valley. During a steep turn the right wing hit the high canopy treetops, tearing off the wingtip and the outboard engine. Losing altitude quickly, the plane nosed into the forest, shredding the fuselage from front to back, while the tail section hit a high embankment, broke off, and slid down the hill.

Considering the condition of the plane, the scatter of human remains and personal effects, and the abundance of untouched survival gear, the crew undoubtedly crashed with the plane and died instantly. An officer's watch recovered from the site had stopped at fifteen seconds after eleven o'clock in the morning (11:00:15), probably the exact time of the crash. A large piece of the tail section discovered intact at the site preserved the plane's serial number.

Study of the human remains showed that at least ten men had flown the plane's final flight. The forensic team could positively identify few of the remains, owing to their deteriorated condition. Nevertheless, through the extraordinary efforts of archaeology, ten crewmen made their final trip home, bringing closure to unwritten chapters of their families' histories.

Historical archaeologists continue to participate proudly in special projects like this one, whenever possible. But most United States archaeologists of World War II have recently become engaged in another monumental, although perhaps more mundane, undertaking. In 1991, military installations dating to the beginning of U.S. involvement in the war turned fifty years old. That anniversary made them potentially eligible for the National Register of Historic Places, a listing of buildings, sites, structures, and objects significant in the nation's history. Federal law requires that archaeologists survey and evaluate all such properties located on federal land. Those associated with important people and events in World War II may be listed in the National Register, as well as those with innovative or representative construction or technological features, and those that can teach us more about the war. Surveying the more than 25 million acres administered by the Department of Defense and the armed services has proven a staggering undertaking, and will take years to complete. In the end, the U.S. government will preserve and document the most significant of these sites and installations for future generations of Americans. Indeed, the military's primary role of "keeping the peace" involves protecting our heritage, including our democratic government and way of life, and the material legacy of that heritage. Through these efforts, our descendants too will learn firsthand of the tremendous investment in land, resources, technology, and human lives that World War II cost the nation.

At Eglin Air Force Base in Florida, for example, lie the remains of important developments in World War II strategic technology and the beginnings of the Army Air Corps. Two parallel rows of concrete pillars protrude from the sand dunes on Santa Rosa Island, extending fifteen hundred feet toward the Gulf of Mexico. Not far away, nine huge concrete structures stand in ruin. Conceived and built in secret, used, and then abandoned soon after the war, they are all that remains of Operation Crossbow. In 1944 the Allies learned of sprawling concrete complexes along the French coast. Intelligence revealed that the Axis powers used them to store, assemble, and fire long-range missiles. At Eglin AFB the army replicated the structures in order to test various means of destroying them without interfering with the planned European invasion. Minimum-altitude attacks by fighter planes proved most effective. Political debate over the efficacy of the approach prevented implementing it in this setting, but Allied forces used it successfully against bridges, railways, and similar targets for the duration of the war.

Later in 1944 the U.S. tested the nation's first operational guided missile, the predecessor of the modern cruise missile. Spread over fourteen bomb-pocked acres at Eglin, missile launching ramps, storage buildings, launch-preparation buildings, assembly facilities, and other support buildings survive in various states of preservation. Archaeologists have identified these shattered concrete skeletons. We now understand better their important role in the war effort, and will preserve them as documents of the tragedy and costs of war.

Many thousands escaped the ultimate cost of war—death—through captivity. By the middle of 1945, more than 425,000 prisoners were held in some 650 prisoner-of-war camps across the United States. Not all stood on land still owned by the Department of Defense today. An example is Camp Hearne in Texas, which operated from 1943 to 1946. Michael Waters of Texas A&M University is concerned that these camps are disappearing along with an entire generation of people who experienced them firsthand. So he and his students have worked for several years to record the history of Camp Hearne before it is lost forever. Overgrown and largely invisible on the surface, the camp still houses fascinating evidence coming to light through the archaeologists' fieldwork. To fully tell the camp's many stories, the team has studied the extensive historical record of documents, drawings, and photographs. They have talked to former prisoners and local residents, and collected objects made or used by the prisoners and associated with the camp. Excavations have uncovered the remains of three prisoner compounds with mess halls, a compound for American administrators, and a hospital complex.

Local citizens had petitioned the federal government to build the camp, imagining prisoners working on local farms to replace farmworkers gone to war. Eventually 4,800 soldiers, mostly of Germany's Afrika Korps captured in Tunisia, arrived at the camp, where they resided in two groups, pro- and anti-Nazi. Only 20 percent were enlisted men, assigned work repairing blankets and raincoats or harvesting cotton, onions, and pecans. Most were noncommissioned officers and thus not required to work under the rules of the Geneva Convention. They passed the time playing sports, taking classes, reading, and embellishing the camp buildings and landscape. Members of a German military orchestra gave concerts, and movies and theatrical performances were regular features. Some locals felt the prisoners received better treatment than their prisoner status warranted, and dubbed the camp the Fritz Ritz. Prisoners tried to escape nonetheless, and conflict between pro- and anti-Nazi groups ended in at least one murder. The army closed the camp early in 1946 after the United States repatriated the German POWs to Europe.

Waters's team has unearthed the concrete slabs of a mess hall and lavatories designed by the federal government to meet the prisoners' basic needs. In the yards around these buildings, they found Luftwaffe uniform buttons, belt buckles, and soldier identification disks. Prisoners had cast some uniform insignia from lead and cut them from aluminum, copying army, air force, and other German national emblems and military badges. They often traded these insignia with guards, but many ended up in the ground, along with the waste from their manufacture. Other lost items remind us of the global nature of the war, including coins from the United States, Germany, France, Tunisia, Italy, and Britain. German mess kits and canteens lay in trash pits where the POWs threw them as they prepared to return home. One prisoner had carefully etched his canteen with views of home, then left it behind with the others.

The prisoners left behind other reminders that the human spirit can survive even war and imprisonment. Photographs and excavated remains record a cement-lined pond for turtles surrounding a flower garden and a decorative fountain in the form of a moated miniature castle with clay figurines. These and another fountain adorned with water-spraying frogs introduced whimsical memories of home into the landscape. And in the theater, complete with orchestra pit, archaeologists found tubes of makeup from wartime performances. For many Americans, these mundane and dramatic finds at Camp Hearne offer a new perspective on the war and its legacy.

As POWs returned home from United States camps at war's end, captured war prizes arrived in the States. One of these, a German submarine (U-1105) commissioned in 1944, was one of fewer than ten submarines outfitted with an experimental synthetic rubber skin designed to counter Allied sonar. Success in evading detection during combat earned it the nickname Black Panther. U.S. engineers carefully studied this early attempt at stealth technology, then used the sub for explosives testing. In 1949 it sank in the Potomac River in Maryland. Rediscovered in 1985, the Black Panther was designated as Maryland's first historic shipwreck preserve, in conjunction with the U.S. Navy–Department of Defense Legacy Resource Management Program. Now future archaeologists, historians of technology, military enthusiasts, and sport divers will have the chance to explore and study this landmark vessel.

Across the country, out in the Pacific at Pearl Harbor, the navy has teamed with the National Park Service to preserve another compelling scar on the global landscape of World War II. On December 7, 1941, the Imperial Japanese fleet attacked U.S. installations on the Hawaiian island of Oahu. Even before bombs fell on Pearl Harbor that Sunday morning, many Americans knew that they would soon be at war with Japan. But they did not expect a seemingly apocalyptic sneak attack. It emblazoned itself in the minds of millions of Americans, a passionate, inflamed response alive even today, spanning generations. The single most powerful image of the Pearl Harbor attack was the twisted, smoking metal and mast of the USS *Arizona*. When it sank, it became the tomb of more than eleven hundred sailors and marines.

In 1962 a memorial was built over the ship's hull, and three years later the secretary of the interior designated the naval base at Pearl Harbor a National Historic Landmark. The National Park Service took over operation of the USS *Arizona* Memorial in 1980, although the navy retains ownership of the ship by law. In 1989 the USS *Arizona* and the USS *Utah* were also designated National Historic Landmarks. In 1983 the NPS tasked its Submerged Cultural Resources Unit (now Submerged Resources Center) with mapping and photodocumenting the remains, and with removing the thousands of coins visitors had tossed from the memorial over the years. The coins formed a carpet over the ship, and the copper they contained was poisoning marine organisms that cover the ship with a protective coral glaze. The team began

Fig. 20.1. USS *Arizona* ablaze after Japanese attack of December 7, 1941. (Courtesy of National Park Service.)

to study how the *Arizona* was deteriorating in the biochemical soup in which it lay. Within a few years NPS underwater archaeologists, assisted by navy divers, had expanded the project to a full study of the World War II remains submerged in the waters of Pearl Harbor.

Even before the first dives, the team raised many questions. What are the conditions of the shipwrecks? Is there any unexploded ordnance on or near the ships? Should we be doing anything to preserve the shipwrecks in place? What about the fact that both the *Arizona* and the *Utah* are also the tomb for more than one thousand servicemen? Should we be diving on these submerged gravesites? Should we penetrate them? Should we be looking for means to slow or stop deterioration? Should we be retrieving significant artifacts? Some people, including navy officials, argued that diving on these wrecks disturbs the final resting place of those who perished. But if we don't dive them, how do we learn enough to make responsible decisions about the appropriate use of this submerged heritage by the public, and ensure their safety? Ultimately the NPS agreed that divers would avoid entering the hull in order to ensure their safety and respect the navy's and the public's concerns about the sanctity of the *Arizona*.

Fig. 20.2. Archaeologist using trilateration—measuring a specific feature to two known points on a baseline—to accurately reproduce the feature's location on a shipwreck site map. (Photo by Brett Seymour, National Park Service.)

The team used a low-tech and labor-intensive approach from the beginning. No one had ever attempted a detailed mapping of a 608-foot battleship in water of six-foot visibility—a diver even one body-length away could not see the ship. There were no guidelines to follow and no black-box technology that could significantly help. The methods centered on string, clothespins, measuring tapes, and a lot of mapping savvy on the part of the dive teams. Their efforts were rewarded with the finding of the turret still outfitted with its 14-inch guns believed salvaged during the war, along with a profusion of

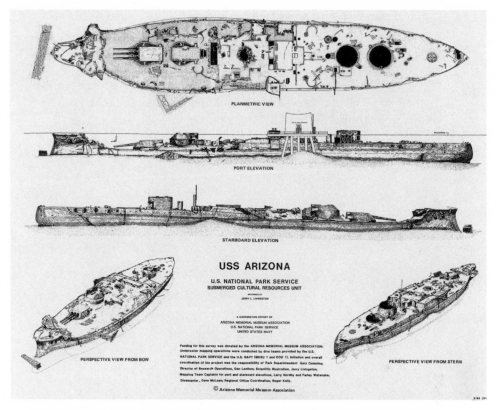

PLANMETRIC VIEW

PORT ELEVATION

STARBOARD ELEVATION

USS ARIZONA

U.S. NATIONAL PARK SERVICE
SUBMERGED CULTURAL RESOURCES UNIT

DRAWINGS BY
JERRY L. LIVINGSTON

A COOPERATIVE EFFORT OF
ARIZONA MEMORIAL MUSEUM ASSOCIATION
U.S. NATIONAL PARK SERVICE
UNITED STATES NAVY

Funding for this survey was donated by the ARIZONA MEMORIAL MUSEUM ASSOCIATION.
Underwater mapping operations were conducted by dive teams provided by the U.S.
NATIONAL PARK SERVICE and the U.S. NAVY (MDSU 1 and EOD 1). Initiation and overall
coordination of the project was the responsibility of Park Superintendent Gary Cummins;
Director of Research Operations, Dan Lenihan; Scientific Illustration, Jerry Livingston;
Mapping Team Captains for port and starboard elevations, Larry Nordby and Farley Watanabe;
Divemaster, Dave McLean; Regional Office Coordination, Roger Kelly.

© Arizona Memorial Museum Association

PERSPECTIVE VIEW FROM BOW

PERSPECTIVE VIEW FROM STERN

Fig. 20.3. Five-part line drawing of the current USS *Arizona,* created by the Submerged Resources Center after two years and hundreds of dives during mapping operations. (Courtesy of National Park Service, Submerged Resources Center.)

live shells directly under the memorial structure! The public safety concerns of the project planners almost became their worst nightmare, but a highly trained Navy Explosive Ordnance Disposal team immediately removed the shells. The divers discovered no evidence of explosion in the vicinity of the stack, where a bomb reportedly dropped into the ship. Most attack-related damage occurred in the bow, supporting the contention that a bomb detonated the forward magazine, sinking the ship. Despite the damage, divers could easily identify such spaces as the galley. There they swam over oven bases and table legs poking up from the intact tiled floor, strewn with long-forgotten coffee cups, plates, and silverware.

Naval memorial, war grave, and on occasion still the burial site for survivors of the attack, the *Arizona* signifies tragedy, triumph, and heroism. The ship and its harbor symbolize the social trauma of war, and remind us of the need for vigilance and preparedness, an object lesson for those who vow "never again." Archaeologists work with pride to ensure Pearl Harbor will continue to serve as a shrine and place of remembrance for Americans and visitors from around the world.

Part 6

Unlock the Past for the Future

From the Past in the Present to the Future

Lu Ann De Cunzo

Archaeologists have a hard enough time "predicting" the past, let alone trying to predict the future. Nevertheless, we have asked four North American archaeologists early in their careers to imagine what the future of historical archaeology might look like. Or at least to share with us what it is that has compelled them to a life in archaeology.

They all agree that archaeology is as much about the present as it is about the past. Audrey Horning has worked in Northern Ireland, where centuries-old tensions still punctuate the rhythm of everyday life, and has studied folks in the Appalachian Mountains of Virginia during the Depression. Maria Franklin is concerned with other centuries-old tensions that grew out of the diverse origins of North Americans and out of such institutions as slavery. Both women bear witness to the relevance of the past to our actions and beliefs today. John Triggs, an archaeologist committed to Canada's urban heritage, advocates community-based archaeology programs. Our archaeological heritage preserves the voices of everyone who contributed to the diversity of the past, and community archaeology programs bring diverse people together to work toward the common goal of protecting that heritage.

Archaeology is about the present in other ways too. The people that we study from the past have descendants today. In the case of African Americans and Native Americans, among others, archaeologists in the past did not acknowledge the rights and responsibilities of these descendant communities to participate in determining the fate of their ancestors and writing the histories of their lives, a point John Jameson returns to in the epilogue.

Both Audrey Horning and Lisa Young, an archaeological conservator, see the future of archaeology as learning, and sharing, the stories of objects and the meanings they held. These objects, they argue, communicate about the past in powerful and unique ways. I am reminded of this point even as I write these words. On the radio this morning I heard the composer of an opera about the Battle of Gettysburg speak of holding bullets from the battlefield to get a feeling for the soldiers who fought and died there. Lisa Young reminds us that without an ongoing commitment to conserve the objects we have excavated, we will lose that tangible, powerful link to our past. But the objects themselves, without the information from their archaeological context, John Triggs asserts, are virtually meaningless. And so the future of archaeology still lies in the soil, and in the techniques we develop to capture more of the information locked in each soil layer and feature we dig.

These archaeologists write of archaeology's future with a voice that, given the diversity that characterizes the field today, is surprisingly unified. Protect and preserve archaeological sites. Conserve archaeological objects. Hear all people's voices, and see all their lives, in the material record they left behind. Include, don't exclude. Work locally, and compare localities around the globe to understand the diversity as well as the commonalities of the human experience.

21

Conserving Our Past

Lisa Young

To look ahead, we must begin by looking back. In 1981 archaeological conservator Katherine Singley published an article in the SHA journal *Historical Archaeology* entitled "Caring for Artifacts After Excavation—Some Advice for Archaeologists." Let me focus on one quote: "Due to the lack of trained archaeological conservators in the USA, many artifacts may wait years for treatment, however, this situation will change in the future as awareness of endangered collections grows, co-operation between archaeologists and conservators increases and support for conservation and curation is mandated."

I could publish an article on archaeological conservation today, repeating this same quote, and the underlying message would not be outdated. Archaeological conservation has been a part of historical archaeology for more than sixty-five years, yet many archaeological projects still do not include conservation, and curation and conservation are still not required on many archaeological excavations in the United States and elsewhere. But things have started to change as awareness of conservation increases among archaeologists. Initially, conservators placed emphasis on making sure artifacts were aesthetically pleasing, and treatments were hurried and mass-produced. Many earlier treatments involved chemicals hazardous not only to the artifacts but to the conservator as well. While the techniques and aims of archaeological conservation may have changed over time, the emphasis on "preserving the past" has always remained the primary goal. Today treatments emphasize the long-term stability of an object and retaining the information attached to it. Archaeological conservation is more than cleaning rust off iron, making objects look shiny and new for exhibition, and placing artifacts in clean plastic bags. Archaeological conservation is slowing down or halting further deterioration to artifacts during and after excavation. Conservators examine, document, and treat objects, conduct research, and teach others about our work. Archaeological conservation is essential to historical archaeology, since the primary goal of any archaeological project is to preserve history and safeguard our past.

Fig. 21.1. Conservator Lisa Young at work on iron fishing trident found at the Tolle-Tabbs site in Historic St. Mary's City, Maryland. (Courtesy of Sue Wilkinson.)

I started my career in archaeological conservation almost fifteen years ago, sitting in a dark, damp basement going through boxes of artifacts excavated over a thirty-year period. While not glamorous, the project was certainly necessary and timely. Many of the artifacts were deteriorating in their damp paper boxes and bags, packing materials no longer supported the artifacts, and labels were illegible. This situation is common to many older archaeological collections, where excavation was the priority and funding rarely provided for cataloging, analysis, curation, and conservation.

As I sat there day after day repackaging boxes, I began to wonder why anyone would leave artifacts in conditions that jeopardized their survival. Overcrowded artifact boxes, ceramics crushed under larger objects, damp artifacts covered in mold, and metals corroded beyond recognition faced me in box after box. The physical damage to the artifacts was very visible, but something worse was happening: the data and information, the *stories* inherent in the artifacts, were disappearing as well. Information about past peoples—what they ate, where they traveled, what toys their children and grandchildren played with—would soon be gone.

As a conservator, I think the most important question I began to ask myself was: Why should a fragile object survive three hundred years of being buried in the ground only to disappear after thirty years of sitting on a storage shelf? I knew I had to do something to stop this from happening, but where would I start? The situation was something most archaeologists faced, but little training was available for archaeologists to learn how to store artifacts in order to ensure their long-term preservation.

And that is when I decided to pursue the field of archaeological conservation. One of the biggest hurdles is that not very many trained archaeological conservators work in the United States. Archaeological conservation is primarily taught and practiced in Europe, with only a few programs in the United States and Canada. Archaeological conservation requires training, background, and experience in anthropology, art, and science. Practical experience is required as well, yet there are very few conservators to apprentice with in order to gain this experience.

I volunteered and worked with archaeological conservators in the United States and abroad, and studied at the University of Wales in Cardiff. It soon became evident that not many conservators work in the United States because many archaeologists are unaware of the benefits of conservation. Even more surprising, most archaeological training in North America does not include classes on conservation, or lectures, or even exposure to the subject. Communication between archaeologists and conservators was somewhat nonexistent, and this needed to change if anyone was going to really accept the fact that conservation *is* a part of archaeology.

As more people become aware of the benefits of conservation, more are starting to do it. Locally, I have done presentations to archaeological field school students, and I participate in archaeological conferences, symposiums, and archaeology summer camps. I have developed and taught workshops to archaeological professionals in order to pass on skills, expertise, and information about conservation. Several years ago the American Institute for Conservation established an archaeological conservation discussion group. We try to find better ways of reaching out to archaeologists. In cooperation with the SHA, the group has created a traveling exhibit on archaeological conservation in order to dispel some of the myths about conservation—such as that it is too expensive, that it is necessary only on wet sites, and that once an object is conserved it is stable forever.

Collections care guidelines and standards have recently become more common within archaeological organizations, such as the Alexandria Archaeology Museum. The United States government requires the curation and conservation of federally owned and administered archaeological collections. In 1999 the state of Maryland became one of the first to require a conservator on every archaeological project. Professional archaeological societies such as the SHA have implemented their own standards and guidelines, and several conservation manuals and Web sites now assist archaeologists in the field.

I feel very fortunate to be practicing archaeological conservation at a time when awareness of conservation is growing exponentially within the archaeological community. As students become educated in all facets of archaeology—including conservation—the process of preserving our past will become much easier, with conservation beginning *before* artifacts are taken out of the ground and not after they have been stored on a shelf for thirty years. The information, secrets, and stories attached to those artifacts will survive for future students, archaeologists, children, and adults to rediscover once again. And most important, we will know we have all done our part toward securing the survival of our past for future generations.

22

Historical Archaeology
That Matters Beyond Academics

Maria Franklin

I choose to practice historical archaeology because I can't think of a more suitable, captivating, or innovative way to study people in the past than by considering the material remains they left behind. I am probably guilty of giving more thought and energy to a pork dinner consumed some time in the late eighteenth century than the family who prepared and ate it did. And I am certain that they would be mystified that anyone two centuries later would carefully excavate, record, and study—at great expense and with much labor—the butchered bones they tossed out. But studying the remains of meals discarded over a forty-year period by an enslaved community that once lived at Rich Neck Plantation on the outskirts of Williamsburg, Virginia, has told us much about early Afro-Virginian lifeways. Archaeological evidence indicates that community members hunted, fished, gardened, raised livestock, and collected shellfish, wild berries, and nuts for their families. They actively cultivated a unique foodways system that combined knowledge of West African, English, and Native American cultural practices. If you have ever had greens, black-eyed peas, or ham hocks, you have had a taste of the culinary ingenuity that enslaved Africans contributed to southern foodways. Through historical archaeology we have been able to write about a long-neglected part of American history—that involving enslaved African Americans—and to learn about how identity and culture are constructed and transformed within a matrix of complex social relationships.

This research has helped me understand how these same phenomena, identity and culture, operate today in a diverse social environment. Moreover, archaeological research allows us to challenge myths about people in the past that are discriminatory and injurious, especially to their descendants. For example, it is assumed that enslaved blacks simply adopted the culture of their owners, but the research at Rich Neck and other slave-related sites has demonstrated that they actively participated in creating their own cultural practices. Thus I find historical archaeology to be a powerful tool in investigating issues that are relevant to our understanding of ourselves and others, and a means by which we can bridge our differences through knowledge of the past.

In envisioning the future of historical archaeology, its potential to contribute new perspectives on history is great indeed. It is an important vehicle through which we can gain insights into a fuller spectrum of lived experiences in the past. This volume alone has contributions on subjects ranging from cultural exchange and identity to labor and industry. As an interdisciplinary field, historical archaeology has the advantage of a wider body of evidence to research, informed by approaches from related disciplines. Martha Zierden's essay on Charleston offers an example of an interdisciplinary archaeology. Further developments in geophysical surveying, Geographic Information Systems, and pollen, faunal, and botanical analyses will increasingly help historical archaeologists to tackle challenging questions about the past. The project in Jamestown, Virginia, shows the potential of these techniques. Yet in projecting historical archaeology's future outlook, our contributions of new knowledge will matter little in the grand scheme of things if we fail to consider what is relevant about our work to the society within which we will live. The central issue to me is relevance, both social and political, and we must look to the public to determine what questions will count the most. Within an increasingly diverse society such as America's, the conflict generated by our social differences is one area where historical archaeology can make a difference. In this, I agree with Terry Weik's eloquent argument in his essay on Maroon freedom fighters.

Within the United States, divisions along the lines of race, gender, ethnicity, religion, class, and sexuality persist. To discover the roots of our differences and conflicts, we must consider the historical forces that shaped our society: colonialism, slavery, cultural contact, the Industrial Revolution, urbanism, and the rise of the modern world. The past informs us of identity, social relations, and the political, economic, and cultural transformation of the United States to which historical actors from a range of backgrounds contributed. Yet history is too often represented exclusively through the eyes of the dominant elite, or as events that have little bearing on the present. This is a problem, since history has a major influence on how we perceive others and ourselves and justifies the workings of our social order. For example, think about the implications of an American history of the settlement of the West that erases the contributions of women who worked the land and raised families, and Asian immigrants who built railroads and ran businesses. Consider an American history of colonialism that fails to address its dependence upon the labor of enslaved Africans. Can you imagine the Industrial Revolution in the North taking place without the poor immigrants who worked in the factories? Through the lens of public history the American past is often presented in ways that suggest that people without political, social, or economic clout were but minor footnotes with no historical agency in what we often assume to be a representative history. Visitors to museums and historic sites are sometimes presented with versions of the past that focus on male gunslingers and goldminers, railroad magnates and bankers, and wealthy slaveowners. Not only do they learn very little about the descendants of people who also made significant contributions to American society, but they come to believe that the past and *current* social ladder built upon differences of race, gender, class, and ethnicity is one that is natural, credible, and inevitable.

Scholars, including historical archaeologists, are debating how our representations of people in the past influence today's society. This debate is partly fueled by the recognition that despite our expertise and training, our personal backgrounds and the social environment within which we live still influence our research interpretations. In short, the past is created in the present, and it would be impossible to reconstruct a past capturing all of its complexities. Even an accurate renovation of a historic structure is extremely difficult to achieve, as Martha Zierden's work in Charleston demonstrates. It follows that coalescing the competing perspectives and "truths" that represent all the experiences of varied individuals living in eighteenth-century Charleston is impossible.

Does this mean that archaeologists are unable to divulge any important insights into the past? I believe firmly that the answer to that question is "no." Otherwise, I would hang it all up and start using my trowel as a pie server. I do believe that rigorous research can lead to meaningful interpretations of the past that can also be used as an instrument to strive for positive social change in today's world. Examples presented in this volume allude hopefully to the future prospect of historical archaeology. This would be a discipline fully engaged in writing inclusive histories and challenging traditional views of the past. One great example is the time-honored myth of Custer's Last Stand. It is part and parcel of a triumphant "history" that weaves together American nationalism and manifest destiny while justifying the exploitation and genocide of Native Americans. Richard Fox's careful analysis of archaeological evidence, however, directly challenges the dominant storyline of the battle of Little Bighorn. Importantly, it brings into focus Sioux Indian oral traditions that have historically contested mainstream America's version of the events.

Historical archaeology is well positioned to contribute fresh perspectives on the past that compete with dominant narratives, especially those that omit the life stories of historically oppressed peoples. As case studies in this volume demonstrate, much can be learned through archaeology about the experiences of groups typically marginalized or erased from history. This would include immigrants, the poor and working class, women, African Americans, and Native Americans. On a global level, historical archaeologists are working to write more inclusive histories not only in the United States but also in Australia, South Africa, Canada, Latin America, and the Caribbean. Presenting diverse historical voices begins the work of dismantling contemporary stereotypes by demonstrating that all kinds of people contributed to our history.

Archaeologists are challenging other stereotypes and myths as well. As a case in point, both Terrance Weik and Kathleen Deagan discuss how common it was for Africans, Native Americans, and Europeans in early Florida to interact culturally and socially. Marriages between Africans and native men and women, as well as Europeans and natives, were not infrequent, giving rise to creole generations who forged new lifeways informed by their diverse heritages. These kinds of interactions are largely erased from traditional histories, which prefer to represent different groups as culturally "pure" and static.

Oftentimes ethnic and racial groups are represented in history as homogeneous and one-dimensional, an erroneous myth of the past that negates the diversity and diverse life histories of people. The history of African Americans, for example, is largely represented through slavery. But black Americans have lived in North America for four centuries, and enslavement does not define their experiences in full. Even during the era of slavery there were blacks whose lives were not circumscribed by plantation bondage. These included free blacks such as the residents of Alexandria, Virginia, about whom Pamela Cressey wrote, Fort Mose's free blacks, and the Maroons at the center of Terrance Weik's essay. When we think of diversity, we have to consider differences not only between groups but also among them, even when considering a particular time and place. For example, Mary Praetzellis's work in West Oakland indicates that African Americans occupied different status positions. Likewise, Roberta Greenwood's study of a Los Angeles Chinatown disputes the assumption that the residents were mainly poor, single men. Diversity exists within a group, now as then, since differences in class, gender, age, religion, and so on variously shape individual experiences even among people who share the same ethnic or racial identity.

Some of the more powerful examples of historical archaeology are those that expose historical continuities between the past and present in order to reveal how relationships of power are continuously reproduced over time. Given archaeology's ability to study long-term settlement and land use patterns, racial segregation is one socially relevant topic that can be addressed. Martha Zierden observes that the opulent homes, as well as the associated outbuildings, of Charleston's wealthy slave owners were once occupied by both slave owner and enslaved. Today these expensive properties belong mostly to upper-class whites. African Americans, many descended from the city's enslaved blacks, are now relegated to the edges of town. This indicates that racial segregation in residential space was unnecessary until after emancipation. Whites could no longer use slavery as a form of social control over blacks. Thus began the process of excluding blacks from white social spaces. Diana Wall and Nan Rothschild state that New York City's population has always maintained its ethnic and racial diversity, which largely influenced its residential patterns. They note that new European arrivals formed ethnic enclaves, but succeeding generations successfully integrated into mainstream society. African Americans were unable to follow the same pattern of residential integration, strongly suggesting that race was the key factor influencing both settlement patterns and the related phenomenon of social mobility.

If we are to establish what issues are relevant to addressing the concerns of a diverse public, and to work toward bridging chasms that divide American society, future historical archaeology must emphasize community-based research. In theory, as John Triggs explains, the past belongs to us all, and we must take responsibility for ensuring that participation in studying and preserving it is shared broadly. If the present rise in programs like Alexandria Archaeology's are any indication, community partnering and public education (particularly through the World Wide Web) will become routine. There is already strong advocacy within archaeology for both to become standard archaeological practice, which will help to boost support for the preservation of our cultural resources. Unfortunately, the vestiges of our heritage are increasingly destroyed at alarming rates, largely through development. We cannot hope to secure sites for future generations without your help.

To conclude, as Lu Ann De Cunzo suggests in introducing this volume, archaeologists share a "crucial goal" in presenting the past in ways that promote public involvement and heritage preservation. In projecting the future of historical archaeology, this will be an important goal. We need to present the past in ways that demonstrate the discipline's relevance in contemporary society. Authors in this volume shed light on some of the major directions that future research will increasingly take: writing inclusive pasts, challenging traditional, dominant views of history, and wiping out divisive myths and stereotypes. I hope you discover that these new insights speak to central concerns in your lives, and will help to promote understanding between diverse peoples. I also hope you will find historical archaeology absorbing enough to get actively involved by supporting our research endeavors and the goals of our discipline.

23

The Past Belongs to Us All

John Triggs

It has been said that if all children followed their adolescent aspirations, the world would be populated with archaeologists, paleontologists, and professional athletes. The fascination with what came before, the mystery of what lies buried below—like the allure of thousands of people cheering our athletic prowess—is a shared human trait. Only later in life, when the reality of making a living forces itself upon us, do most folks choose to follow other career paths. But a handful doggedly pursue their youthful passion for the past. To those few the rewards are great. We are allowed the luxury of realizing our lifelong ambition. Despite rather minimal material rewards, we have the great benefit of engaging in a study aimed at answering the questions in which we all share a common interest.

As we have seen, the scope of historical archaeology is as broad as it is diverse, incorporating a variety of disciplines in the search for answers to questions not found in the written record alone. The unique approach offered by historical archaeology, where documents, artifacts, and the context of the site comprise the material for study, distinguishes it from other types of archaeology and traditional historical approaches. The combined study of all these sources of information allows the historical archaeologist not only to answer questions about the past but also to pose other questions not considered beforehand. This latter point, described by William Fitzhugh as "new avenues into the past," makes the discipline both exciting and challenging. There is nothing so exhilarating as when all the information comes together in a way that suggests a completely new perspective on the past—and the more so when this is at odds with accepted historical interpretations.

However, epiphanies do not occur nearly as often as we would like, and in many cases our findings merely corroborate the written record or provide supplementary details to a particular historical question. Indeed, many of the early studies mentioned in the preceding chapters, such as those at Jamestown and Fort Necessity, were directed toward answering the basic questions of location, size, and layout of the sought-after features. This is not always as easy as it seems: the shape of Fort Necessity, for example, remained in doubt even after the preliminary archaeological excavations in the 1930s. This is largely due to the techniques used at that time. Today we recognize the need to use manual excavation (rather than backhoe) regardless of the type of site we investigate, as both David Starbuck, working on rural industrial sites, and Martha Zierden of Charleston so rightly point out. The quantity and quality of information we obtain relates directly to the methods used in excavation. My experience on several sites has provided ample evidence that it is better to excavate a small section of the site carefully than to go for the big picture using mechanical equipment or inappropriately gross excavation methods.

Some of my earliest work was in the city of Kingston, Ontario, at the site of Fort Frontenac, a late-seventeenth-century fur trade post at the eastern end of Lake Ontario. This urban archaeology project sought to locate the walls of the masonry fort and any artifacts that would provide insight into one of the earliest European settlements west of Quebec City. The Ontario Heritage Foundation funded the excavation, designed purely as a research project; no development or other activities threatened the land for the foreseeable future. From the beginning we used careful excavation techniques, removing each layer separately by trowel, and we drew, photographed, and documented all layers and features with copious notes. We did not use mechanical equipment.

Perhaps the most memorable aspect of the Fort Frontenac project was the stunning revelation that the walls, which everyone had assumed that railways, roads, and other urban encroachments would have completely eradicated, lay only twenty-five centimeters (about ten inches) below the ground surface. The story at many urban sites is the same: archaeological remains of the city's earliest inhabitants lie intact often only inches below our feet. Mary Praetzellis, working in West Oakland, California, and Bill Moss, working in Quebec, found similar cases of archaeological survival in surprisingly shallow contexts.

It seemed remarkable at the time that the Fort Frontenac project lasted as long as it did, continuing for four seasons from 1982 to 1985. During that period about ten professional archaeologists and forty excavators (who received on-the-job training) as well as a host of volunteers were employed in one form or another. Community involvement and municipal support allowed the outgrowth of that project to survive today as the Cataraqui Archaeological Research Foundation, a nonprofit organization dedicated to investigating and preserving the region's archaeological resources. In many ways the project served as a model for the type of urban archaeological research organizations that every major Canadian city should establish. We know from past experience that archaeological remains do survive below city streets and in the most unexpected places, and it is our responsibility to preserve or record these before they are lost to urban encroachment.

To this end there is a need for archaeological units such as that described by Pamela Cressey in Alexandria, where a city archaeologist and a small number of professional assistants working with a large number of volunteers comprise a community-oriented research team dedicated to preserving the city's heritage resources. Unfortunately, this is a rarity in Canadian cities, with the exception of Quebec and, until recently, Toronto. All too often, urban archaeological sites are slated for rescue and salvage archaeology under existing provincial heritage legislation. Salvage of resources is always preferable to destruction, but a preemptive approach whereby cities have a heritage plan and a professionally trained archaeological staff would ensure that urban archaeological resources are considered far in advance of construction and that appropriate methods of study are employed.

A similar approach was carried out on a smaller scale in the city of Hamilton, Ontario. Beginning in 1991 the city initiated a program of historical archaeology at Dundurn Castle, the impressive residence built by Sir Allan MacNab in 1832, now a National Historic Site. The plans called for a three-year archaeological project designed to retrieve as much information as possible about life at Dundurn Castle in the nineteenth century before construction destroyed the site. Three levels of government funding supported the project, which represented the largest-ever archaeological undertaking in the country in association with a municipal museum. More than ten years later the project continues. It has evolved into a research-oriented program focusing on the restoration of the nineteenth-century picturesque landscape and formal gardens (much like the Nathaniel Russell House project in Charleston), a fur-trade site excavated by a university field school since 1992, a War of 1812 military encampment, and various early- to mid-nineteenth-century structures situated within the thirty-two-acre park. The project has thrived on community involvement since its inception, and more than one hundred volunteers have done everything from washing artifacts to conducting historical research, surveying, and excavation. In fact, the single most important reason for the success of the project is the support received from the community. People have a genuine pride in "the gem of Hamilton," as Dundurn is often called. In lectures, publications, media stories, and educational programs, the archaeologists have shared the ways that the archaeological findings have changed our understanding of Hamilton's history. In these ways the archaeology program at Dundurn Castle stands as a model of what should be done in North American cities.

Fig. 23.1. Student archaeologist Joel Bourne excavating an 1840s midden deposit from the military establishment at Penetanguishene on Georgian Bay, Ontario. (Courtesy of John Triggs.)

Perhaps one of the greatest contributions of historical archaeology is illuminating the past by giving voice to people who, for various reasons, are absent in the written record. In Kathleen Deagan's words, these people have been excluded from society and the American dream: they have been disenfranchised on the basis of ethnicity, gender, or socioeconomic position. My own research at a War of 1812 British naval base on Georgian Bay, conducted with university field schools since 1991, has focused on such people. We have examined the social relationships of the enlisted men and officers, women, civilians, and native people who comprised the highly transitory population during the first three decades of the nineteenth century. We don't know the names of many of these people, others appear only as entries on muster rolls, but the artifacts they made and used provide a tangible link to the past; to paraphrase James Deetz, the material culture contains "messages," which it is our task to decipher. Reconstructing this naval base society using both archaeological and historical sources provides a richer picture of this particular place and, just as important, a picture that has relevance beyond the site.

The "stories" constructed by historical archaeologists are not simply vignettes of a particular time and place. We must situate these individual historical episodes within a larger context to fully appreciate their significance, whether on a regional or a global scale. They stand nonetheless as individual segments of a much larger story, which everyone can identify with in one way or another. You may make this connection to the past by virtue of being a newly arrived immigrant, or on the basis of your ethnicity, gender, or class. However each of us makes the connection, it is these shared experiences that remind us that the past belongs to us all.

24

Does Historical Archaeology Really Matter in Today's World?

Audrey Horning

Like all archaeologists, I am often asked, "What's the best thing you have ever found?" And, like most, I invariably find this question difficult to answer. For me, the genuine excitement of unearthing an unusual or unexpected find, while intoxicating enough at the time, is a fleeting pleasure. Besides, while an archaeologist for the Colonial Williamsburg Foundation, I worked at sites in the restored colonial capital and at Jamestown and Martin's Hundred where most newly uncovered objects pale into insignificance beside the impressive existing archaeological collections amassed through the work of pioneering historical archaeologists Ivor Noël Hume, J. C. Harrington, and John Cotter. What lingers in my mind is the human stories that emerge from the totality of field, laboratory, and historical research, and the way those stories resonate today.

Fundamentally, the study of material culture from any time or place, whether buried in an archaeological site, stored in an old trunk, or revered as a glass-encased *objet d'art,* is about the people who interacted with those objects—the producers, the consumers, the discarders, the hoarders, the admirers—all of whom have consciously or unconsciously attached meaning to material. How we tease out these disparate meanings from seemingly mute objects in our efforts to interpret and understand the past is the true challenge of archaeology—regardless of the intrinsic "neatness" or monetary worth of any individual excavated object. Having said that, I deeply respect the power of a single artifact to silently yet powerfully convey an important message.

So then, what *is* the best artifact I have ever found? A rusted, fragmentary toy ray gun, uncovered with a colleague, Elizabeth Jordan, in the rubble of an abandoned log house high up on a forested mountain slope in Virginia's Shenandoah National Park. What is so special about this ray gun, tangible proof of the rocketing popularity of the youthful and heroic Buck Rogers during the Depression era? It is not so much the surviving details of its futurist

Fig. 24.1. "33 Repeater" toy ray gun, produced in the 1930s by the All Metal Products Company of Wyandotte, Michigan, found at the former home of Wesley and Adelaide Corbin, Corbin Hollow, Shenandoah National Park, Virginia. (Courtesy of Audrey Horning.)

styling, nor the way it comfortably fits into the palm of my hand, nor even the fact that I can document its manufacture in Wyandotte, Michigan between 1934 and 1941 (hardly an ancient treasure!). What is significant about this compelling artifact is where it was found and what greater meaning it holds for the past and, more important, for the present. Let me explain. . . .

In the 1930s, Shenandoah National Park was created out of a patchwork of family farms, pastures, mines, and lumber operations. Inhabitants were described as "not of the twentieth century" and living a poverty-stricken, medieval lifestyle in isolated log cabins in the Appalachian hollows. Families were removed from park lands, in a move celebrated by outsiders as a positive step toward "civilizing the mountaineer," which understandably left many of the displaced embittered. Surface collection and excavations carried out during a recent National Park Service–sponsored archaeological study of three former settlements within the park uncovered Coke bottles, watch faces, Bakelite toys, 78-rpm record fragments, cologne, hair tonic, face cream, and Tabasco bottles—all in addition to the tin ray gun. These objects, combined with intensive research in local courthouses and interviews with former residents, clearly reveal the extensive involvement of hollow dwellers in the wider social and economic world even as they highlight a vibrant local identity. The ray gun on its own, an innocuous piece of pop culture reflecting a deep-seated twentieth-century American faith in technology and progress, clearly demonstrates the ridiculous and insidious nature of the mountain isolation myth. It also clearly acknowledges the identity of the 1930s mountaineers as twentieth-century Americans—an acknowledgment critical to the identity of the surviving displaced and their descendants as twenty-*first* century Americans.

What the ray gun and the hollows study convey to me is the true excitement, power, and relevance of historical archaeology in the present. The past *does* matter, and often at a very personal level. But sites do not have to date a century back to still hold meaning for people's lives today. Historical archaeology, as discussed throughout this book, has long been concerned with the continuing impact of European colonization. The lasting legacy of the slave trade, the relations between natives and newcomers, the environmental changes wrought by the movement of peoples into unfamiliar lands—all of these issues hold immediate relevance for contemporary society. Four years of living in Northern Ireland, where the events of four hundred years ago are routinely employed as a rationale for present-day bloodshed, convinced me that historical archaeologists must continue to foster a dialogue about the global impact of sixteenth- and seventeenth-century colonization. The centrality of this concern can be read in Jim Deetz's classic definition of historical archaeology as the "*archaeology of the spread of European cultures throughout the world since the fifteenth century, and their impact upon and interaction with the cultures of indigenous people.*"

In 1607, at the same time that England gained a slippery toenail-hold in the New World by dumping 104 quarrelsome men and boys on the mosquito-ridden shores of Jamestown Island, King James announced his Ulster Plantation scheme, designed to colonize the north of Ireland with loyal British subjects. Both colonial ventures struggled with economic dependency, and both were embroiled in conflict and warfare; they employed a similar range of material culture, and they found only similarities between the "wild Irish" and the "savages" of North America. Not surprisingly, scholars on both sides of the Atlantic have long recognized that the links between British colonial North America and the Ulster Plantation are readily reflected in the archaeological record. But despite the archaeological similarities, our interpretation of colonization and plantation remains divergent. The English roots of America are commemorated at sites up and down the eastern seaboard, with the value of archaeology and of public education assumed. By contrast, public interest in the archaeology of British expansion in Northern Ireland is far from implicit, in a land where present-day army posts and police stations mimic the defensive architecture of seventeenth-century fortified settlements.

In 1998 I directed an excavation at Movanagher, an English village established in 1611 that was destroyed by the Irish during the 1641 Rebellion. Historical documents and contemporary local memory present the site as insular, suggesting the only possible relationship between natives and newcomers was one of conflict. Yet the archaeology revealed a surprising degree of Irish influence in the material culture used by the English inhabitants. Soil stains and ceramics indicate that settlers slept in oval Irish-style houses with open hearths and walls of woven saplings, cooking and eating their meals from a mishmash of hand-built Irish ceramic pots as well as wheel-thrown English wares. Linking us to the seemingly mundane daily lives of the past inhabitants of the short-lived village, the finds suggest a degree of interaction and adaptation between the settlers and the native Irish that is too often denied in the present. The medium of archaeology itself allowed for an open discussion of these issues with local schoolchildren and residents. Ideally, continued archaeological research exposing the complexity of Ireland's modern history will help to strengthen the fragile discussion between Northern Ireland's long-polarized communities, now slowly treading the rocky road toward peaceful coexistence.

Yet back in the United States, our early English colonial sites seldom inspire similarly delicate discussion, even though natives and newcomers in both lands were caught up in the same global process. From a young age, we are taught that the significance of sites like Jamestown and Plymouth is their role in the creation of an independent, democratic nation. We almost forget that these towns were the timber, brick, stone, and mud superstructure of human communities riddled by conflict as well as cooperation, destabilized by disease and yet strengthened by good fortune, and wholly comprised of living, breathing human beings with all their flaws, foibles, and individual identities. But it is only through addressing the incredible diversity of these individual stories, readily brought to life through archaeology, that we will ever be able to understand why and how the "idea" of America continues to provide national cohesion in an unsettled world. That cohesion will only be sustained through the belated acknowledgment of the contributions made by all participants in the momentous events of the past five hundred years, and through the recognition that the past and present of North America do not exist in a vacuum.

Does this mean that we should stop examining venerable sites like Jamestown? Absolutely not. If archaeology can teach us something new about life in the 1930s, then surely it retains the capacity to change our understanding of the 1630s and to inform our outlook and identity in the 2030s. As the twenty-first century progresses, American historical archaeologists must continue to learn from colleagues in other lands to better understand the place of North America in the world today. We must also continue to find new ways to interpret an "old" American history in its global context and to engage you—the increasingly diverse and sophisticated public—in the process. After all, it is your past and it is your future.

Epilogue

John H. Jameson Jr.

Archaeology as Inspiration

In this book we have set out to introduce you to the exciting world of archaeology and what it contributes to the rich fabric of North American history. We have concentrated on the historical periods beginning with the early contacts between Europeans and Native Americans. We have taken you on a journey to important archaeological sites and projects from Canada to the Caribbean, from the early Viking voyages through World War II. We have told the stories of pioneering archaeologists working in rural and urban North America, on the land and under water, at forts, shipwrecks, missions, farms, city lots, and sites of industry. We have shown how historical archaeology is important. The contributors have shared their findings and encourage you to join in preserving and studying our common cultural heritage.

We have noted that "historical archaeology" differs from "prehistoric archaeology" in that it concentrates on periods of human history when written records are part of the physical remains of a culture. Some scholars see historical archaeology as a method of comparing archaeological, documentary, and oral data, which complement each other to reveal a more complete picture of the past. Taking a broad perspective, they distinguish historical archaeology as the archaeology of literate societies. By examining both the places people lived and the documents some left behind, historical archaeologists attempt to discover the fabric of everyday life in the past and seek a greater understanding of the historical development of societies. Thus, as James Deetz pointed out, historical archaeology can provide insights into historical processes that written records *by themselves* cannot. Historical archaeology deals with the unintended, the subconscious, the worldviews, and the mindsets of individuals. An important contribution of historical archaeology, he contended, is to illuminate the undocumented details and context of cultural history beyond diluted and incomplete recordings of a minority of "deviant, wealthy, white males." To Deetz, the most important outcome of historical archaeology is to democratize history.

Archaeologists deal with three-dimensional artifacts that people can feel, smell, touch, dream about, and care about. We use archaeology to teach concepts of culture and to learn important things about ourselves, about who we have been, who we are, and where we are going. While archaeology makes important contributions to history and social studies, remember also its power to inspire people. We believe that historical archaeologists today perform much of the best and most recognized research in archaeology. Our colleagues in academia, museums, cultural resource management (CRM), and government increasingly provide leadership in these endeavors by amplifying history and making it more meaningful to people.

Historical archaeology embraces the interests of a diverse group of scholars in anthropology, history, historical architecture, geography, and folklore. In the New World, historical archaeologists work on a broad range of sites preserved on land and under water. These sites document early European settlement and its effects on Native American peoples as well as the subsequent spread of the frontier and later urbanization and industrialization. They also record the spread and influence of Asian and African cultures. Internationally, historical archaeologists turn their attention to issues such as colonization that have worldwide implications.

Preservation and Protection

Public concern about protecting archaeological sites has a long history in North America stemming from the conservation movement of the late nineteenth century and a tradition of public stewardship of resources. Since the 1930s in the United States, Congress has charged the National Park Service with preserving and interpreting nationally significant historic sites. Parks Canada and other conservation agencies in Canada have played a similar role. Mounting concerns about wanton looting and destruction of sites led to a bevy of protection laws in the 1960s and 1970s. In the United States, perhaps the most important of these was the National Historic Preservation Act of 1966, which established the National Register of Historic Places (NRHP) and State Historic Preservation Offices. Although not a perfect system, the NRHP has protected hundreds of thousands of historic and archaeological sites.

National Historic Landmarks are nationally significant historic places designated by the U.S. secretary of the interior because they possess exceptional value or quality in illustrating or interpreting the heritage of the United States. Fewer than three thousand historic places have been designated as National Historic Landmarks. Working with citizens throughout the nation, the National Historic Landmarks Program draws upon the expertise of National Park Service staff working to nominate new landmarks and provide assistance to existing landmarks.

In Canada, the federal government has recently launched the Historic Places Initiative, resulting in the establishment of the Canadian Register of Historic Places, publication of "Standards and Guidelines for the Conservation of Historic Places in Canada," and a certification process to promote private-sector preservation. These programs intend to encourage and assist communities across Canada to conserve historic places. Similar to the U.S. National Register, the Canadian Register is Canada's list of historic places of local, provincial, territorial, and national significance. It includes a searchable database, accessible on the Internet, and encompasses gardens, fortresses, archaeological sites, grain elevators, theaters, churches, and historic districts among its many historically significant places.

Emphasis on Public Outreach

Public interpretation at sites such as parks and museums succeeds when archaeologists carry out their research imaginatively with a strong public component. People have become activists on behalf of significant archaeological sites that they cherish because they have directly experienced them. Where communities value their cultural legacy, government authorities receive public support to deal with development more sensitively, and tourism is booming in places that retain their distinctive heritage values. Significant archaeological sites are preserved, attracting private and government funding for conservation and interpretation, along with thousands of local and international visitors each year.

Today most professional archaeologists in North America recognize the importance of archaeology education and are working with teachers, tour guides, museum educators, park rangers, artisans, members of the media, government officials, and community leaders to develop innovative programs.

A large number of private CRM firms expend considerable resources in promoting educational opportunities for volunteers and students. An example is the full-time public programs division at Statistical Research, Inc., in Tucson, Arizona. SRI produces the USDA Forest Service's publication *PIT Traveler,* which advertises nationwide programs and volunteer opportunities. Through PIT (an acronym for Passport in Time), volunteers work with professional archaeologists and historians on projects including archaeological excavation, rock art restoration, survey, archival research, historic structure restoration, gathering oral histories, and writing interpretive brochures.

The Heritage Education Program of the U.S. Bureau of Land Management has also made important contributions to archaeology education at the federal level. The bureau's Project Archaeology has produced high-quality educational materials and teacher workshops. For example, *Intrigue of the Past: A Teacher's Activity Guide for Fourth through Seventh Grades* contains twenty-eight classroom-tested lesson plans that use history and archaeology to teach science, math, history, social studies, art, language arts, and such higher-level thinking skills as problem solving, synthesis, and evaluation.

Among federally sponsored programs, the National Park Service has been the traditional leader in promoting education by developing partnerships and initiatives both within and outside the government. The NPS publication *Common Ground,* for example, is a quarterly magazine distributed to more than twelve thousand members of the public as well as archaeologists, land managers, preservation officers, museum professionals, law enforcement agents, and educators. The NPS Southeast Archeological Center in Tallahassee, Florida, has helped to develop archaeology-related curricula, both in formal school settings and at more informal settings such as national parks and museums. The center has organized and coordinated many public-oriented publications, academic symposia, workshops, and training programs.

The NPS has also been a leader in developing performance standards for educational programming, such as the Essential Competencies for archaeologists, which require knowledge and understanding of interpretation philosophy and techniques. In 2000 the NPS finalized the Effective Interpretation of Archaeological Resources "shared competency" training module. An interagency, interdisciplinary work group developed the module over the course of three years. It outlines a unique course of study for cross-training employees in the three NPS career fields of archaeology, interpretation, and education. Specialists in these fields are trained together in the skills and abilities (shared competencies) needed to carry out a successful public interpretation program.

At the state level, the Arizona State Historic Preservation Office developed exemplary standards for public archaeology education in the 1980s and 1990s. Arizona Archaeology Month now features more than one hundred public events. Innovative volunteer programs such as the Arizona Site Steward Program and the State Archaeology Fair have opened new opportunities for learning and stewardship.

Our contributors have introduced you to many notable examples at the\
municipal level, including Charleston, South Carolina; Alexandria, Virginia;
and Quebec City. In these cases, local communities have taken the initiative
in historic preservation, education, and archaeological protection. Professional organizations, especially the Society for Historical Archaeology, the
Society for American Archaeology, and the Archaeological Institute of
America, plus regional, state, and local groups, have also played important
roles in emphasizing education in archaeology. The SHA has sponsored and
copublished this book and is developing an accompanying Web site.

In Canada, public education programs have been a priority of Parks
Canada, where public education and involvement are important elements in
historic site restoration efforts from coast to coast. The agency has established notable interpretive and living history centers at historic military sites
such as the Fortress of Louisbourg. Early coordination and support by
agency staff were critical to the successes of these public archaeology programs. Some programs dependent upon government funding and political
goodwill have been less fortunate, such as the late and much-lamented Archaeological Resource Centre, the Province of Ontario's joint archaeology
education venture with the Toronto schools. Another loss was the excellent
educational program developed by the Archaeological Survey of Alberta.
Both programs were victims of the mid-1990s cash crunch, despite demonstrated popularity among students, teachers, and the general public.

Combined professional and avocational groups in Canada such as the
Ontario Archaeological Society have long operated public education programs in conjunction with excellent archaeological research using volunteers. The provincewide archaeological program and the provincial museum
in Saskatchewan have thrived with the enthusiasm and backing of societies
such as the Saskatchewan Archaeological Society. Likewise, the Canadian
Archaeological Association, founded in 1968, has made public education a
priority in recent years. Beginning in the 1980s, the CAA engaged in a series
of discussions aimed at developing public and political support for national
archaeological protection legislation. Other notable examples of education
initiatives are Quebec's provincewide network Réseau archéo-Québec, which
promotes public access to information about Quebec's multicultural and archaeological heritage. For more than fifteen years, the City of Quebec has
sponsored an impressive program of site recording and public education that
has greatly illuminated the rich cultural history of the city. Pointe-à-Callière,
the Montreal Museum of Archaeology and History, is another leader in public outreach, offering a wide array of workshops, tours, and multimedia exhibits.

21

Unlocking the Past: Painting by Martin Pate
John H. Jameson Jr.

The Southeast Archeological Center, National Park Service, produced this oil painting for the SHA's Unlocking the Past project. The image was developed through a conceptual collaboration between SEAC staff member John Jameson and the artist, with input from John Ehrenhard of SEAC, Lu Ann De Cunzo, and members of the SHA Public Education and Information Committee. It depicts a metaphor of modern archaeological practice that emphasizes the importance of research and public interpretation of objects made, used, and discarded by people from the many cultures that have made North America. The four figures at the base represent the four main cultural groupings addressed in the Unlocking the Past project and book: European Americans, Native Americans, African Americans, and Asian Americans.

Reaching Out

Archaeologists are increasingly concerned with how the past is presented to, and consumed by, North Americans, and so we are looking into new ways of communicating about our finds through our national parks, museums, popular literature, film and television, music, and various multimedia formats. Many of us are not content to rely solely on traditional techniques. We want to venture beyond explanations of what things were and how they worked. Archaeological information and objects can inspire a wide variety of artistic expressions ranging from computer-generated reconstructions and traditional artists' conceptions to such art forms as poetry, playwriting, and opera.

Developments in Native American Archaeology

In the 1990s a new era of American Indian archaeology emerged in the United States with the passage of the Native American Graves Protection and Repatriation Act of 1990. NAGPRA addresses the rights of Native Americans, Indian tribes, and Native Hawaiian organizations to their ancestral human remains, funerary objects, sacred objects, and related cultural items. It requires federal agencies and museums that receive federal funds to provide information about Native American cultural items. It also requires that these objects and remains, upon presentation of a valid request, be returned or repatriated. Accordingly, many archaeologists, historians, and cultural resource managers have been forced to rethink their assumptions about how to

Epilogue. 1. *Unlocking the Past,* oil painting by Martin Pate (Digital image courtesy of Southeast Archeological Center, National Park Service.)

conduct research and interpret our findings. We have learned that we are no longer the sole proprietors and interpreters of the American Indian past—nor should we be—whether in pre- or post-European contexts. In fact, the definition of "cultural resources" in the archaeological sense has broadened from a focus on objects, features, and architectural elements to less tangible items such as "place" and "traditional cultural property." This is due primarily to the effects of new federal mandates and policies that have made American Indians integral players in cultural resource management policies, and our reconsidering what constitutes "data" and who owns or controls the data.

Challenges for the Future

Successful efforts in archaeology education have overcome political and social obstacles to inform and involve the public. Isn't public inspiration the ultimate goal of archaeology? Innovative approaches encourage dialogues, establish partnerships, and work toward more inclusive, participatory archaeology. We measure our success by how well we earn your trust as curators of the written as well as the unwritten record. Posterity will judge how effectively we have used archaeological finds for the education and enjoyment of present and future generations.

The Society for Historical Archaeology plays a key role in promoting these efforts. We hope that the Unlocking the Past project encourages historical archaeologists to share their findings and inspires readers like you and the public at large to join us in studying and preserving our common historical heritage.

For Further Reading and Viewing

Introduction: The Stuff of Histories and Cultures

Advisory Council on Underwater Archaeology. www.acuaonline.org.

Bass, George F., ed. 1988. *Ships and Shipwrecks of the Americas: A History Based on Underwater Archaeology.* London: Thames and Hudson.

Brauner, David R., comp. 2000. *Approaches to Material Culture Research for Historical Archaeologists.* 2nd ed. California, Pa.: Society for Historical Archaeology.

Cotter, John L. 1998. *A Bibliography of Historical Archaeology in North America, North of Mexico.* www.sha.org/cot2intr.htm.

Cotter, John L., Daniel G. Roberts, and Michael Parrington. 1992. *The Buried Past: An Archaeological History of Philadelphia.* Philadelphia: University of Pennsylvania Press.

Deagan, Kathleen A. 1983. *Spanish St. Augustine: The Archaeology of a Colonial Creole Community.* New York: Academic Press.

———. 1987. *Artifacts of the Spanish Colonies of Florida and the Caribbean, 1500–1800.* Vol. 1, *Ceramics, Glassware, Beads.* Washington, D.C.: Smithsonian Institution Press.

———, ed. 1995. *Puerto Real: The Archaeology of a Sixteenth-Century Spanish Town in Hispaniola.* Gainesville: University Press of Florida.

Deagan, Kathleen, and José María Cruxent. 2002. *Archaeology at La Isabela, America's First European Town.* New Haven: Yale University Press.

Deetz, James. 1977. *In Small Things Forgotten: An Archaeology of Early American Life.* Garden City, N.Y.: Anchor Press / Doubleday. (Rev. ed. 1996.)

———. 1993. *Flowerdew Hundred: The Archaeology of a Virginia Plantation, 1619–1864.* Charlottesville: University Press of Virginia.

Deetz, James, and Patricia Scott Deetz. 2000. *The Times of Their Lives: Life, Love, and Death in Plymouth Colony.* New York: W. H. Freeman.

Egan, Geoffrey, and Ronald L. Michael, eds. 1999. *Old and New Worlds.* Oxford: Oxbow.

Falk, Lisa, ed. 1991. *Historical Archaeology in Global Perspective.* Washington, D.C.: Smithsonian Institution Press.

Historical Archaeology. Quarterly publication of the Society for Historical Archaeology.

Leone, Mark P., and Neil Asher Silberman, eds. 1995. *Invisible America: Unearthing Our Hidden History.* New York: Henry Holt.

Ludlow Collective. 2002. "The Colorado Coal Field War Archaeology Project." *SAA Archaeological Record* 2 (2): 21–23.

Miller, George L., Ann Smart Martin, and Nancy S. Dickinson. 1994. "Changing Consumption Patterns: English Ceramics and the American Market from 1770 to 1840."

In *Everyday Life in the Early Republic,* edited by Catherine E. Hutchins, 219–39. Winterthur, Del.: Winterthur Museum.

Noël Hume, Ivor. 1970. *A Guide to Artifacts of Colonial America.* Philadelphia: University of Pennsylvania Press.

———. 2001. *If These Pots Could Talk: Collecting 2,000 Years of British Household Pottery.* Milwaukee, Wis.: Chipstone Foundation.

Orser, Charles E., Jr., ed. 2002. *Encyclopedia of Historical Archaeology.* London: Routledge.

Praetzellis, Adrian. 2000. *Death by Theory: A Tale of Mystery and Archaeological Theory.* Walnut Creek, Cal.: AltaMira.

———. 2003. *Dug to Death: A Tale of Archaeological Method and Mayhem.* Walnut Creek, Cal.: AltaMira.

Society for Historical Archaeology. www.sha.org.

South, Stanley, ed. 1994. *Pioneers in Historical Archaeology: Breaking New Ground.* New York: Plenum.

Part 1. Cultures in Contact

Melting Pots or Not?

Dawdy, Shannon Lee, ed. 2000. "Creolization" issue. *Historical Archaeology* 34 (3).

Lister, Florence C. 1997. *Pot Luck: Adventures in Archaeology.* Albuquerque: University of New Mexico Press.

Viola, Herman J., and Carolyn Margolis, eds. 1991. *Seeds of Change: A Quincentennial Celebration.* Washington, D.C.: Smithsonian Institution Press.

Chapter 1. Spaniards and Native Americans at the Missions of La Florida

Hann, John H., and Bonnie G. McEwan. 1998. *The Apalachee Indians and Mission San Luis.* Gainesville: University Press of Florida.

Milanich, Jerald T. 1999. *Laboring in the Fields of the Lord: Spanish Missions and Southeastern Indians.* Washington, D.C: Smithsonian Institution Press.

Milanich, Jerald, and Charles Hudson. 1993. *Hernando de Soto and the Indians of Florida.* Gainesville: University Press of Florida and Florida Museum of Natural History.

Milanich, Jerald T., and Susan Milbrath, eds. 1989. *First Encounters: Spanish Explorations in the Caribbean and the United States, 1492–1570.* Ripley P. Bullen Monographs in Anthropology and History, No. 9, Florida Museum of Natural History. Gainesville: University Press of Florida.

Wenhold, Lucy L., trans. and ed. 1936. *A 17th Century Letter of Gabriel Díaz Vara Calderón, Bishop of Cuba.* Miscellaneous Collections 95, no. 16. Washington, D.C.: Smithsonian Institution.

Worth, John E. 1998. *The Timucuan Chiefdoms of Spanish Florida.* 2 vols. Gainesville: University Press of Florida.

Chapter 2. Bioarchaeology of the Spanish Missions

Larsen, Clark Spencer. 2000. "The Bones of La Florida." *Scientific American* 282 (6): 80–85.

———. 2000. *Skeletons in Our Closet: Revealing Our Past through Bioarchaeology.* Princeton: Princeton University Press.

———, ed. 2001. *Bioarchaeology of Spanish Florida: The Impact of Colonialism.* Gainesville: University Press of Florida.

Chapter 3. African Americans on Southern Plantations

Fennell, Christopher C. 2000. "Conjuring Boundaries: Inferring Past Identities from Religious Artifacts." *International Journal of Historical Archaeology* 4 (14): 281–313.

Ferguson, Leland G. 1992. *Uncommon Ground: Archaeology and Early African America, 1650–1800.* Washington, D.C.: Smithsonian Institution Press.

Heath, Barbara J. 1999. *Hidden Lives: The Archaeology of Slave Life at Thomas Jefferson's Poplar Forest.* Charlottesville: University Press of Virginia.

Yentsch, Anne Elizabeth. 1994. *A Chesapeake Family and Their Slaves: A Study in Historical Archaeology.* Cambridge: Cambridge University Press.

Chapter 4. Black Seminole Freedom Fighters on the Florida Frontier

Deagan, Kathleen, and Darcie MacMahon. 1995. *Fort Mose: Colonial America's Black Fortress of Freedom.* Gainesville: University Press of Florida and Florida Museum of Natural History.

Katz, William Loren. 1986. *Black Indians: A Hidden Heritage.* New York: Atheneum.

Landers, Jane. 1999. *Black Society in Spanish Florida.* Urbana: University of Illinois Press.

Porter, Kenneth W. 1996. *The Black Seminoles.* Gainesville: University Press of Florida.

Price, Richard, ed. 1979. *Maroon Societies: Rebel Slave Communities in the Americas.* 2nd ed. Baltimore: Johns Hopkins University Press.

Chapter 5. The Chinese in the Cities of the West

Chinese Historical Society of Southern California. www.chssc.org.

Greenwood, Roberta S. 1996. *Down by the Station: Los Angeles Chinatown, 1880–1933.* Los Angeles: Institute of Archaeology, University of California, Los Angeles.

———. 1999. "The Hing Lung Laundry in Santa Barbara." In *Chinese America: History and Perspectives,* 71–79. San Francisco: Chinese Historical Society of America.

Hoo, Judy Soo. 1997. *American Journey: The Asian-American Experience.* CD. Primary Source Media in association with the UCLA Asian American Studies Center.

Metropolitan Transportation Authority of Southern California. www.MTA.net/laund/index.htm

Origins and Destinations: 41 Essays on Chinese America. 1994. Los Angeles: Chinese Historical Society of Southern California, UCLA Asian American Studies Center.

See, Lisa. 1995. *On Gold Mountain.* New York: St. Martin's Press.

Wegars, Priscilla, ed. 1993. *Hidden Heritage: Historical Archaeology of the Overseas Chinese.* Amityville, N.Y.: Baywood.

Part 2. Challenging and Changing Environments

Exploring New Lands and Exploiting New Environments

Shackel, Paul A., and Barbara J. Little, eds. 1994. *Historical Archaeology of the Chesapeake*. Washington, D.C.: Smithsonian Institution Press.

Chapter 6. Early Encounters with a "New" Land: Vikings and Englishmen in the North American Arctic

Alsford, Stephen, ed. 1993. "The Meta Incognita Project: Contributions to Field Studies." Mercury Directorate Series paper 6. Ottawa: Canadian Museum of Civilization; Washington, D.C.: Arctic Studies Center, Smithsonian Institution.

Fitzhugh, William W., and Jacqueline S. Olin, eds. 1993. *Archeology of the Frobisher Voyages*. Washington, D.C.: Smithsonian Institution Press.

Fitzhugh, William W., and Elisabeth I. Ward, eds. 2000. *Vikings: The North Atlantic Saga*. Washington, D.C.: Smithsonian Institution Press.

McDermott, James. 2001. *Martin Frobisher: Elizabethan Privateer*. New Haven: Yale University Press.

Ruby, Robert. 2001. *The Unknown Shore: The True Story of How the First English Colony in the New World Was Founded, Lost, and Found Again*. New York: Henry Holt.

Symons, Thomas, Stephen Alsford, and Chris Kitzan, eds. 1999. "Meta Incognita: A Discourse of Discovery; Martin Frobisher's Arctic Expeditions, 1576–1578." Mercury Directorate Series. 2 Vols. Ottawa: Canadian Museum of Civilization.

Chapter 7. Jamestown, Virginia

Association for the Preservation of Virginia Antiquities, Jamestown Rediscovery project. www.apva.org.

Bridenbaugh, Carl. 1980. *Jamestown, 1544–1699*. New York: Oxford University Press.

Cotter, John L. 1958. *Archeological Excavations at Jamestown Colonial National Historical Park and Jamestown National Historic Site, Virginia*. Archeological Research Series no. 4. Washington, D.C.: National Park Service.

———. 1994. *Archaeological Excavations at Jamestown, Virginia*. Rev. ed. Special Publication no. 32. Richmond: Archeological Society of Virginia.

Curtin, Philip D., Grace S. Brush, and George W. Fisher, eds. 2001. *Discovering the Chesapeake: The History of an Ecosystem*. Baltimore: Johns Hopkins University Press.

Jamestown Rediscovery: A World Uncovered. 1997. Video. Association for the Preservation of Virginia Antiquities.

Kelso, William M., ed. 1995–2001. *Jamestown Rediscovery*. 7 vols. Richmond: Association for the Preservation of Virginia Antiquities.

Noël Hume, Ivor. 1963. *Here Lies Virginia: An Archaeologist's View of Colonial Life and History*. Charlottesville: University Press of Virginia. (Rev. ed. 1994.)

———, and Audrey Noël Hume. 2001. *The Archaeology of Martin's Hundred*. 2 vols. Philadelphia: University of Pennsylvania Museum of Archaeology and Anthropology; Williamsburg: Colonial Williamsburg Foundation.

Stahle, David W., Malcolm K. Cleaveland, Dennis B. Blanton, Matthew D. Therrell, and David A. Gay. 1988. "The Lost Colony and Jamestown Droughts." *Science* 280:564–67.

Chapter 8. The Shipwreck of La Salle's *La Belle*

Bruseth, James E., Layne Hedrick, and John de Bry. 2000. "Découverte et Fouille de 'La Belle.'" In *Cavelier de La Salle, L'Expédition de 1684: La Belle,* edited by Jean Boudriot: 22–34. Paris: Collection Archéologie Navale Française.

Texas Historical Commission. www.thc.state.tx.us/lasalle/lasbelle.html.

"*Voyage of Doom.*" 1999. *NOVA* presentation produced by WGBH Boston. www.pbs.org/wgbh/nova/lasalle/

Weddle, Robert S. 2001. *The Wreck of the Belle, the Ruin of La Salle.* College Station: Texas A&M University Press.

Chapter 9. Mining the West

Dixon, Kelly. 2003. *Boomtown Saloons: History and Archaeology in Virginia City, Nevada.* Reno: University of Nevada Press.

Hardesty, Donald L. 1988. *The Archaeology of Mining and Miners: A View from the Silver State.* Special Publication no. 6. California, Pa.: Society for Historical Archaeology.

Holliday, J. S. 1999. *Rush for Riches: Gold Fever and the Making of California.* Berkeley and Los Angeles: University of California Press.

Lanyon, Milton, and Laurence Bulmore. 1991. *Cinnabar Hills: The Quicksilver Days of New Almaden.* 5th ed. Los Gatos, Cal.: Village Printers.

Smith, Grant H. 1998. *The History of the Comstock Lode: 1850–1997.* With new material by Joseph V. Tingley. Reno: Nevada Bureau of Mines and Geology.

Part 3. Building Cities

Tales of Many Cities

Desjardins, Pauline, and Geneviève Duguay. 1992. *Pointe-à-Callière: From Ville-Marie to Montreal.* Translated by Kathe Roth. Sillery, Quebec: Le Vieux-Port de Montréal and Septentrion.

Mrozowski, Stephen A., Grace H. Ziesing, and Mary C. Beaudry. 1996. *Living on the Boott: Historical Archaeology at the Boott Mills Boardinghouses, Lowell, Massachusetts.* Amherst: University of Massachusetts Press.

Shackel, Paul A. 2000. *Archaeology and Created Memory: Public History in a National Park.* New York: Kluwer.

Chapter 10. Quebec City, Canada

Larocque, Robert. 2000. *La Naissance et la mort à Québec autrefois: Les Restes humains des cimetières de la basilique Notre-Dame-de-Québec.* Cahiers d'archéologie du CÉLAT no. 5. Quebec: Université Laval, Ville de Québec, and Ministère de la Culture et des Communications.

Rouleau, Serge, and Anne Desgagné. 1995. *Recherches archéologiques: Le Site des jardins du Séminaire de Québec*. Quebec: Ville de Québec.

Rouleau, Serge, Dominique Lalande, Catherine Fortin, and l'Ostéothèque de Montréal (under the direction of William Moss). 1988. *L'archéologie du monastère des Récollets à Québec (CeEt-621)*. Cahiers d'archéologie du CÉLAT no. 4. Quebec: Université Laval, Ville de Québec, and Ministère de la Culture et des Communications.

Simoneau, Daniel. *Rapport d'inventaire archéologique: Les Jardins du Séminaire de Québec*. Quebec: Ville de Québec.

Ville de Québec. 1994. *Travelling Back in Time: 5 Archaeological Sites to Discover, Recreate, Understand*. Quebec: Ville de Québec.

———. 1996. *Recherches archéologiques dans la cour des petits du Séminaire de Québec (CeEt-32)*. Quebec: Ville de Québec.

Chapter 11. New York City

Archaeological Institute of America. Interactive dig at Brooklyn's eighteenth-century Lott House. www.archaeology.org/magazine.php?page=online/features/lott/index.

Cantwell, Anne-Marie, and Diana diZerega Wall. 2001. *Unearthing Gotham: The Archaeology of New York City*. New Haven: Yale University Press.

Gilbert, Allan S., ed. 2004. *Archaeology in the Bronx*. New York: Bronx County Historical Society.

Hansen, Joyce, and Gary McGowan. 1998. *Breaking Ground, Breaking Silence: The Story of New York's African Burial Ground*. New York: Henry Holt.

Moore, Christopher. 1994. *The African Burial Ground: An American Discovery*. Directed by David Kutz. Video. Brooklyn, N.Y.: Kutz Television.

Rothschild, Nan A. 1990. *New York City Neighborhoods: The Eighteenth Century*. San Diego: Academic Press.

Update: Newsletter of the African Burial Ground. New York: Office of Public Education and Interpretation of the African Burial Ground.

Wall, Diana diZerega. 1994. *The Archaeology of Gender: Separating the Spheres in Urban America*. New York: Plenum.

———, and Anne-Marie Cantwell. 2004. *Archaeological Tours of New York City*. New Haven: Yale University Press.

Chapter 12. Community Archaeology in Alexandria, Virginia

Alexandria Archaeology Museum. City of Alexandria, Virginia, Office of Historic Alexandria. http://oha.ci.alexandria.va.us/archaeology.

Blomberg, Francine. 1992. *African American Heritage Park: Archaeological Investigations*. Alexandria Archaeology Publications no. 39. Alexandria, Va.: Office of Historic Alexandria.

Blomberg, Francine, Steven J. Shephard, Barbara H. Magid, Pamela J. Cressey, Timothy Dennee, and Bernard K. Means. 2001. *"To Find Rest from All Trouble": The Archaeology of the Quaker Burying Ground, Alexandria, Virginia*. Alexandria Archaeology Publications no. 120. Alexandria, Va.: Office of Historic Alexandria.

Cressey, Pamela J. 1993. *To Witness the Past: African American Archaeology in Alexandria, Virginia*. Alexandria, Va.: Office of Historic Alexandria.

Landes, Robin S., and Joanna T. Moyar. 1996. *Archaeologists at Work: A Teacher's Guide to Classroom Archaeology*. 2nd ed. Alexandria Archaeology Publications no. 48. Alexandria, Va.: Office of Historic Alexandria.

Shephard, Steven J. 1988. *Development of a City-Site: Alexandria, Virginia, 1750–1850*. Alexandria Archaeology Publications no. 16. Alexandria, Va.: Office of Historic Alexandria.

Chapter 13. Urban Life in Colonial Charleston, South Carolina

Edgar, Walter. 1998. *South Carolina: A History*. Columbia: University of South Carolina.

Honerkamp, Nicholas, and Martha Zierden. 1989. *Charleston Place: The Archaeology of Urban Life*. Leaflet no. 31. Charleston, S.C.: Charleston Museum.

Joseph, J. W., and Martha A. Zierden, eds. 2001. *Another's Country: Archaeological and Historical Perspectives on Cultural Interaction in the Southern Colonies*. Tuscaloosa: University of Alabama Press.

Panter, Rich. 1999. *When Rice Was King*. Video. Columbia: South Carolina Educational Television.

Poston, Jonathan H. 1997. *The Buildings of Charleston: A Guide to the City's Architecture*. Columbia: University of South Carolina Press.

Chapter 14. "A Place to Start From": West Oakland, California

Anthropological Studies Center, Sonoma State University. "Cypress/West Oakland Historical Archaeology Project." www.sonoma.edu/asc/ongoingprojects/cypress/cypress.htm.

London, Jack. 1913. *Valley of the Moon*. New York: Macmillan.

Stewart, Suzanne, and Mary Praetzellis, eds. 1997. *Sights and Sounds: Essays in Celebration of West Oakland*. Cypress Project Interpretive Report no. 1, Anthropological Studies Center, Sonoma State University. Sacramento: California Department of Transportation.

Part 4. Making a Living in Rural America

Chapter 15. The Archaeology of Agricultural Life

Baugher, Sherene, and Terry Klein, eds. "Historic Preservation and the Archaeology of Nineteenth-Century Farmsteads in the Northeast" 2001–2002 issue. *Northeast Historical Archaeology* 2003:30–31.

Delaware Department of Transportation. "Archaeological Exploration and Historic Preservation in Delaware." www.deldot.net/static/projects/archaeology/index.html.

Hardesty, Donald L., with Brodhead, Michael. 1997. *The Archaeology of the Donner Party*. Reno: University of Nevada Press.

McClelland, Linda F., et al. n.d. *Guidelines for Evaluating and Documenting Rural Historic Landscapes*. National Register Bulletin no. 30. Washington, D.C.: National Park Service.

McMurry, Sally. 1988. *Families and Farmhouses in Nineteenth-Century America: Vernacular Design and Social Change.* New York: Oxford University Press.

Orser, Charles E., Jr., ed. 1990. "Historical Archaeology on Southern Plantations and Farms." *Historical Archaeology* 24 (4): i–vi, 1–126.

Spector, Janet D. 1993. *What This Awl Means: Feminist Archaeology at a Wahpeton Dakota Village.* St. Paul: Minnesota Historical Society Press.

Stewart-Abernathy, Leslie C. 1986a. *The Moser Farmstead: Independent but Not Isolated; The Archaeology of a Late Nineteenth Century Ozark Farmstead.* Research Series 26. Fayetteville: Arkansas Archeological Survey.

———. 1986b. "Urban Farmsteads: Household Responsibilities in the City." *Historical Archaeology* 20 (2): 5–15.

———. 1987. "From Memories and From the Ground: Historical Archeology at the Moser Farmstead in the Arkansas Ozarks." In *Visions and Revisions: Ethnohistoric Perspectives on Southern Cultures,* edited by George Sabo III and William M. Schneider, 98–113. Athens: University of Georgia Press.

Stine, Linda F., Martha Zierden, Lesley M. Drucker, and Christopher Judge, eds. 1997. *Carolina's Historical Landscapes: Archaeological Perspectives.* Knoxville: University of Tennessee Press.

Yamin, Rebecca, and Karen Bescherer Metheny, eds. 1996. *Landscape Archaeology: Reading and Interpreting the American Historical Landscape.* Knoxville: University of Tennessee Press.

Chapter 16. The Archaeology of Rural Industry

Claassen, Cheryl. 1994. "Washboards, Pigtoes, and Muckets: Historic Musselling in the Mississippi Watershed." *Historical Archaeology* 28 (2): 1–145.

Council, R. Bruce, Nicholas Honerkamp, and M. Elizabeth Will. 1991. *Industry and Technology in Antebellum Tennessee.* Knoxville: University of Tennessee Press.

Evans, Oliver. 1850. *The Young Mill-Wright and Miller's Guide.* 13th ed. Reprint, New York: Arno Press, 1972.

Gordon, Robert B., and Patrick M. Malone. 1994. *The Texture of Industry: An Archaeological View of the Industrialization of North America.* New York: Oxford University Press.

Light, John D., and Henry Unglik. 1984. *A Frontier Fur Trade Blacksmith Shop: 1796–1812.* Studies in Archaeology, Architecture, and History. Ottawa: Parks Canada.

Robbins, Roland Wells, and Evan Jones. 1959. *Hidden America.* New York: Alfred A. Knopf.

Starbuck, David R. 1986a. "The New England Glassworks: New Hampshire's Boldest Experiment in Early Glassmaking." *New Hampshire Archeologist* 27 (1): 1–148.

———. 1986b. "The Shaker Mills in Canterbury, New Hampshire." *IA: The Journal of the Society for Industrial Archeology* 12 (1): 11–38.

Part 5. Cultures in Conflict

Chapter 17. The Archaeology of America's Colonial Wars

Armour, David A. 2000. *Colonial Michilimackinac*. Mackinac Island, Mich.: Mackinac State Historic Parks.

Boal Janssens, Cynthia. 2000. "Unearthing the History of Colonial Michilimackinac." *American Archaeology* 4 (1): 18–23.

Calver, William Louis, and Reginald Pelham Bolton. 1950. *History Written with Pick and Shovel*. New York: New York Historical Society.

Fry, Bruce W. 1984. *"An Appearance of Strength": The Fortifications of Louisbourg*. 2 vols. Studies in Archaeology, Architecture, and History. Ottawa: Parks Canada.

Hanson, Lee, and Dick Ping Hsu. 1975. *Casemates and Cannonballs: Archeological Investigations at Fort Stanwix, Rome, New York*. Publications in Archeology 14. Washington, D.C.: National Park Service.

Mackinac State Historic Parks, Michigan. www.mackinacparks.com.

Parks Canada. "Fortress of Louisbourg." www.fortress.uccb.ns.ca/.

Starbuck, David R. 1999. *The Great Warpath: British Military Sites from Albany to Crown Point*. Hanover, N.H.: University Press of New England.

Stone, Lyle M. 1974. *Fort Michilimackinac, 1715–1781*. East Lansing: The Museum, Michigan State University.

Chapter 18. The Civil War Under Water

Friends of the *Hunley*. www.hunley.org.

"*Maple Leaf* Shipwreck: An Extraordinary American Civil War Shipwreck, Jacksonville, Florida 1864." www.mapleleafshipwreck.com.

Geier, Clarence R., Jr., and Susan E. Winter, eds. 1994. *Look to the Earth: Historical Archaeology and the American Civil War*. Knoxville: University of Tennessee Press.

History Channel. *Raise the Hunley*. VHS, 50 min. store.aetv.com.

———. *Raise the Monitor*. VHS, 100 min. store.aetv.com.

Monitor National Marine Sanctuary. www.monitor.nos.noaa.gov.

U.S. Naval Historical Center. www.history.navy.mil.

Chapter 19. Native and "Newcomer": Battle of Little Bighorn

El Conejo Productions. 1995. *Archaeology, History, and Custer's Last Battle*. Video. Norman: University of Oklahoma Press.

Fox, Richard Allan, Jr. 1993. *Archaeology, History, and Custer's Last Battle*. Norman: University of Oklahoma Press.

Haecker, Charles M., and Jeffrey G. Mauck. 1997. *On the Prairie of Palo Alto: Historical Archaeology of the U.S.-Mexican War Battlefield*. College Station: Texas A&M University Press.

Scott, Douglas D., Richard A. Fox, Melissa Connor, and Dick Harmon. 1989. *Archaeological Perspectives of the Battle of the Little Bighorn*. Norman: University of Oklahoma Press.

Scott, Douglas D., and Richard A. Fox. 1987. *Archaeological Insights into the Custer Battle*. Norman: University of Oklahoma Press.

Secrets of the Little Bighorn. 1992. Learning Channel Archaeology Series. Video. Films for the Humanities and Sciences. www.films.com.

U.S. National Park Service. "American Battlefield Protection Program." www.cr.nps. gov/abpp.

———, Midwestern Archaeological Center. "Archeology at the Battle of the Little Bighorn." www.cr.nps.gov/mwac.

Chapter 20. A Global Contest: World War II

Delgado, James P. 2001. *Lost Warships: An Archaeological Tour of War at Sea.* Vancouver: Douglas and McIntyre.

Jasper, Joy Waldron, James P. Delgado, and Jim Adams. 2001. *The USS Arizona: The Ship, the Men, the Pearl Harbor Attack, and the Symbol That Aroused America.* New York: St. Martin's Press.

Lenihan, Daniel, ed. 2001. "USS *Arizona* Memorial: Submerged Cultural Resources Study: USS *Arizona* Memorial and Pearl Harbor National Historic Landmark." www.nps.gov/usar/scrs/scrs.htm.

Lenihan, Daniel. 2002. *Submerged: Adventures of America's Most Elite Underwater Archaeology Team.* New York: Newmarket.

Linenthal, Edward Tabor. 1991. *Sacred Ground: Americans and Their Battlefields.* Urbana: University of Illinois Press.

Wright, Newell O., and Mathilda Cox, eds. 1997. "A Challenge for the Military Mission: Preservation in the Armed Forces" issue. *CRM* 20 (13). www.cr.nps.gov/crm.

Part 6. Unlock the Past for the Future

Chapter 21. Conserving Our Past

Bourque, Bruce J., Stephen W. Brooke, Ronald Kley, and Kenneth Morris. 1980. "Conservation in Archaeology: Moving Toward Closer Cooperation." *American Antiquity* 45 (4): 794–99.

Conservation OnLine. palimpsest.stanford.edu.

Magid, Barbara H., and Carol E. Snow. 1991. *Buried in Storage: The Alexandria Archaeology Collections Management Project.* Nashville, Tenn.: American Association for State and Local History Technical Leaflet 178, vol. 46, no. 5.

Robinson, Wendy. 1998. *First Aid for Underwater Finds.* London: Archetype Publications; Portsmouth: Nautical Archaeological Society.

Singley, Katherine R. 1981. "Caring for Artifacts after Excavation: Some Advice for Archaeologists." *Historical Archaeology* 15 (1): 36–48.

U.S. National Park Service. "Managing Archaeological Collections." www.cr.nps.gov/ aad/collections.

Watkinson, David. 1996. *First Aid for Finds.* 2nd ed. Hereford: RESCUE; London: Archaeology Section, U.K. Institute for Conservation.

Chapter 22. Historical Archaeology That Matters Beyond Academics

Delle, James A., Stephen A. Mrozowski, and Robert Paynter, eds. 2000. *Lines That Divide: Historical Archaeologies of Race, Class, and Gender.* Knoxville: University of Tennessee Press.

Little, Barbara J., ed. 2002. *Public Benefits of Archaeology.* Gainesville: University Press of Florida.

Singleton, Theresa A., ed. 1999. *"I, Too, Am America": Archaeological Studies of African-American Life.* Charlottesville: University of Virginia Press.

Wilkie, Laurie A. 2000. *Creating Freedom: Material Culture and African American Identity at Oakley Plantation, Louisiana, 1840–1950.* Baton Rouge: Louisiana State University Press.

Chapter 24. Does Historical Archaeology Really Matter in Today's World?

Horning, Audrey. 2004. *In the Shadow of Ragged Mountain: Historical Archaeology in Nicholson, Corbin, and Weakley Hollows.* Luray, Va.: Shenandoah National Park Association.

U.S. National Park Service. 2001. *The Jamestown Archeological Assessment.* Washington, D.C.: Department of the Interior.

Epilogue

Edgar, Blake. 2000. "Whose Past Is It, Anyway?" Review of *Skull Wars,* by David Hurst Thomas. *Scientific American,* July, 106–7.

Jameson, John H., Jr., ed. 1997. *Presenting Archaeology to the Public: Digging for Truths.* Walnut Creek, Cal.: AltaMira.

———, ed. 2004. *The Reconstructed Past: Reconstructions in the Public Interpretation of Archaeology and History.* Walnut Creek, Cal.: AltaMira.

Jameson, John H., Jr., John E. Ehrenhard, and Christine A. Finn, eds. 2003. *Ancient Muses: Archaeology and the Arts.* Tuscaloosa: University of Alabama Press.

Merriman, Nick, ed. 2004. *Public Archaeology.* New York and London: Routledge.

Parks Canada. 2003. Canada's Historic Places Initiative. www.pc.gc.ca

U.S. Bureau of Land Management. "Project Archaeology." www.blm.gov/heritage/project_archaeology.htm.

U.S. National Park Service. *Common Ground.* www.cr.nps.gov/aad/cg.

———. "Module 440: Effective Interpretation of Archaeological Resources," Interpretive Development Program. www.nps.gov/idp/interp/440/module/htm.

———. "National NAGPRA." www.cr.nps.gov/nagpra.

Zimmerman, Larry J., Karen D. Vitelli, and Julie Hollowell-Zimmer, eds. 2003. *Ethical Issues in Archaeology.* Walnut Creek, Cal.: AltaMira.

Contributors

Rebecca Allen is president of Past Forward, Inc., Garden Valley, California.

R. Scott Baxter is historical archaeologist at Past Forward, Inc., Garden Valley, California.

James E. Bruseth is director of the Archaeology Division at the Texas Historical Commission.

David Clark is lecturer in anthropology at Catholic University.

Pamela J. Cressey is city archaeologist for the city of Alexandria, Virginia, and adjunct associate professor at George Washington University.

Gary Cummins is manager of the U.S. National Park Service's Harpers Ferry Center.

Lu Ann De Cunzo is associate professor of anthropology at the University of Delaware.

James P. Delgado is executive director of the Vancouver Maritime Museum.

Andrew Edwards is a staff archaeologist with the Colonial Williamsburg Foundation.

Leland Ferguson is Distinguished Professor Emeritus in the Department of Anthropology, University of South Carolina.

William Fitzhugh is curator of Arctic anthropology at the National Museum of Natural History, Smithsonian Institution.

Richard A. Fox is professor of anthropology at the University of South Dakota.

Maria Franklin is an assistant professor with the Department of Anthropology and the Center for African and African American Studies at the University of Texas at Austin and a senior research fellow with the Department of Archaeological Research at the Colonial Williamsburg Foundation.

Roberta S. Greenwood is research associate with the Los Angeles County Museum of Natural History and president of the consulting firm Greenwood and Associates.

Audrey J. Horning is assistant professor of anthropology at the College of William and Mary and director of the Achill Archaeological Field School in the Republic of Ireland.

John H. Jameson Jr. is Senior Archaeologist, Public Interpretation and Public Outreach Lead, National Park Service Southeast Archeological Center in Tallahassee.

Clark Spencer Larsen is Distinguished Professor of Social and Behavioral Sciences and chair of the Department of Anthropology at Ohio State University.

Daniel J. Lenihan is an underwater archaeologist with the National Park Service Submerged Resources Center in Santa Fe, New Mexico.

Kim A. McBride is codirector of the Kentucky Archaeological Survey at the University of Kentucky.

Sarah McDowell is an education graduate student at the University of Delaware.

Sara Mascia is vice president of the cultural resources management firm Historical Perspectives, Inc., Westport, Connecticut.

Jerald T. Milanich is curator in archaeology at the Florida Museum of Natural History.

William Moss is principal archaeologist for the City of Quebec.

Mary Praetzellis is a historical archaeologist and administrative manager of the Anthropological Studies Center at Sonoma State University in California.

Margaret Purser is professor of anthropology at Sonoma State University.

Nan A. Rothschild is Ann Whitney Olin Professor of Anthropology at Barnard College, Columbia University.

David R. Starbuck is assistant professor of anthropology at Plymouth State University.

Leslie "Skip" Stewart-Abernathy is a station archaeologist with the Arkansas Archeological Survey and an associate professor of anthropology at the University of Arkansas at Fayetteville.

John Triggs is assistant professor of archaeology and classical studies at Wilfrid Laurier University.

Diana diZerega Wall is professor of anthropology at City College of the City University of New York.

Terrance Weik is assistant professor of anthropology at the University of South Carolina.

Lisa Young is an archaeological conservator and president of Alexandria Conservation Services, Ltd.

Martha Zierden is curator of historical archaeology at the Charleston Museum.

Index

Abraham (Black Seminole), 40, 41
Abraham's Old Town (Fla.), 11, 36, 37, 40–44
Adam, William, 123
Africa, 30, 31, 33–34, 35, 38, 44, 95
African Americans: and agriculture, 36, 124; in California, 111, 113, 115, 192; and cemeteries, 100; clothing of, 5; and Colono Ware, 31, 38; culture of, 16, 30–32, 33, 106, 124; depictions of, 210; and diet, 115; free, 30, 39, 100, 192; historical documentation on, 72; and labor movement, 111; and literacy, 115; material culture of, 32, 106, 113; memorials to, 100; as Pullman porters, 112, 115; and religion, 34–35; residences and households of, 113, 115; scholarship on, 31, 183, 192; in South Carolina, 11, 106, 193; in Spanish colonies, 38; stereotypes of, 30; treatment of, 36; in Virginia, 11, 33, 97, 100, 189. *See also* Slaves, African and African American
African Burial Ground (New York, N.Y.), 94–95
Africans: and agriculture, 33, 40, 120; Bakongo, 34–35; in Barbados, 33; in the Caribbean, 8; and creolization, 32–33; and cultural interaction, 6–7, 31; cultures of, 10, 16, 40, 206; and Europeans, 192; in Florida, 8; forced immigration of, 31, 45; hairstyles of, 39; historical documentation on, 40; and Indians, 40, 192; and ironworking, 40; material culture of, 35; in North America, 6–7; and religion, 34–35, 39; and scarring, 39; as servants, 9; in South Carolina, 31, 33; and warfare, 40. *See also* Slaves, African and African American
Age of Exploration, 58
Agriculture: activities for, 127, 129, 130, 132; Africans and, 33, 40, 120; and agribusiness, 130; in California, 77, 112; culture of, 119, 128, 129, 130, 143; and development, 131; and economy, 118, 121; and environment, 143; and everyday life, 128; in Florida, 19, 21, 39, 41, 143;

Indians and, 119, 126, 127; as industry, 134; and irrigation, 77; labor for, 129; lands for, 76, 86, 87, 117, 118, 120, 126, 130; Maroons and, 39, 40, 41; methods of, 119, 121, 124, 128; in Middle Atlantic colonies, 128; in New England, 11; New York City and, 89; orchards, 76, 112, 134; and progressive farm movements, 130; publications on, 119, 128, 132; in Quebec, Can., 83, 86–87; scholarship on, 124–25; Shakers and, 135; slaves and, 31, 32, 40; in South Carolina, 30, 31, 33, 102; southern, 32; and technology, 130; Thomas Jefferson on, 119; tools and machinery for, 129, 130, 132; in Virginia, 30, 32; work camps for, 49. *See also* Crops
Airplanes, 4, 174–75, 176
Akron, Ohio, 137
Alaska, 51, 72
Albany, N.Y., 89, 155, 156
Alberta, Can., 209
Albuquerque, N.M., 63
Alexandria, Va.: African Americans in, 97, 100; archaeology in, 80, 100, 102, 197; cemeteries and burials in, 97, 100; City Council of, 97; environment in, 99, 100; free blacks in, 192; historical documentation on, 98; industry in, 97, 100; landfills in, 103–4; landscape of, 97; on maps, 11; material culture in, 99; museums in, 98, 99; as National Historic District, 97; neighborhoods in, 97, 98; as port, 99; preservation in, 97, 99; public education in, 98, 99, 209; public works in, 97; Quakers in, 97; and trade, 97; volunteers in, 99, 100, 197; waterfront of, 97, 98, 99
Alexandria African American Heritage Park (Va.), 100
Alexandria Archaeological Commission (Va.), 97, 98, 100
Alexandria Archaeology (Va.), 97–101, 106, 193
Alexandria Canal Tide Lock (Va.), 99
Alexandria Heritage Trail (Va.), 98, 100

All Metal Products Company (Wyandotte, Mich.), 201

Alpine County, Calif., 73

Ambler (family), 64

Amelia Island, Fla., 26

American Agriculturist (periodical), 132

American Battlefield Protection Program, 173

American Institute for Conservation, 187

Animals: birds, 51, 105, 109, 129; bones of, 19, 38, 103, 105–6, 114, 124, 129, 158, 189; boreworms, 93; cattle, 41, 53, 105, 106, 107, 109, 119, 123, 125, 129, 158; chickens, 19, 109, 121, 128, 129; deer, 39; dogs, 1, 3; European, 10; and fences, 125; fish, 53, 106, 142, 159; foxes, 128; game and wildlife, 51, 53, 60; goats, 53; horses, 53, 105, 125, 145, 166; Indians and, 119; insects, 52, 68, 83; livestock, 53, 104, 119, 123, 124, 128, 129, 189; mules, 128; muskrats, 129; oppossums, 129; ownership of, 105; oxen, 128; pens for, 55; pigs, 53, 105, 128, 129; rabbits, 39; rats, 112; reptiles, 52, 68; seals, 60; slaves and, 189; snails, 85; squirrels, 129; turtles, 39, 129; uses of, 51, 53; waste from, 112

Annapolis, Md., 16, 80

Anthony, Ronald, 108

Anthropological Studies Center (Sonoma State University, Calif.), 80, 110, 113

Anthropologists and anthropology, 6, 12, 15, 58, 95, 187, 206

Antietam, Md., 173

Appalachian Mountains, 183, 201

Appalachian Spring (Copland), 136

Archaeological collections, 186

Archaeological conservation and conservators, 68, 69, 70, 109, 150, 163, 184, 185–88

Archaeological education and training, 196, 197, 203, 207–8, 209, 212

Archaeological features: canals, 117, 134; cellars, 64–65, 120, 121, 146, 154, 156; cisterns, 104, 109, 120, 125; courtyards, 85; as cultural resources, 212; dams, 122, 135, 136; depressions, 146; ditches, 52, 123, 135, 146; drains, 104, 106, 108, 109; dumps, 59, 127, 130, 135, 139, 140, 144, 156; earthworks, 155; fences and fence lines, 47, 52, 125, 130; fireplaces and hearths, 85, 145; floorboards, 84; flumes, 122; furnaces, 141; gardens, 107; gates, water, 122; headraces, 135; housing lots, 110; impressions, 64;

iron by-products, 144; kilns and ovens, 63, 140; in landfills, 92; landscapes, 49; latrines, 151, 159; locations of, 152; on maps, 76; middens, 198; military lines, 158; palisades, 38, 154; paving, 108; pens, 130; pits, 3, 47, 58–59, 64, 66–67, 103, 110, 122, 127, 135, 158; plotting of, 152, 196; privies, 47, 103, 104, 109, 110, 111, 113, 114, 115, 117; quarry marks, 59; raceways, 138; roadways, 47, 52, 85; sidewalks, 47; smokestacks, 134; spillways, 135, 138; stains, 38–39, 42, 154, 203; stratigraphic, 61, 66, 74, 196; systems for, 122, 130; trash, 159; trash racks, 135, 136; trenches, 58, 59, 111; walls, 58, 84, 90–93; wells, 58, 103, 104, 109, 110, 111, 115, 143, 159; woodsheds, 125; workshops, 58; work yards, 104, 106, 107, 108. *See also* Building foundations and remains

Archaeological Institute of America (Boston), 209

Archaeological Resource Centre (Ont.), 209

Archaeological sites: components of, 10; contexts of, 195, 212; of elites, 121–23; farms, 119, 120, 125, 205; fur trade, 197; hazardous, 76, 110; homesteads, 119, 122; industrial, 76, 117, 138, 140, 141, 142, 143–46, 147; interpretation of, 143; Inuit, 56, 60; military, 120, 152, 156, 159, 197; models for, 124; rural, 124, 125, 134, 138, 139, 140, 196; tenant homes, 119; underwater, 11, 68, 69, 150, 160–65, 205, 206. *See also specific sites and locations*

Archaeological Survey of Alberta, 209

Archaeological techniques and tools: analysis, botanical, 190; analysis, DNA, 70, 71; analysis, faunal, 190; analysis, forensic, 74, 156, 167, 175; analysis, laboratory, 44, 110; analysis, microscopic, 167; analysis, pollen, 190; analysis, soil-layer, 104; backfilling, 88; backhoeing, 91, 196, 104; bulldozing, 8, 140, 141; cataloging, 98; cofferdams, 69; computer imaging, 163; conductivity testing, 63; cranes, 163; development of, 184; diving, 162, 165; documentation, 185, 196; excavation, 8, 63, 64–66, 135, 197, 201; excavation, hand, 74, 104, 196; excavation, salvage, 103; excavation, test, 38, 83, 123, 166; exhibits on, 154; fieldwork, 63, 110, 152, 168, 177; Geographic/geophysical Information Systems, 152, 190; grids, 175; ground truthing, 63; heavy equipment, 74; illustrating, 65, 93, 98, 164, 196; magnetometry, 63, 162; mapping, 135, 152, 157–58, 163, 164, 165, 168, 175; mapping programs, 73; measured drawing, 134; measuring, 93; mechanical equipment, 140; metal detectors, 166, 167; micromorphology, 66; microstratigraphy, 66, 67; of 1930s, 196; nondestructive, 67; paleobotany, 66, 67; peels, 66; photography, 38, 93, 134, 196; radar, ground-penetrating, 63, 152; reconstructions, computer-generated, 210; recording, 94, 189, 197, 209; refinements in, 152; remote sensing, 67, 152, 157; resistivity testing, 63; restoration, 208; rigging, 162; robotic submarines, 160; sampling, 66–67, 84, 85, 87; screening, 44, 99; site plans, 134; surface collecting, 201; surgical incisions, 63, 64, 65; surveying, 59, 134, 166, 174, 175–76, 197, 208; surveying, geophysical, 63, 190; survey instruments, computerized, 73; trenching, 65, 66; underwater, 150

Archaeologists: activities of, 5; and agricultural sites, 117; and archaeological conservation, 187; and civil rights movement, 16; collaboration by, 26, 82, 138; community, 97; on cultural interaction, 15; and farms, 118, 119, 131, 133; and Fort Mose (Fla.), 38; goals of, 10, 193; and hazardous materials, 76; and historical archaeology, 62; and homesteads, 119; industrial, 117, 134–37, 140; and Jamestown, Va., 62, 63; and material culture, 4; military-site, 156, 159, 172–73; and myth busting, 65; and National American Graves Protection and Repatriation Act, 210–11; pioneering, 205; and plantations, 119; publications for, 208; and ranches, 118, 119; and tenant homes, 119; testing for, 208; underwater, 68, 162, 164, 165; urban, 12, 17; women as, 7–8
—, historical: and battlefields, 172–73; as curators, 212; goals of, 5, 10, 13; and industrial historians, 134–37; on influence of the past, 191; and myth busting, 139; and oral history, 134; pioneering, 200; and rural industrial sites, 134, 146–47; and urban archaeology, 45; and wars and uprisings, 149, 175

Archaeology: and anthropology, 58; challenges of, 200; and collections care, 188;

and colonialism, 19; community, 97–101, 102, 109, 111, 183, 193, 196–97, 207; and cultural landscapes, 52; and cultural resources, 212; and diversity, 184; and economy, 100; and environmental history, 51–52; feminist, 126, 127; goals of, 185, 212; government and, 197; and historical archaeology, 195; and historical documentation, 22, 24; and history, 58, 206; Indians and, 210–11; industrial, 134, 141; legislation on, 138, 175; military-sites, 152, 156, 157, 159; and natural science, 58; prehistoric, 6, 118, 205; and racism, 44, 100; and religion, 34; roles of, 1; rural, 120, 205; significance of, 3; and slavery, 16, 30, 35; stereotypes of, 1; underwater, 150, 160, 205, 206; videos on, 111
—, historical: archaeologists and, 62; and artifacts, 137, 195, 206; in Australia, 192; and Battle of Little Bighorn (Mont.), 166; characteristics of, 6; and civil rights movement, 8; and class, 8, 10; and collaboration, 6, 12, 24, 52, 83–84, 190, 195, 204, 205, 206; components of, 195; and conservation, 185–88; and consumerism, 8; and culture, 15, 189; definitions of, 202, 205; and diversity, 8, 12, 103, 195, 203–4, 206, 212; and documentary research, 137; early period of, 62, 120, 121–23; and environment, 8, 12, 202; and European colonization, 202; and everyday life, 6, 205; and feminist movement, 8; and Fortress of Louisbourg (Cape Breton Island), 153; future of, 183–84, 193–94; geographical scope of, 205; global, 192, 198; goals of, 212; historians and, 62; and historical documentation, 6, 7, 8, 134, 195, 205; and history, 12, 195; and humanism, 16; and identity, 189; and imperialism, 8; and Indians, 192; and industrialization, 206; as inspiration, 206; and the Internet, 12; James Deetz and, 12, 202, 205–6; and Jamestown, Va., 62; John Cotter and, 12; Kathleen Deagan and, 8, 12; and labor history, 10; and material culture, 5, 6, 8; and military history, 152; and myth busting, 189–90, 191, 192, 194, 195, 202, 203; and oral history, 6, 8, 205; perspectives on, 195, 205; and power relationships, 193; and prehistoric archaeology, 205; and race, 8; relevance of, 183–84, 189–90, 193–94, 198,

Archaeology, historical—*continued*
202, 203–4; rewards of, 195–96; and scientific view, 16; scope of, 195, 205; and segregation, 193; and settlement patterns, 193; and site contexts, 195; and slavery, 8; and slaves, 189; and slave trade, 202; study of, 1, 2; subfields of, 159; support for, 194, 196; and urbanization, 206
—, urban: in Albany, N.Y., 155; in Alexandria, Va., 80, 97–101, 102; in Annapolis, Md., 80; and archaeological remains, 45, 49, 80, 102, 109, 196, 197; aspects of, 88; in Canada, 83, 196–97; in Charleston, S.C., 80, 102–9; collaborations in, 79, 109; and community involvement, 95; developers and, 106; focus of, 79; at Fort Frontenac (Ont.), 196–97; government and, 97, 102, 106; at Jamestown, Va., 80; and landfills, 46, 80–81, 103–4; and landscaping, 82, 83; in Los Angeles, Calif., 80; models for, 196–97; and museums, 106; and natural disasters, 110; in New York City, 89, 90, 93, 94, 95, 96; in Philadelphia, Pa., 80; and preservation, 102, 106; and public education, 98, 100, 104; public participation in, 98; and reconstruction, 82; and redevelopment, 99; and renovation, 102; research organizations for, 196; scope of, 79, 110; in St. Augustine, Fla., 80; support for, 89; and transportation, 110; and urban development, 45, 46, 47, 97, 102; in West Oakland, Calif., 80, 110, 196; in Williamsburg, Va., 80
Architects, 100, 109
Architecture: adobe, 45, 122; African Americans and, 32, 33; armories and armorers' shops, 139, 157; artisans' quarters, 157; assembly facilities, 176; barns, 55, 121, 128, 129, 130; barracks, 156, 157, 158; battery areas, 158; bellows houses, 144; blacksmith shops, 147; blockhouses, 158; brick, 64, 66, 106, 107; British, 156; bunkhouses, 123; cabins, 140; changes in, 7; chicken houses, 121; Chinese and, 48–49; churches and temples, 19, 20, 28, 49, 54, 57; concrete, 176; corncribs, 128; craft shops, 147; as cultural resources, 212; dating of, 54; dirt, 145; Dutch, 92; English, 65–66, 156; European, 39; farmhouses, 117, 120, 121, 123, 124, 125, 128, 129, 131, 132; fences, 117; filing and machine shops, 139; fireplaces and hearths, 85, 145, 154, 156, 157, 159, 203; flats, 113; floorboards, 84; forges, 139, 144; forts and citadels, 87, 151; French, 85, 156; functions of, 48–49; furnaces, 143, 144, 145, 146, 147; gables, 92; glasshouses, 140, 141; hide-covered, 126; Hispanic, 45; historical, 206; hospitals, 156, 158; huts, 151, 156, 157, 158, 159; Indian, 39, 126, 127; industrial, 143; Irish, 203; kilns, 143, 145, 146; kitchens, 87, 104, 106, 107, 108, 120; on Kodlunarn Island (Can.), 60; at L'Anse aux Meadows (Newfoundland), 54–55; launch-preparation buildings, 176; laundries, 115; layout of, 195; log, 120, 121, 156, 200; lookout posts, 151, 158; Maroons and, 42; masonry, 196; materials for, 51, 55; mills, 117, 135, 138, 143, 147; miners and, 73; missile launching ramps, 176; naval bases, 198; ornament on, 114–15; pens, 130; permanence of, 49, 55; pigeon houses, 85; pillars, 145; on plantations, 123; plaster, 65; porches, 120; potteries, 146; powder magazines, 154; in Quebec, Can., 84–85, 87, 88; on ranches, 118, 122, 123; redoubts, 158; renovation and restoration of, 108–9, 191, 208; rentals, 113; restrictions on, 85; rural, 117, 118, 134; and separation of spaces, 7, 93, 104, 107, 193; servant quarters, 32; service buildings, 104, 120, 121, 124, 156, 158, 176; shapes of, 195, 196, 203; shops, 112; slaves and, 31, 107, 108; smokehouses, 120; and socioeconomic status, 84, 85, 92, 103, 107, 108, 112, 113, 114–15, 123, 193; in South Carolina, 33, 104, 106; of Spanish missions, 20; stables, 55; stockades, 152, 156; stone, 90–93, 122, 145, 154; suburban, 120; symbolism of, 35; tenant, 123, 125, 129; timber and daub, 85; townhouses, 80, 104; trading posts, 126; wagon sheds, 121; walls, 84, 90–93, 196, 203; washhouses, 136; wooden, 122, 129, 145, 154, 155; woodsheds, 125; work camps, 123; workshops, 58
Archivo General de Indias (Seville, Sp.), 22
Arctic, 52, 56, 58, 61
Arizona, 118, 207, 208
Arizona, USS (ship), 150, 178–82
Arizona Archaeological and Historical Society, 118
Arizona Archaeology Month, 208

Arizona State Historic Preservation Office, 208
Arkansas, 11, 120
Arkansas Archeological Survey, 120
Arkansas State Highway and Transportation
    Department, 120
Army Air Corps, U.S., 176
Army Central Identification Laboratory, U.S.,
    174, 175
Army Corps of Engineers, U.S., 165
Artifacts: age of, 201; armor, 5; beads, 5, 39,
    42, 44, 68, 85, 86, 106, 107, 115, 155;
    boards, 163; bottles, 5, 37, 38, 42, 114,
    123, 159, 161, 202; bowls, 96; boxes,
    wooden, 69; bricks, 5; buttons, 5, 39, 85,
    87, 107, 115, 142, 152, 164, 166; cans,
    123; casks, wooden, 69; chamber pots, 5;
    coins, 52, 69–70, 85, 86, 106; combs, 85,
    164; cosmetics, 48; dating of, 5, 20, 54, 58,
    60; decanters, 96; deterioration of, 185,
    186–87; Dutch, 5; English, 5; face cream,
    202; funerary, 210; furnishings, 49; furni-
    ture hardware, 107; gaming pieces, 87,
    165; glass, 103, 106, 118, 140; glassware,
    96, 155; handkerchiefs, 116; historical
    documentation as, 205; ID tags, 164;
    inkstands, 115; inscriptions on, 159; inter-
    pretation of, 10, 110; iron, 58, 59, 60, 61,
    144, 145, 186; jewelry, 44, 48, 114; kettles,
    143; lanterns, 164; leather, 115; lumber,
    122; marks on, 139; meanings of, 200;
    medals, religious, 19, 24, 38, 39; medical
    supplies, 165; memorabilia, 115; mess
    equipment, 165; metal, 187; military, 151,
    156, 165; milk pans, 118; mortar, 59; name
    bracelets, 174; Norse, 56; paper, 165; par-
    lor items, 113, 115; personal belongings,
    85, 164, 165, 175; pewter, 69, 71; picket
    pins, 166; pins, 39, 85; pipes, 5, 42, 103,
    104, 136–37, 138; porringers, 69, 71;
    quartz crystals, 106; records, 78 rpm, 202;
    repatriation of, 210; saloon-related, 74;
    shells, 129; ships' cargoes, 161, 165; silk,
    116; silver, 44, 116; slag, 59, 144, 145;
    slave tags, 107; and socioeconomic status,
    48, 113; spindle whorls, 55; spurs, 166;
    storage of, 187; survival gear, 175;
    tablewares, imported, 121; teacarts, 115;
    toiletries, 202; tools, 1, 38; tops, 87; trees,
    122; trivets, 3; value of, 200; wallets, 165;
    watches, 116, 166, 175, 202; wig curlers,
    5; wood, 59; writing utensils, 165. See also

Animals: bones of; Ceramics; Human re-
    mains; Tools and machinery; Weapons and
    ammunition
Asians and Asian Americans, 6–7, 210
Association for the Preservation of Virginia
    Antiquities, 62
Athens, Greece, 63
Auger, Reginald, 59, 61
Australia, 192

B-17 bomber (Papua New Guinea), 174–75
Baffin Island (Can.), 11, 57, 60
Ballard, Robert, 160
Baptizing Spring (Fla.), 20, 21, 24
Barange, C., 69, 70–71
Barbados, 33
Barbary Coast (Virginia City, Nev.), 74
Battison, Edwin, 139
Bear Lying Down (Lakota Sioux warrior), 173
Beaudry, Mary, 125–26, 141–42
Bevan, Bruce, 63
Bianchi, Leonard, 96
Bioarchaeologists and bioarchaeology, 16, 24,
    25–29, 63, 83
Bird's-eye View of Oakland (Snow and Roos),
    112
Black history, 36
Black Legend, 25, 28
Black Seminoles. *See* Maroons
Blakey, Michael, 95
Blankets, 134
Bloomery Forge (N.Y.), 144
Bluff Furnace (Tenn.), 144, 145
Boarders, 113, 115
Boott Mills boarding houses (Mass.), 141–42
Boston, Mass., 10, 90
Boston Women's Heritage Trails, 10
Bourne, Joel, 198
Bow, N.H., 143
Brenman, Ben, 100
Brennan, Louis, 125
Bridges, 176
British. *See* English and British
British Columbia, 142
Broadwater, John, 150
Brooklyn (N.Y.), 95
Brooks, Hervey, Pottery Shop and Kiln
    (Conn.), 143
Brown, Jeffrey, 145
Brown, Jeffrey L., Institute of Archaeology,
    145

Brown, Marley, 63
Building foundations and remains: in California, 47, 49; in Canada, 80, 84–85, 87; in Charleston, S.C., 103; in Florida, 24, 38; at Jamestown (Va.), 64–65, 67; on Kodlunarn Island (Can.), 58; in New York City, 90; at rural industrial sites, 134, 144. *See also* Architecture
Bureau of Land Management, U.S., 208
Burials, 25, 28, 97, 115–16, 126, 210. *See also* Cemeteries; Gravestones
Burning of Pilaklikaha by Gen. Eustis (painting), 40–41

California: agriculture in, 77; Chinese in, 45; and communication, 111; environment in, 72, 73–74, 76–77; government of, 110; Indians in, 76; on maps, 11; Mexicans in, 76; mining in, 11, 76–77; museums in, 76; and Spanish colonization, 19; and transportation, 110, 111; urban archaeology in, 80, 196
California Department of Transportation, 110
California Gold Rush, 76
Cambria, Calif., 48–49
Camino real (road, Fla.), 20, 23, 24
Camp followers, 152
Camp Hearne (Tex.), 11, 176–78
Camps, military, 11, 151–52, 156, 159, 176–78, 197
Canada: and American Revolution, 158; archaeological conservation in, 187; archaeology in, 183, 197, 205; colonization in, 68; community archaeology in, 196–97; English culture in, 156; and English law, 156; farms in, 87; forts in, 196–97, 209; frontiers of, 155; fur trade in, 196; government of, 153, 207; historical archaeology in, 192; historic sites in, 153, 207, 209; languages in, 156; museums in, 197; public education in, 209; rural industry in, 134; and trade, 86; urban archaeology in, 196–97; urban heritage of, 183. *See also* Montreal, Can.; Ontario, Can.; Quebec, Can.
Canadian Archaeological Association, 209
Canadian Register of Historic Places, 207
Canterbury, N.H., 135, 136, 137
Cape Breton Island, Can., 11, 153, 155
Captives, 57, 176

Cardiff, Wales, 187
Caribbean: Africans in, 8; archaeology in, 16, 192, 205; boreworms in, 93; ceramics in, 16; environment of, 10; Europeans in, 10; Indians in, 8; maps of, 11; as place of origin, 38; plantations in, 89; rural industry in, 134; Spanish and, 8, 10, 19; sugar processing in, 11, 142; and trade, 89, 153
"Caring for Artifacts After Excavation—Some Advice for Archaeologists" (Singley), 185
Carolinas, 38. *See also* Charleston, S.C.; North Carolina; South Carolina
Carson, Cary, 63
Carter, James, 115
Carter, Nellie, 115
Cataraqui Archaeological Research Foundation (Ont.), 196
Cathay Company, 57
Cathédrale Notre-Dame (Quebec, Can.), 87
Catholics and Catholicism, 16, 19–24, 25, 38, 39, 85, 87. *See also* Religion
Catoctin Furnace (Md.), 144
Cavender, Chris, 126, 127
Cemeteries, 1–3, 4, 87, 94–95, 100, 156. *See also* Burials; Gravestones
Ceramics: in Africa, 35; African Americans and, 31; American, 121; annular ware, 107; banks, 96; bowls, 33, 107; British, 121; butter pots, 129; Caribbean, 16; Chinese, 34, 45, 48, 107, 115; Colono Ware, 31, 33, 34, 38, 106, 107; as consumer goods, 5, 31, 129; costs of, 129, 146; crocks, 43; dating of, 20; decoration on, 20, 33, 34, 42, 43, 45, 95, 145; delft, 155; dishes, 95, 96, 121; dolls, 128; economic analysis of, 5; English, 115, 203; European, 31, 34, 43; European Americans and, 33; German, 155; handles, 3; imported, 129; Indian, 20, 31, 32, 38, 43; Irish, 203; ironstone, 42, 43; Italian, 16; jars, 33, 34, 39; local, 129; majolica, 20; makers' marks on, 123; manufacture of, 31, 33, 82, 97, 134, 143, 145–46, 203; milk pans, 129, 130; modern production of, 16; Moroccan, 16; mugs, 43; Panamanian, 16; pearlware, 43; Peruvian, 16; plates, 33, 42, 43; platters, 43; porcelain, 45, 48, 95, 107, 160; pots, 5, 31, 32, 33, 34, 35, 38, 39, 42, 145; on ranches, 123; redware, 3, 96; regional, 129; and religion, 35; in rural America, 118; scholarship

on, 146; serving pieces, 96; shapes of, 20, 33, 43, 129, 145; shaving basins, 160; slaves and, 107; and socioeconomic status, 95, 96, 129; Spanish, 20; Spanish-tradition, 16; stoneware, 43, 155; storage of, 186; symbolism of, 35; Taiwanese, 16; teapots, 128; tea sets, 95; and technology, 146; tenant farmers and, 129; and tools, 35; on urban sites, 106; uses of, 31, 39, 43, 129, 134, 203; vessels, 134; wall tiles, 155; wasters, 145–46

Champlain, Samuel de, 82, 83, 87

Charles II, king of Spain, 38

Charleston, S.C.: animals in, 104, 105, 106, 107; archaeology in, 80, 102–9, 190, 191, 196; architecture in, 103, 104, 106, 107, 108–9, 193; class in, 107, 109; consumer goods in, 103; everyday life in, 102–3, 104, 107, 109; foodways in, 105–6, 109; gardens in, 103, 107, 108; historical documentation on, 103; historic district of, 109; and historic preservation, 102, 109; history of, 102; industry in, 103; landfills in, 103–4; on maps, 11; Martha Zierden and, 190, 191; material culture in, 104–5, 107; museums in, 103, 109, 197; population in, 103; as port, 106; public education in, 106–8, 109, 209; restoration in, 108; settlement patterns in, 193; sewage in, 104; and slavery, 16, 104–5, 106, 107, 109, 193; wealth in, 193. See also South Carolina

Charleston Place (hotel/convention center, S.C.), 103, 104

Charlotteburg Middle Forge (N.J.), 144

Chattanooga, Tenn., 11

Chee Kung Tong, 49

Chemistry, 140

Children: Arapaho, 173; Chinese, 48; and education, 118; and Fortress of Louisbourg (Cape Breton Island), 153; Indian, 126, 173; rural, 118, 126; and Sand Creek Massacre (Colo.), 173; scholarship on, 118; as subordinates, 15; in West Oakland, Calif., 113–14, 115

China, 57

Chinatowns, 11, 45–49

Chinese: and burials, 115–16; in California, 45–49, 113, 115–16, 192; and cities, 16, 45, 49; and class, 49; and clothing, 115–16; culture of, 47; diet of, 115; and diversity, 45, 192; and foodways, 49; historical documentation on, 72; and languages, 48, 49; lifeways of, 49; material culture of, 16, 115; occupations of, 16, 45, 47–48, 115, 142; and opium, 115; and oral history, 48–49; and politics, 48; and racism, 49; and religion, 49; relocation of, 45–46; rural, 49; scholarship on, 47, 49; and tobacco, 115; and trade, 48, 49; treatment of, 115; and work camps, 45, 48–49

Churches and temples: and Canadian Register of Historic Places, 207; Catholic, 16, 28; in Florida, 19, 20, 28; in Greenland, 54; immigrants and, 112; in New York City, 93; Norse, 54, 57

Civil rights movement, U.S., 8, 16, 30, 36

Claassen, Cheryl, 142

Class: Chinese and, 49; and discrimination, 80; and diversity, 192; and historical archaeology, 8, 10, 192; immigrants and, 112–13; Irish and, 74; and living conditions, 80; middle, 95, 107, 112; and neighborhoods, 95–96; poor, 107, 192; and scholarship, 197; in 21st-century America, 190, 191; women and, 95; working, 80, 95–96, 109, 112–13, 192

Clintonville, N.Y., 144

Clothing: African American, 5; belts, 115, 152; boots and shoes, 115, 166; buckles, 39, 87, 107, 115; care of, 114; Chinese, 48, 115–16; corsets, 114; English and, 60; European, 5; flight gear, 174, 175; Indians and, 5, 40, 60; manufacture of, 134; Maroons and, 39, 40, 44; materials for, 51; in Michigan, 154; production of, 114; trousers, 116; turbans, 44; undergarments, 116; winter, 60; wool, 116

Cloutier, Céline, 85

Clovis, 2

Coffin, Jethro, site, 119

Colleges and universities: Appalachian State University, 142; Binghamton University, 10; Boston University, 130, 140, 141; Brown University, 4; Collège des Jésuites, 87; College of William and Mary, 4, 63; Harvard University, 4; Howard University, 95; Johns Hopkins University, 28; Laval University, 59; Séminaire de Québec, 83, 84–88; Sonoma State University, 80, 110; SUNY-Plattsburgh, 144; Texas A&M University,

Colleges and universities—*continued*
69, 176; University of British Columbia,
142; University of California at Berkeley, 4;
University of California at San Diego, 26;
University of Cape Town, 4; University of
Denver, 2; University of Florida, 8, 21, 22;
University of Maryland, 80; University of
Massachusetts-Boston, 141; University of
Michigan, 70; University of Nevada, 74;
University of Nevada at Reno, 75; University of Pennsylvania, 2; University of Tennessee at Chattanooga, 103, 145; University of Virginia, 4; University of Wales, 187;
Yale University, 139
Colonialism and colonization: archaeology
and, 19; British and, 32, 58, 62, 82, 173,
202–3; and conflict, 202; and cultural interaction, 12; and economic dependency, 202;
and environment, 51, 62, 202; Europeans
and, 62, 202, 206; French and, 52, 68, 69,
71, 82, 87, 149–50, 154; historical documentation on, 6; impact of, 202, 206; Indians and, 206; interpretation of, 150, 203;
in Ireland, 202–3; James Deetz on, 202;
legacy of, 190; and rural life, 118; scholar-
ship on, 149–50, 190–91; and slavery, 190–
91; in South Africa, 173; Spanish and, 8,
15–16, 19, 37–38, 58; Viking, 53, 56
Colonial National Historical Park (Va.), 62
Colorado, 72, 173
Colorado Coal Field War Archaeology Proj-
ect, 10
Colorado National Guard, 10
Columbus, Christopher, 8, 15, 52, 53, 56
Common Ground (periodical), 208
Comstock Lode, 74
Concord, N.H., 146
Confederate States of America, 165
Congress, U.S., 206
Connecticut, 139, 143
Conservation manuals, 188
Conservation Research Laboratory (Texas
A&M University, Tex.), 69
Consumer revolution, 5
Consumers and consumerism, 8, 118, 121,
123, 124, 130, 200
Continental Artillery Cantonment (N.J.), 157
Convents, 87
Cooper, James Fenimore, 156
Copland, Aaron, 136
Corbin, Adelaide, 201

Corbin, Wesley, 201
Corbin Hollow (Va.), 200–202
Cotter, John L.: and American historical ar-
chaeology, 1; biography of, 2; and cemeter-
ies, 1–3; and historical archaeology, 2, 12;
and Jamestown, Va., 62, 64, 65, 66, 67; in
Philadelphia, 1–3, 80; photo of, 3; as pio-
neer, 200
Cotter, John L., Award, 2
Couillard, Guillaume, 83, 84, 85–86, 87, 88
Council, R. Bruce, 145
Countess of Warwick Island. *See* Kodlunarn
Island (Can.)
County of Santa Clara, Calif., 76
Cranmer, Leon, 137
Creolization, 9, 15, 30–33, 192
Cressey, Pamela, 80, 192, 197
Crimes, 36, 46, 68, 72, 157, 206
Crops: beans, 41; cash, 33; choice of, 124;
corn, 39, 41, 119, 126, 127, 129; cotton,
102; fruit, 119; grain, 128, 134; hay, 123,
128, 130; rice, 30, 33, 39, 41, 102; sugar
cane, 143; tobacco, 4, 30, 32, 119; wheat,
119, 128, 129. *See also* Agriculture
Crowley's Ridge (Ark.), 120
Cuba, 20
Cudjo (Black Seminole), 40
Cudjo (Jamaican), 40
Cudjo (surname), 40
Cultural resource management (CRM), 143,
206, 207, 210–11
Culture and Communications Department
(Quebec, Can.), 83
Currie, Doug, 66
Custer, George A., 13, 166, 168, 170–71

Dallas, Tex., 70
Dancing, 136
Darford, Eng., 60
Databases, 207
Deagan, Kathleen A., 1, 7–10, 12, 38, 80,
192, 198
De Cunzo, Lu Ann, 193, 210
Deetz, James J. F.: biography of, 4; on colonial
Anglo-Americans' worldview, 7; on coloni-
zation, 202; on dogs, 1, 3; on gravestones,
1, 3, 4; and historical archaeology, 12, 202,
205–6; on interpreting the past, 13; on
Massachusetts, 4; on material culture, 3–4,
198; photos of, 6, 9; on Virginia, 4
Delaware, 11, 124–25, 128–29

Delaware Department of Transportation, 124–25

Department of Agriculture, U.S., 207

Department of Defense, U.S., 175–76

Depression, 76, 183, 200

Detyens Shipyard (S.C.), 163

Development: agriculture and, 131; airports, 131; archaeological sites and, 146; community archaeology and, 207; and destruction of cultural resources, 193; farms and, 130, 133; highways, 131; sewers, 131; urban archaeology and, 82, 83, 89, 90, 95, 96, 100, 102, 196, 197

Dickens, Charles, 96

Diet: in Africa, 33; African Americans and, 115; in California, 113, 114, 115; changes in, 28; Chinese and, 115; and economic status, 118; in Georgia, 28; in Hispaniola, 9–10; historical documentation on, 72; Indians and, 24, 26–28; at military sites, 159; reconstruction of, 26–28; in rural America, 124; in South Carolina, 105

Dikes, 128

Discovery Channel, 160

Diseases and medical conditions: amputations, 156; arthritis, 70; back problems, 70; cholera, 112; in cities, 81; common cold, 25; dehydration, 71; dysentery, 67, 112; epidemics of, 87, 112; European, 9, 23, 25; French and, 52, 68; herniated discs, 156; hypothermia, 71; Indians and, 9, 23, 24, 25, 29; infections, 156; infectious, 29; influenza, 25; iron deficiency anemia, 28; at Jamestown, Va., 203; knowledge of, 87; malnutrition, 28, 29; measles, 25; at Plymouth, Mass., 203; and sanitation, 112; scalpings, 156; skeletal evidence of, 70–71; smallpox, 25, 156; stress, 156; strokes, 113; tooth decay, 28, 70; tuberculosis, 156; typhoid, 112; venereal disease, 114; yellow fever, 25

Diversity: African Americans and, 192; archaeology and, 12, 103, 184, 195, 203–4, 206, 212; Chinese and, 45, 192; class and, 192; cultural interaction and, 15; ethnicity and, 192; gender and, 192; historical archaeology and, 12, 195; material culture and, 184; in New York City, 193; race and, 192; religion and, 192; scholarship and, 184, 190. See also Ethnicity; Race and racism

Documentation, historical: on Abraham's Old Town (Fla.), 43; on African Americans, 72; agricultural publications, 119; on Alexandria, Va., 98; on archaeological features, 76; archaeologists and, 62; archaeology and, 22, 24, 134; archives and, 110, 170, 208; as artifacts, 205, 212; on battlefields, 151; on Battle of Little Bighorn (Mont.), 168, 170–71; on Black Seminole Maroons, 36; census rolls, 48; on children, 118; on Chinatowns, 46, 48; on Chinese, 72; city plans, 84, 85; and colonization, 6; construction plans, 151; on consumer choices, 124; on Corbin Hollow, Va., 202; corroboration of, 195; courthouses and, 202; diaries, 37, 151; drawings and sketches, 127, 151, 165; on drug use, 72; elites and, 103; and exploration, 6; on farms, 120, 133; on Fort Mose (Fla.), 38; on Fortress of Louisbourg (Cape Breton Island), 153; on forts, 151; on Frobisher expedition, 58; government records, 72; historians and, 62; and historical archaeology, 6, 7, 8, 62, 134, 195, 205; Icelandic, 56; on Indians, 72, 126, 127; inventories, 61; on Jamestown, Va., 67; journals, 137; on La Belle artifacts, 68; and labor history, 10; land grants, 87; letters, 137, 151; libraries and, 110, 170; limitations of, 7, 72, 195, 198, 205; and literacy, 72; on Maple Leaf, 165; maps, 76; and material culture, 4; Mexicans and, 72; military, 37, 151, 152, 159, 198; on mining and miners, 72, 75, 76; on minorities, 118; on Movanagher (Ire.), 203; on musseling, 142; newspapers, 37, 46, 47, 76; notarized, 84; photographs, 10, 46, 48, 110, 113, 120, 133, 161; on pipes, 137; plans, 153; on Pleasant Hill, Ky., 137; on prostitution, 72; on Quebec, Can., 85, 87; reliability of, 37, 40, 47, 48, 61, 72, 151; on rural America, 117, 134; Shakers and, 137; sheepskin parchment, 53–54; by Soto's army, 21; on Spanish-Indian contact, 25; on Spanish missions, 20–22, 23; on Stewart Redman, 129; on stores, 129; travelers' accounts, 37; value of, 161; on Viking exploration and colonization, 53–54, 56; on West Oakland, Calif., 110; on women, 72, 118

Dorset, Can., 56

Drugs and medicines, 35, 51, 67, 72, 96, 114, 115, 132

Dundurn Castle (Ont.), 197
Dunne, Adele, 98
Duquesne, Fort (Pa.), 152
Dutch, 89, 91, 92, 93–94, 152, 155
Dutch West India Company, 155

Earthquakes, 110
East Coast, 139, 142, 203
East Dorset, Vt., 146
Eaton (Hopewell) Furnace (Ohio), 144
Economy: in Alexandria, Va., 100; in Annapolis, Md., 80; and archaeology, 100; capitalist, 122, 128; colonial, 12; in Delaware, 128, 129; 18th-century, 7; in Florida, 19, 37; free enterprise, 7; frontier, 37; Indians and, 19, 127; at Jamestown, Va., 52; maritime, 153; Maroons and, 37; and ranches, 122, 123; role of, 12; seasonal, 123; Shakers and, 135; and specie, 123; subsistence, 127; in Tennessee, 145; and transportation, 111; and wars and uprisings, 149
Edward, Fort (N.Y.), 156, 157
Eglin Air Force Base (Fla.), 176
Egypt, 120
Ehrenhard, John, 210
Elizabeth I, queen of England, 57
Emancipation, 193
Emerson Bixby Blacksmith Shop, 143
Engineering, 117
England and Great Britain: archaeology in, 67; and colonization, 82, 202–3; entertainment in, 74; and Florida, 19–20, 21, 38; and Ireland, 74; and Jamestown, Va., 65; landowners in, 74, 75; Martin Frobisher in, 57; and Spain, 19–20; trees in, 60, 61; wealth in, 74, 75
English and British: in Arctic, 52; and Baffin Bay (Can.), 60; and clothing, 60; and colonization, 58, 173; and environment, 57–58; and exploration, 57–59; and farmsteads, 120; in Florida, 21; and foodways, 189; and Indians, 57; at Jamestown, Va., 52; and Kodlunarn Island, Can., 57–58; and Michilimackinac, Mich., 154; in New York City, 93–94; in New York State, 155; occupations of, 112; and slaves, 37–38; and Spanish, 37–38; and technology, 57
Englishtown (Calif.), 76
Environment: adaptation to, 72, 76; Africans and, 6–7; and agriculture, 143; in Alaska,

72; Arctic, 62; Asians and, 6–7; in California, 72, 73–74, 76–77; in Canada, 57–58, 87, 89; Caribbean, 10; and climate, 56; and colonization, 12, 51, 62, 202; in Colorado, 72; English and, 57–58; Europeans and, 6–7, 62; exploitation of, 51; farms and, 124; in Florida, 37, 39, 40, 143; and Frobisher expedition, 59; in Great Basin, 72; in Hispaniola, 10; and historical archaeology, 8, 12, 202; and ice, 57, 60; Indians and, 6–7, 40; and industry, 12, 52, 76–77, 100, 117, 143; and landfills, 93; management of, 51, 63; Maroons and, 39, 40; and material culture, 4; modification of, 51; in Mojave Desert, 72; in New York City, 90; in North America, 6–7; in Papua New Guinea, 174; and pollution, 81; and railroads, 112; on ranches, 122, 123; settlers and, 52; shaping of, 76; specialists in, 83; in South Carolina, 33; and technology, 57; in Texas, 68; urban, 80, 81; Vikings and, 56; in Virginia, 52, 62, 63, 67, 99, 100; and wealth, 51; and weather, 52; and westward expansion, 127
Ericson, Leif, 53, 54
Eric the Red, 53
Ethnicity: and cuisines, 15; and discrimination, 94; and diversity, 192; and economy, 17; and everyday life, 118; and historical archaeology, 7; Irish and, 74; and material culture, 16–17; in New York City, 93–94, 193; and politics, 17; in rural America, 118; scholarship on, 192, 198; in 21st-century America, 15, 190, 191; and value systems, 15; in Virginia, 32. See also Diversity; Race and racism
Ethnobotanists, 109
Europe, 56, 76, 176, 187
European Americans, 72, 112, 124, 210
Europeans: and Africans, 192; in the Caribbean, 10; clothing of, 5; and colonization, 62, 202, 206; and cultural interaction, 6–7, 31; depictions of, 210; and environment, 62; and exploration, 15; and Indians, 192; and Maroons, 37; and mining, 72; and New York City, 89; in North America, 6–7; Northern, 56–57; and Quebec, Can., 87
Evans, Lynn, 154
Evans, Oliver, 139
Everyday life: in Charleston, S.C., 80, 102–3,

104, 107, 109; in Delaware, 128; domestic, 141–42; at Dundurn Castle (Ont.), 197; and ethnicity, 118; family life, 118; on farms, 121; at Fort Mose (Fla.), 38; at Fortress of Louisbourg (Cape Breton Island), 153; and gender, 10; of glassblowers, 140; and historical archaeology, 6, 205; on *H. L. Hunley*, CSS, 164; of industrial workers, 117; in Ireland, 183, 203; and living standards, 159; in Lowell, Mass., 141–42; and material culture, 4; in Michilimackinac, Mich., 154; at military sites, 159; of miners, 10, 72, 73; at Mount Independence (Orwell, Vt.), 158–59; in Quebec, Can., 82; on ranches, 118; and religion, 118; in Silver Mountain City, Calif., 73; of slaves, 16; of soldiers, 82, 152; and technology, 117; urban, 121

Exhibits, 12, 111, 187–88, 209

Explorers and exploration: Arctic, 52, 61; De Soto and, 21; English and, 57–59; Europeans and, 6, 15, 61, 119; France and, 52, 68; goals of, 56; in Gulf of Mexico, 52, 69; historical documentation on, 6; La Salle and, 68; Norwegian, 54; scholarship on, 58, 61; in Southeast, 52; in Texas, 68, 69; Vikings and, 51, 53, 55, 56–57

Fairbanks, Charles, 16

Family Dig Day (Alexandria, Va.), 99

Farming, 119, 121, 127, 128, 130, 143

Farms: activities on, 126; African Americans and, 124; Africans and, 120; and agricultural press, 132; archaeologists and, 118, 133; archaeology of, 120, 130, 205; in Arkansas, 120; company, 139; corn, 119; dairy, 119; decrease in, 131–33; in Delaware, 125, 128–29; and development, 130, 133; elites and, 121–23; English and, 120; and environment, 124; European Americans and, 124; everyday life on, 121; family, 119, 126, 131–33, 201; feature systems on, 125; French and, 120; fruit, 119; gardens on, 129; Germans and, 120; in Greenland, 54; Hispanics and, 120; historical, 120, 130–31; historical documentation on, 120, 133; improvements on, 130; Indian planting villages, 126; and industry, 134; labor on, 124; layout of, 128; in Massachusetts, 130; Midwestern, 120; migration from, 30, 120; models for, 123–24; in New England, 120, 124; in New Hampshire, 124; in New York, 125; Norse, 54, 55, 57; and oral history, 120, 133; preservation of, 131; in Quebec, Can., 83, 86–87; as rural landscapes, 124; scholarship on, 125; southern, 30, 120, 123; tenant, 125, 128–29; tobacco, 119; trade goods on, 121; urban, 124; in Virginia, 201; and westward expansion, 127; wheat, 119; women and, 132; work areas of, 125, 129; yards of, 118

Federal Highway Administration, U.S., 120

Feminist movement, 8

Fences, 104, 122, 124, 128, 129, 130

Ferguson, Leland, 16, 36, 106

Fiegel, Kurt, 137

Fires, 19, 20, 42, 43, 87

Fitzhugh, William, 195

Five Points (New York, N.Y.), 96

Florida: Africans in, 8; agriculture in, 143; Black Seminoles/Maroons in, 11, 36, 38, 41–42; creolization in, 192; environment in, 37, 143; as frontier, 37, 39; Great Britain and, 19–20, 21, 38; Gulf Coast of, 143; Indians in, 8, 21, 22, 26–28, 36, 41–42; industry in, 143; interaction in, 192; maps of, 11; migration from, 41; military installations in, 176; as place of origin, 38; plantations in, 41; roads in, 20, 23; runaway slaves in, 30; Soto in, 21; Spanish in, 8, 16, 19–24, 26–28, 58; sugar processing in, 11, 142, 143; underwater archaeology in, 164–65

Florida Bureau of Archaeological Research, 26

Flowerdew Hundred (Va.), 6

Folklore, 206. *See also* Oral history

Fontana, Bernard, 118

Food and drink: in Africa, 33; alcoholic, 57, 72, 74, 75, 115; arrowroot, 43; beans and legumes, 39, 189; beef, 4, 53, 105–6, 107, 129, 135, 158; berries, 39, 53, 128, 189; chicken, 19, 128, 129; Chinese, 115; condiments, 33, 96, 121, 161, 202; coontie plant root, 43; corn, 19, 28, 39, 127; dairy products, 128, 129, 134, 135; deer, 39; ethnic, 15; European, 10, 19; fish, 33, 39, 53, 106, 112, 142, 153, 159, 189; from Frobisher expedition, 61; fowl, 105; Freaky cereal, 4; fruits, 4, 39, 55–56, 114, 135; game, 53, 60; geese, 129; goats, 53; gourds,

Food and drink—*continued*
39; government rations, 39; grain, 207;
greens, 189; ham, 189; and historical archaeology, 8; honey, 135; Hostetter's Bitters, 115; imported, 115; from *La Belle,* 69;
Maroons and, 43; and material culture, 4;
meats, 10, 33, 51, 109, 114, 121, 128, 129;
muskrat, 129; nuts, 55–56, 189; oppossum,
129; plants, 51; pork, 53, 105, 128, 129,
135, 189; rabbits, 39; rice, 33, 39, 127;
seals, 60; sheep, 53; shellfish, 39, 129, 189;
soffkee, 43; Spanish, 19; squashes, 39; squirrels, 129; storage of, 121; sugars, 135, 142,
143; tea, 115; tortillas, 16; as trade goods,
32, 71, 86–87, 153; turtles, 39, 129; vegetables, 33, 51, 86–87, 114, 128; waterfowl,
129; wheat, 19; working class and, 96
Foodways: in Africa, 33, 189; African Americans and, 33, 189; breweries, 67; butchering, 105–6, 107, 109, 129, 158, 189; butter
churning, 126, 128; canning, 114, 118, 121,
128; Chinese, 49; cooking, 39, 59, 104, 105,
113, 129; dairying, 129; English, 189;
equipment for, 43; on farms, 124; fishing,
39, 112, 129, 142; food production, 124; at
forts, 39, 158; fuels for, 59; gathering, 39,
127; and gender, 128, 129; hunting, 37, 39,
60, 69, 74, 112, 127, 129; Indian, 39, 40,
127, 189; Maroons and, 39, 40; networks
for, 129; oystering, 129; preparation, 129;
processing, 129; and refrigeration, 121;
slaves and, 105; smoking, 121; southern,
189; and Spanish colonization, 19; storage,
39, 121, 127, 129; trapping, 129, 131
Forests, 127
Forest Service, U.S. Department of Agriculture, 207
Forts: and archaeology, 151; British, 151, 155,
156; Canadian, 152, 155; characteristics of,
156, 159, 195, 196; colonial, 150; construction of, 151, 159; Dutch, 152, 155;
English, 152, 154, 156; exhibits on, 154;
foodways in, 158; French, 151, 152, 154,
155, 156; of French and Indian War, 156;
and frontiers, 159; George I. Quimby on,
149; historical documentation on, 151;
hospitals in, 158; National Park Service
and, 157; provisioning of, 156, 159; Revolutionary War, 156, 158; scholarship on,
149, 150; Spanish, 151, 152; and trade
goods, 159; U.S., 152. *See also specific forts*

Fox, Richard, 191
France: architecture in, 85; 21st-century, 70;
and World War II, 176
Franklin, Maria, 183
Freemont Mine (Calif.), 73
French: in Canada, 155; and colonization, 52,
68, 69, 71, 87; and disease, 52; and explo-
ration, 52, 68; and farmsteads, 120; and
forts, 155; and fur trade, 154; in Michigan,
154, 155; and Quebec, Can., 84, 88; and
Spanish, 152; and Texas, 69; and trade, 69,
71, 83; and transatlantic voyages, 69
Friends of Alexandria Archaeology (Va.), 97,
100
Frobisher, Martin, 11, 57–61
Frontenac, Fort (Ont.), 196–97
Frontiers, 37, 39, 119, 155, 156, 159, 206
Fuels: charcoal, 58, 59, 60, 144; coal, 4, 59,
60, 61; petroleum, 76; on Shaker sites, 135;
timber, 53; uses of, 59–60

Gangs of New York, The (film), 96
Gardens and gardening: in Annapolis, Md.,
80; and Canadian Register of Historic
Places, 207; in Charleston, S.C., 103, 104,
107, 108; at Dundurn Castle (Ont.), 197;
18th-century, 7; on farms, 129; at Fortress
of Louisbourg (Cape Breton Island), 153;
market, 119; and material culture, 4; resto-
ration of, 197; slaves and, 189; specialists,
109; as symbols, 7; and symmetry, 7
Gender: and diversity, 192; and everyday life,
10; at military sites, 159; roles of, 128;
scholarship on, 198; and 20th-century ar-
chaeology, 7–8; in 21st-century America,
190, 191
Geneaology, 123
Geography, 93, 206
Geologists, 67
Geophysicists, 63
Georgia, 11, 19, 25–29, 37, 42
Germans, 120, 176–78
Ghana, 40
Gorman, Frederick, 140
Governor's Palace (Williamsburg, Va.), 65
Gracia Real de Santa Teresa de Mose. *See*
Mose, Fort (Fla.)
Grand Banks, 153
Gravestones, 1–3, 4, 7, 100. *See also* Burials;
Cemeteries
Great Basin, 72

Great Britain. *See* England and Great Britain

Great Plains, 127

Greece, 120

Greenland, 11, 53–54, 56, 57

Greenwich Village (New York, N.Y.), 95

Greenwood, Roberta, 16–17, 80, 192

Greenwood and Associates, 45, 46–48

Guide to Artifacts of Colonial America, A (Noël Hume), 5

Gulf Archaeology Research Institute (Fla.), 143

Gulf Coast (Tex.), 52

Hacienda (Calif. settlement), 76

Hall, Charles Francis, 58, 60

Hamden, Conn., 139

Hamilton, Ont., 197

Hardesty, Donald, 75, 122, 130

Harpers Ferry, W. Va., 80, 142

Harrington, J. C., 62, 140, 152, 200

Harrington, J. C., Medal in Historical Archaeology, 2, 4

Harrison, David A., Professorship of Historical Archaeology, 4

Harvey, John, 66, 67

Hawaiians, 210

Hayti (Alexandria, Va., neighborhood), 100

Hazeltine, Joseph, 146

Hébert, Anne, 83

Hébert, Guillaume, 83

Hébert, Guillemette, 83, 85

Hébert, Louis, 83, 85–87

Henn, Roselle, 92

Heritage Education Program (U.S. Bureau of Land Management), 208

Hickam Air Force Base (Hawaii), 174

Hill, James, 159

Hispanics, 120

Hispaniola, 1, 8–10

Historians: architectural, 63, 64, 65; on cultural interaction, 15; and Fort Mose (Fla.), 38; garden, 109; and historical archaeologists, 83; and historical archaeology, 62; industrial, 134–37, 138; and Jamestown, Va., 62, 63, 66; and Native American Graves Protection and Repatriation Act, 210–11; social, 117; on Spanish-Indian contact, 25; of technology, 117, 141; and West Oakland, Calif., 110

Historical Archaeology (periodical), 185

Historic Annapolis, Inc. (Md.), 80

Historic Charleston Foundation (S.C.), 102, 107

Historic districts, 76, 83, 84, 86, 97, 109, 207

Historic Places Initiative (Canada), 207

Historic St. Mary's City, Md., 186

History: and anthropology, 58; and archaeology, 58, 206; cultural, 206; environmental, 51–52, 67; and historical archaeology, 195, 206; living, 153, 209; and natural science, 58; public, 67, 98, 99, 104, 106–8, 109, 111, 140, 191, 203, 206, 207

Hobbs, Carl, 67

Homesteads, 119, 122, 123–24

Homosassa, Fla., 143

Honerkamp, Nicholas, 103, 145

Hopewell Furnace (Pa.), 144

Hopewell Village National Historic Site (Pa.), 144

Horning, Audrey, 183, 184

Housatonic, USS (ship), 162

Human remains: African American, 95; of B-17 bomber crew, 174, 175; bones, 25–28, 163, 164; British, 156; Chinese, 115–16; forensic analysis of, 70, 156, 174, 175; from Fort William Henry (N.Y.), 156; French, 69, 70–71; on *H. L. Hunley*, CSS, 163, 164; identification of, 70, 163; Indian, 25–29, 210; and Native American Graves Protection and Repatriation Act, 210; reconstructions of, 70; skeletons, 25–28, 69, 70–71, 115–16, 156; teeth, 26–28, 70

Hunley, H. L., CSS (ship), 160, 162–64, 165

Iceland, 53, 56

If These Pots Could Talk (Noël Hume), 5

Immigrants: activities of, 112–13, 190; African, 33, 120; Asian, 190; children of, 112; Chinese, 16, 45–49, 115–16, 142; and cities, 45; and class, 112–13; communities of, 17, 94, 193; and cultural interaction, 15; English, 120; European, 10; French, 69, 120; German, 113, 120; Greek, 113; Hispanic, 120; historical archaeology and, 192; and industry, 80, 142, 191; Irish, 52, 74–75; Italian, 112, 113; and land ownership, 119; Mexican, 113; occupations of, 52, 112, 142; and politics, 17; Portuguese, 112; and saloons, 113; scholarship on, 190; Shakers, 135; Slovenian, 113; Spanish, 16; and unions, 112; and wealth, 17

Immigration: Africans and, 31; forced, 8, 12, 15, 31, 41–42, 45; French and, 83; and historical archaeology, 7; increases in, 119; Irish and, 74; and land, 119; regulation of, 83; voluntary, 8, 12, 15, 45

Independence, Mount (fortress site, Vt.), 158–59

Independence National Historical Park (Pa.), 2

Indians: activities of, 39, 60, 119, 126, 127; adaptation by, 28; and Africans, 192; appearance of, 57; and archaeology, 210–11; and Battle of Little Bighorn (Mont.), 166–72; and British, 202; and burials, 210; in California, 76; in Canada, 58, 87, 198; in the Caribbean, 8; and ceramics, 31, 32; clothing of, 5, 60; and colonization, 206; and cultural interaction, 6–7, 12, 31; and cultural resource management, 212; cultures of, 10; and diet, 24, 26–28; and disease, 9, 23, 24, 25, 29; displacement of, 40, 41–42, 119; and economy, 19; and English, 57; and Europeans, 15, 192; in Florida, 8, 19, 21, 22–23, 24, 26–28; and foodways, 189; and Frobisher expedition, 59, 60; and gender, 126; and genocide, 191; in Georgia, 25–29; in Greenland, 53; health of, 26, 28, 29; in Hispaniola, 9, 10; historical archaeology and, 192; historical documentation on, 72, 126, 127; and immigrants, 12; and jewelry, 44; and land, 119; and La Salle, 68, 71; in Michigan, 154; in North America, 6–7; occupations of, 9, 10, 28, 76; and oral history, 54, 60, 61, 126, 170, 171, 191; paintings of, 44, 210; population of, 19; and Portuguese, 57; prehistoric, 2, 25–28; and religion, 16, 19, 28; remains of, 24, 25–29; and runaway slaves, 36; scholarship on, 31, 183; and seasonal migration, 127; and Soto's army, 21; and Spanish, 10, 16, 19, 24, 25, 28, 57; and technology, 61; in Texas, 68, 69; and tools, 32; and trade, 31, 69; and U.S. government, 40, 41–42; and Vikings, 53; and westward expansion, 119; working conditions of, 26, 28, 29

Indian tribes: Algonkian, 82; Arapaho, 173; Cheyenne, 172, 173; Dakota, Wahpeton, 126–27; Guale, 26; Inuit, 54, 56, 57, 59, 60; Karankawa, 68; Mohawk, 155; Mohican, 155; Seminole, 36, 40, 41–42,

44; Shawnee, 173; Sioux, 172, 173, 191; Timucua, 20, 21, 22–23

Industrialists, 139

Industrialization, 52, 80, 118, 121, 206

Industrial Revolution, 117, 134, 190, 191

Industry: and American System of Manufactures, 139; archaeology of, 205; and architecture, 134; basketry, 31; blacksmithing, 134, 135, 143, 144–45; boat building, 61; button manufacture, 142; canning, 142; clothing manufacture, 134; cloth production, 134; commercial, 138; and conspicuous production, 130; costs of, 146; craft, 31, 135, 147; and cultural values, 147; and economy, 118, 145; English, 140; and environment, 12, 100, 143; extractive, 134; and factories, 118, 121, 138, 139, 140; and farms, 134; fishing, 142, 147, 153; forges, 66, 139, 144; fuels for, 145, 146; gas plants, 46; glassmaking, 134, 140, 141; gun manufacture, 139; historical reconstructions of, 143; immigrants and, 191; in industrial nations, 117; ironmaking, 11, 55, 60, 61, 143–44; ironworking, 40, 140; and labor, 139, 146; and landscapes, 112, 138; on maps, 11; and markets, 140; at military encampments, 157; modern, 138; modernization of, 145; musseling, 142; periodicals on, 135; pipe production, 137, 138; potteries, 82, 97, 134, 138, 143, 145–46; in preindustrial societies, 117; printing, 135; processes for, 139, 147; ranching, 122–23; raw materials for, 146; reconstructions of, 141; rural, 11, 134–47, 196; scholarship on, 142; sewing, 135; Shakers and, 135–37; shipbuilding, 69, 82, 165; shoemaking, 135; shops for, 118; siting of, 146; spinning, 135; sugar processing, 97, 100, 142, 143; tanneries, 82; and technology, 145, 147; in Tennessee, 144, 145; timber, 123, 142, 201; tool making, 134; toy manufacture, 201; traditions of, 143; and transportation, 140, 146; trash racks, 135, 136; urban, 138; wastes from, 112; weaving, 135; wheelmaking, 135; woodworking, 135. See also Mines and mining

Ingstad, Anne Stine, 54

Ingstad, Helge, 54

Instruments, musical, 43

Interaction: African Americans and, 12; Africans and, 6–7, 9, 31, 37, 40, 44, 192; Anglo Americans and, 48; anthropologists on, 15; Appalachian residents and, 202; archaeologists on, 15; Asians and, 6–7; British and, 57, 60, 203; in Caribbean, 8; Chinese and, 12, 48; and colonization, 12; and conflict, 149–50; cultural, 190; and diversity, 15; economic, 202; Euro-Africans and, 37; Europeans and, 6–7, 26, 31, 32–33, 37, 51, 53, 58, 61, 149–50, 192, 202, 205; farm communities and, 124; in Florida, 8, 192; French and, 71, 149–50; Hispanics and, 48; in Hispaniola, 1, 9–10; historians on, 15; historical archaeologists and, 15; hostile, 51, 53, 56, 58; and immigration, 15; and imperialism, 15; intermarriage, 38, 40, 192; Irish and, 203; Maroons and, 40, 44; and material culture, 15; military alliances, 40, 44; and residence patterns, 40; scholarship on, 61; social, 202; Spanish and, 1, 8, 9, 10, 12, 57; stereotypes of, 25; Vikings and, 53

—, Indian: with Africans, 6–7, 8, 31, 37, 40, 44, 192; with Asians, 6–7; with English and British, 57, 58, 60, 203; with European Americans, 126, 127; with Europeans, 6–7, 26, 32–33, 53, 58, 149–50, 192, 202, 205; with French, 71, 149–50; with other Indians, 51; with Portuguese, 57; with Spanish, 1, 8, 9, 10, 57; with Vikings, 53

Internet, 12, 188, 193, 207, 209
Ireland, 74, 183, 202–3
Irish, 52, 74–75, 202
Iron Hawk (Lakota Sioux warrior), 172
Isandlwana (South Africa), 173
Isle Royale. See Cape Breton Island
Italy, 16
Ivitanayo, Fla., 23

Jacksonville, Fla., 41, 164
Jamaica, 36, 40
James I, king of England, 202
James, Fort (Va.), 63
Jameson, John H., Jr., 183, 210
Jamestown, Va.: anniversaries of, 2, 63; as archaeological site, 62–67, 80, 190, 195, 200; architecture at, 64–66; Association for the Preservation of Virginia Antiquities and, 62, 63; as capital, 62; collaborative research on, 63; and colonization, 2, 52, 58, 202; conflict in, 203; construction at, 64–65; and cultural management, 63; diseases at, 67, 203; and economy, 52; environment at, 62, 63, 67; fort at, 63; historians and, 66; historical documentation on, 67; industry at, 63–64, 66, 140; interpretation of, 64, 67; J. C. Harrington and, 62, 140; John Cotter and, 2, 62, 64, 65, 66, 67; on maps, 11; material culture at, 202; National Park Service and, 62, 65, 67, 140; occupations at, 66, 67; photographs of, 64; scholarship on, 203; significance of, 203; and trade, 52
Jamestown ReDiscovery (Va.), 63
Japanese, 150
Jefferson, Thomas, 119
Johnson, Gerald, 67
Johnson, Kenneth, 21, 24
Jonesboro, Ark., 120
Jordan, Elizabeth, 200
Jumper (Seminole Indian), 41

Karklins, Karlis, 5
Kebec. See Quebec, Can.
Kelso, Gerald, 66–67
Kelso, William, 63
Kemp, Richard, 66
Kentucky, 136, 137
Kenyon, Walter, 58
Kettles, 43, 143
Kilns, 63–64, 66, 134
King, Martin Luther, Jr., 36
King's House Tavern (N.Y.), 90
Kingsley, Fla., 42
Kingsley, Zephaniah, 41
Kingston, Ont., 196
Kodlunarn Island (Can.), 11, 57–58, 59–60, 61

La Belle (ship), 52, 68, 69, 70, 71
Labor: African Americans and, 111; and agriculture, 121, 124, 129; Chinese and, 47, 142; and fort construction, 151; and historical archaeology, 10; historical documentation on, 10; Indians and, 10, 28; industry and, 139, 146; and labor movement, 111; and plantation system, 124; railroads and, 112; on ranches, 124; in rural America, 121. See also Slaves, African and African American

Laboring in the Fields of the Lord (Milanich), 20

Lae, Papua New Guinea, 174

L'Aimable (ship), 68

La Isabela, Hispaniola, 8

La Joly (ship), 68

Lake City, Fla., 21

La Navidad, Hispaniola, 8

Land: agricultural, 125; division of, 128; explorers and, 51; frontier, 119; in Greenland, 56; and homesteading, 123; immigrants and, 119; Indians and, 119; leasing of, 123; managers of, 208; ownership of, 119, 121, 129, 130, 131; settlers and, 51; and squatting, 123; and tenancy, 123; use of, 193; and World War II, 176

Landfills, 80–81, 90–93, 95, 103–4, 110

Landscapes: African Americans and, 32; in Alexandria, Va., 97; and archaeology, 52; in Boston, 10; and Chinatowns, 49; cityscapes, 81; cultural, 52, 90; and ditches, 75; and drainage patterns, 87; at Dundurn Castle (Ont.), 197; and farming, 119, 124, 131; features of, 75–76, 112; formal, 123; frontier, 159; industry and, 112, 138; of Little Bighorn Battlefield (Mont.), 168; mapping of, 73; and military sites, 159; mill systems on, 135; and mining, 72, 73, 75–77, 130; museums and, 80; National Park Service on, 124; in New England, 124; in New York City, 90; preservation of, 97; public services and, 112; in Quebec, Can., 82, 84, 85, 87; railroads and, 112; ranches and, 118, 122; restoration of, 197; rural, 117, 118, 124; Shakers and, 135, 136; of Silver Mountain City, Calif., 73; and socioeconomic order, 81; urban, 82, 109; Western, 72; in West Oakland, Calif., 112; work areas on, 118; yardscapes, 81

Languages, 22, 40, 48, 60, 126, 156

L'Anse aux Meadows (Newfoundland), 11, 54–57

Larsen, Clark Spencer, 16, 24

La Salle, René-Robert Cavelier, sieur de, 52, 68–69, 71

Lasch, Warren, Conservation Center (S.C.), 163

Last of the Mohicans, The (Cooper), 156

Last Stand Hill, Mont., 171

Latin America, 192

Laval, François de, 83

Legislation: Canadian, 197, 209; farm bills (U.S.), 131; heritage, 138, 175

Homestead Act (U.S., 1862), 119–21; National Historic Preservation Act (U.S., 1966), 206; Native American Graves Protection and Repatriation Act (NAGPRA, U.S., 1990), 210–11

Lesson plans and curricula, 100, 143, 208

Librarians, 63

Library of Congress, U.S., 40

Lifeways, 126, 128, 189, 192

Light, John, 144–45

Lincoln, Abraham, 165

Lindenmeier, 2

Lister, Florence, 16

Lister, Robert, 16

Literacy, 72, 115

Literature, 210

Little, Edward, 130

Little Bighorn, Mont., 11, 13, 166–73, 174, 191

Little Rapids, Minn., 11, 126–27

Livingston, Robert, 91, 92

Loma Prieta, Calif., 110

London, Eng., 90, 123

London, Jack, 112

Long Pond Ironworks (N.J.), 144

Los Angeles, Calif., 46–48, 80, 192

Loucks, L. Jill, 21

Loudon, N.H., 147

Louisbourg, Cape Breton Island, 153, 154

Louisbourg, Fortress of (Cape Breton Island), 11, 153, 155, 209

Louisiana Territory, 68

Lovelace, Francis, 90

Lowcountry, 106. *See also* Charleston, S.C.; South Carolina

Lowell, Mass., 80

Lower Canada, 82. *See also* Quebec, Can.

Lower Peninsula, Mich., 154

Ludovica. *See* Quebec, Can.

Machinery. See Tools and machinery

Mackinac Island, Mich., 154

Mackinac State Historic Parks (Mich.), 154

Mackinaw City, Mich., 155

MacNab, Allan, 197

Maine, 155

Malcolm X, 36

Malone, Patrick, 3

Manchester, Eng., 135

Manhattan (New York, N.Y.), 89, 93

Mann, Eunice, 113–14

Mann (family), 113, 114

Maple Leaf (ship), 11, 160, 164–65

Maps, historical: Abraham's Old Town (Fla.) on, 37; archaeological features on, 76; *camino real* (Fla.) on, 21; Chinatowns on, 46, 48; farms on, 133; Fort Mose (Fla.) on, 38; and Fortress of Louisbourg (Cape Breton Island), 153; of Los Angeles, 46; of New York City, 92; of Quebec, Can., 85, 87; surveyor's, 37; of West Oakland, Calif., 110

Maps, modern, 11, 22, 23, 73, 157–58

Marine sanctuaries, 161

Marine scientists, 63

Markets, 93, 123, 128, 140

Maroons, 11, 16, 36–40, 44, 190, 192. *See also* African Americans; Slaves, African and African American

Marriages, 9, 10, 38, 40, 128, 192

Marshes, 68, 128, 129, 130

Martin's Hundred (Va.), 152–55, 200

Maryland, 4, 11, 144, 186, 188

Massachusetts, 4, 131, 141–42, 143, 144

Matagorda Bay, Tex., 11

Material culture: African Americans and, 35, 113; Anglo-American, 7; in Boston, Mass., 10; in Charleston, S.C., 104–5, 107; Chinese, 16; and cultural interaction, 15; and diversity, 184; 18th-century, 7; and environment, 4; and ethnicity, 16–17; and everyday life, 4; George I. Quimby on, 149; and historical archaeology, 5, 6, 8; historical documentation on, 4; of *H. L. Hunley*, CSS, 163, 164; in Ireland, 202, 203; James Deetz on, 3–4, 198; meaning of, 200; museums and, 109; and oral history, 4; and ranches, 122; slaves and, 104–5; and socioeconomic status, 107; study of, 85, 189; of U.S. democracy, 176; in Virginia, 99, 202; in West Oakland, Calif., 113

Mazaokiyewin (Wahpeton Dakota), 127

McEwan, Bonnie, 26

McGuire, Randall, 10

McLean, Shea, 164

Merrimack, USS (ship), 150

Meta Incognita Committee (Can.), 59

Mexico and Mexicans, 19, 26, 41, 72, 76

Micanopy (Seminole chief), 41

Michigan, 11, 142, 154, 155, 201

Michilimackinac, Fort (Mich.), 11, 154, 155

Michilimackinac, Mich., 154

Middle Atlantic, 128

Midwest, 120

Migration, 128, 201. *See also* Immigrants; Immigration

Milanich, Jerald, 16, 26

Miles Brewton house (Charleston, S.C.), 106, 108

Militias, 38, 39, 139, 152, 156

Millennium Trails, 100

Miller, George L., 5

Mills: in Canada, 134; in Caribbean, 11, 134; and crops, 129; dangers to, 138; floor plans of, 143; in Florida, 11, 143; foundations of, 134, 135; grist, 144; lesson plans on, 143; in Massachusetts, 142, 144; and millponds, 135; on plantations, 134; in rural America, 134; sawmills, 134, 143; sites of, 147; Shaker, 135; steam-powered, 143; sugar, 11, 143; textile, 134

Mines and mining: African Americans and, 72; in Appalachian Mountains, 201; Chinese and, 72; cinnabar mining, 76; and Comstock Lode, 74; copper mines, 142; Donald Hardesty on, 122, 130; English and, 52; and environment, 12, 52, 72, 76–77; equipment for, 75; Europeans and, 72; gold mines, 74, 76, 142; and Gold Rush, 76; historical documentation on, 72, 76; Indians and, 72, 76; on Kodlunarn Island (Can.), 57, 58, 59, 60; and landscapes, 72, 73, 75–77; and literacy, 72; mercury mining, 76, 77; Mexicans and, 72, 76; and oral history, 76; pocket mining areas, 72; silver mines, 73–74; sites of, 147; strip mines, 51; technology for, 72, 73, 75–76, 77; and transportation, 76; Western, 52, 72–73, 75–77, 123; women and, 72

Minnesota, 11, 127

Missions, Spanish, 11, 16, 19–29, 69, 205

Modernity, 159

Modernization, 190

Mohney, Chan, 100

Mojave Desert, 72

Monasteries, 85, 87

Monitor, USS (ship), 11, 150, 160, 161–62, 165

Montana, 11, 166–73

Montreal, Can., 80, 155

Morocco, 16

Morristown, N.J., 157

Mose, Fort (Fla.), 30, 38–39, 43, 80, 192

Moser Farmstead (Ark.), 120–21

Moss, William, 79, 196

Movanagher (Ire.), 203

Mrozowski, Stephen, 66–67, 141–42

Mudflats, 68

Murphy, James, 137

Museums: Alexandria Archaeology Museum (Va.), 99, 188; American Museum of Natural History (Washington, D.C.), 25; archaeologists and, 138; and artifacts, 80; in California, 76; in Canada, 58, 80, 83, 197, 209; in Charleston, S.C., 80, 103, 107, 108, 109; Charleston Museum (S.C.), 80, 103, 108; Colonial Williamsburg Foundation (Va.), 5, 62–63, 155, 200; curators of, 109; funding of, 210; Heyward-Washington House (S.C.), 105; historical interpretation in, 191; and landscapes, 80; and living history, 153, 154; Mariners' Museum (Va.), 93, 162; and material culture, 109; municipal, 197; Musée de la Nouvelle-France, 83; and museum educators, 207; Museum of Natural History (Fla.), 8, 20, 26; Nathaniel Russell House (S.C.), 106, 107, 109, 197; and Native American Graves Protection and Repatriation Act, 210; in New England, 137; in New York State, 137; Old Sturbridge Village (Mass.), 124, 143, 144; Plimoth Plantation (Mass.), 4; Pointe-à-Calliere, Montreal Museum of Archaeology and History, 80, 209; publications for, 208; and public education, 206, 207, 209, 210; Royal Ontario Museum, 58; Shaker, 137; Smithsonian Institution (Washington, D.C.), 58; in Texas, 68; and urban archaeology, 79, 106; and virtual technology, 80

Naming practices, 40

National Geographic, 160

National Historic Districts (U.S.), 76, 97

National Historic Landmarks Program (U.S.), 207

National Historic Landmarks (U.S.), 38, 76, 150, 154, 206–7

National Historic Sites (Canada), 197

National Park Service (U.S.): and American Battlefield Protection Program, 173; archaeologists for, 173; and Boott Mills boardinghouses excavations (Mass.), 80, 142; career fields in, 208; and Colonial Williamsburg, 62–63; and education programming standards, 208; and forts, 152, 157; and Fort Stanwix (N.Y.), 157; and Harpers Ferry, W. Va., 80; and historical reconstructions, 152, 157; and Indians, 173; and Jamestown, Va., 52, 62–63, 65, 67, 140; John Cotter and, 2; and Little Bighorn Battlefield (Mont.), 166, 173; and military sites, 152; and National Historic Landmarks Program, 207; and preservation, 206; and public education, 208; repositories of, 63; on rural historic landscapes, 124; and Shenandoah National Park (Va.), 201–2; and Southeast Archaeological Center (Fla.), 208, 210

National Register of Historic Places (NRHP, U.S.), 175, 206, 207

Natural resources: cinnabar, 87; clay, 146; coke, 145; copper, 134, 142; exploitation of, 76; explorers and, 51; fuel, 143; gold, 51, 74, 76, 142; in Hispaniola, 9; hornblende, 60; and industry, 134, 146; iron, 53, 55, 61, 134, 143–44; lime, 134, 143; mercury, 76, 77; metals, 73; ores, 57, 59, 60; pearls, 142; processing of, 134; pyrite, 60; quest for, 72; settlers and, 51; silver, 51, 73, 74; timber, 51, 53, 56, 60, 61, 134, 142, 201; Vikings and, 56; and World War II, 176

Navigation, 53

Necessity, Fort (Pa.), 152, 195–96

Netherlands, 89

Networks, 122

Nevada, 11

New Almaden, Calif., 76

New Almaden Quicksilver Mine (Calif.), 76–77

New Amsterdam. *See* New York, N.Y.

New Brunswick, Can., 55
Newbury, Mass., 130
Newell, Dianne, 142
New England: agricultural sites in, 11, 120,
    124; archaeology in, 11, 137, 146; battle-
    fields in, 150; cemeteries in, 4; ceramicists
    in, 146; colonial wars in, 11; foods in, 56;
    glassware from, 96; industry in, 11, 146;
    investors from, 165; landscapes in, 124;
    modern maps of, 11; timber in, 56, 150
New England Glassworks (N.H.), 140
Newfoundland, 11, 51, 55, 59
New France. See Canada
New Hampshire: archaeology in, 135, 136,
    137, 141, 143; farms in, 124; industry in,
    144, 146, 147; migration from, 113
New Haven, Conn., 139
New Jersey, 11, 130, 144, 157
New Netherland. See New York, N.Y.
New Orleans, La., 82
Newport News, Va., 93, 162
New Spain. See Caribbean; Florida;
    Hispaniola; Mexico
New Town (Va.), 64–65
New York, N.Y.: archaeology in, 11, 12, 79–
    80, 89, 90–93; architecture in, 91, 92; cem-
    eteries in, 94–95; churches in, 93; city halls
    in, 90; class in, 95–96; cultural geography of,
    93–94; cultural landscape of, 90; diversity
    in, 193; Dutch and, 91, 93–94; English and,
    89, 93–94; ethnicity in, 93–94; historical
    maps of, 92; immigrants in, 94, 193; and
    industrial ranching, 123; landfills in, 90–93,
    95, 103–4; markets in, 93; modern maps of,
    11; natural setting of, 89; neighborhoods
    in, 93–94; occupations in, 93; population
    of, 89–90, 94; as port, 82, 89, 90; Scots in,
    92; settlement in, 89, 193; and slavery, 16;
    slaves in, 93, 94–95; slums in, 96; suburbs
    of, 95; and trade, 93; transportation in, 93;
    and West Indies, 93; women in, 95
New York State, 125, 137, 144, 152, 155,
    156, 157–58
Nichols-Colby Sawmill (N.H.), 143
9/11 (terrorist attacks), 79, 96
Noël Hume, Ivor, 5, 200
Nonprofit organizations, 79
Normandy, France, 2

Norse. See Vikings
North Carolina, 160, 161
Northwest Passage, 52, 57, 72
Nova Scotia, Can., 153

Oakland, Calif., 111. See also West Oakland,
    Calif.
O'Brien and Costello's Saloon and Shooting
    Gallery (Nev.), 74
Occupations: African Americans and, 113,
    115; agricultural workers, 49; apothecaries
    and pharmacists, 66, 67, 83, 115; appren-
    tices, 93, 140; armorers, 157; artisans, 10,
    139, 154, 157; assaying, 58, 60; bakers, 93;
    bankers, 191; blacksmiths, 144, 145; brew-
    ers, 66; business owners, 93; canal diggers,
    117; carpenters, 4, 93; clerics, 16, 19, 20,
    23, 24, 83; construction, 16; contractors,
    84; doctors, herbal, 48; engineers, 112; es-
    tate appraisers, 4; farmers, sharecroppers,
    and tenant farmers, 30, 36, 83, 119, 121,
    124, 127, 129, 130, 131; ferrymen, 24;
    fishermen, 45, 49, 153; glassblowers, 140;
    gravestone carvers, 4, 7; gunslingers, 191;
    insurance agents, 115; investors, 102; jour-
    neymen, 93; laborers, 10, 28, 47, 121, 139,
    142, 151; landowners, 74; laundrymen, 48,
    115; Maroons and, 40; masons, 93; me-
    chanics, 115; merchants, 48, 82, 92, 129,
    153; millers, 139; miners, 10, 45, 52, 72,
    73–74, 75, 76, 153, 191; mining managers,
    76; missionaries, 127; musicians, 4, 153;
    pastry chefs, 4; pilots, 175; pirates, 83;
    planters, 30, 31, 32, 41; politicians, 37;
    potters, 16, 20, 33, 145, 146; produce
    workers, 48; Pullman porters, 112, 115;
    railroad magnates, 191; railroad workers,
    16, 45, 49, 112, 113; ranchers, 23; sailors,
    61, 70–71, 164, 165; seaweed-gatherers,
    48, 49; servants, 9, 23, 32, 93, 107, 113,
    153; silversmiths, 93; slave owners, 191,
    193; slavers, 36; surveyors, 21, 37; teach-
    ers, 48; tobacco planters, 4; traders, 37,
    127, 154; translators, 40; whalers, 54, 60;
    workingmen, 115. See also Slaves, African
    and African American; Soldiers and officers
Ohio, 144
Oklahoma, 40, 41

Old Chatham, N.Y., 137
Ontario, Can., 11, 58, 144–45, 196–97, 198, 209. *See also* Canada; Montreal, Can.; Quebec, Can.
Ontario Archaeological Society, 209
Ontario Heritage Foundation, 196
Oral history: and Battle of Little Bighorn (Mont.), 170, 171, 191; and California, 48–49, 111, 113; Chinese and, 48–49; and Corbin Hollow, Va., 202; and farms, 120, 133; and folklore, 206; and Greenland, 53–54; historical archaeology and, 6, 8, 134, 205; Indians and, 54, 60, 61, 126, 170, 171, 191; industrial archaeologists and, 134; and Kodlunarn Island (Can.), 61; and L'Anse aux Meadows (Newfoundland), 54, 55; and material culture, 4; and mining, 76; and Moser Farmstead (Ark.) 120–21; and Movanagher (Ire.), 203; and musseling, 142; Norse, 53–54; and rural America, 117; and Vinland, 56; volunteers and, 208
Orange, Fort (N.Y.), 155
Oregon, 142
Orient, 52, 128, 129
Orr, David, 63
Orwell, Vt., 158–59
Outer Banks (N.C.), 160

Pacific Coast, 142
Paint, 109
Paleobotany, 66
Paleopathology, 26
Palo Alto, Tex., 173
Palynologists, 66–67
Panama, 16
Papua New Guinea, 174–75
Parasites, 83
Parks, 2, 62, 100, 154, 200–202. *See also* National Park Service (U.S.); Parks Canada
Parks Canada, 54, 58, 152, 153, 206, 209
Parris Island, S.C., 152
Passport in Time (PIT, U.S. Forest Service program), 207–8
Pate, Martin, 210, 211
Paterson, N.J., 141
Pearl Harbor, Hawaii, 11, 150, 178, 179, 182
Penetanguishene, Ont., 198
Pennsylvania, 11, 144, 157, 195–96
Pentagoet (fort site, Maine), 155
Pentagon, 79

Peru, 16
Philadelphia, Pa., 1–3, 80, 90, 129, 157
Philipsburg Manor (N.Y.), 125, 140
Phytolith, 100
Pickman, Arnold, 90, 95
Pilaklikaha. *See* Abraham's Old Town (Fla.)
Pilgrims, 4
PIT Traveler (U.S. Forest Service publication), 207–8
Pittsburgh, Pa., 115, 152
Place-names, 16
Plantations: African Americans on, 11, 124; archaeology and, 44, 106, 119, 123, 124; Caribbean and West Indies, 31, 89; ceramics on, 33; in Florida, 41; houses on, 123; interpretation of, 203; James Deetz on, 4; Middleburg (S.C.), 32; mills on, 134; models for, 123–24; slave quarters on, 16; and slavery, 36, 106, 124; in South Carolina, 11, 30, 32, 33, 102, 123; Southern, 16, 124; tobacco, 4; and trade, 31; in Virginia, 4, 11, 30
Plants: as artifacts, 10; cattails, 67; goosefoot, 67; at Jamestown, Va., 67; medicinal, 87; and paleobotany, 66; pollen from, 67, 109, 190; sagebrush, 122; sedges, 67; seeds of, 39, 67; specialists on, 63, 83, 109; sweet woodruff, 67; as trade goods, 86–87; uses of, 67; wax myrtle, 67; weeds, 67
Pleasant Hill, Ky., 11, 136, 137, 138
Plymouth, Mass., 203
Pollard, Gordon, 144
Ports, 82, 99
Portuguese, 57
Powlesland, Dominic, 66, 67
Praetzellis, Mary, 80, 192, 196
Preservation: in Alexandria, Va., 97, 99; of archaeological resources, 79, 122, 146, 184, 196, 197, 206, 207, 209; of burial mounds, 126; in Canada, 206, 207; in Charleston, S.C., 102, 106; and community involvement, 79, 207, 209; and conservation movement, 206; of cultural resources, 131, 193, 205; groups for, 106; of historic sites and places, 13, 122, 133, 157, 176, 197, 212; history of, 109; legislation on, 138, 197, 206, 209, 210–11; at Michilimackinac, Mich., 154; of *Monitor,* USS, 161; officers for, 208; private-sector, 207; publications for, 208; of rural industrial sites, 146–47; of shipwrecks, 150;

states and, 208; of technology, 138; of *Titanic*, RMS, 160
Prisoners of war, 176–78
Province of Quebec. *See* Quebec, Can.
Publications, interpretive, 208
Public Broadcasting Service (PBS), 160
Public education, 98, 99, 100, 143, 193, 209, 210
Puerto Real, Hispaniola, 8–10
Pullman Palace Car Company, 115

Quakers, 1–3, 97
Quebec, Can.: agriculture in, 83, 86–87; archaeology in, 11, 12, 79, 82–88, 196, 197, 209; architecture in, 84–85, 87, 88; British and, 82, 83; cathedrals in, 87; cemeteries in, 87; Champlain and, 82, 87; citadel in, 87; colleges in, 83, 84–88; and colonization, 82, 83, 87; construction in, 83, 87; convents and monasteries in, 85, 87; culture in, 156; diseases in, 87; environment in, 87, 89; Europeans and, 87; everyday life in, 82; fortification of, 82, 155; founding of, 82, 83; French and, 82, 84, 88; historical documentation on, 84, 85, 87; historical reconstructions in, 87; Indians and, 87; industry in, 82; landscape of, 82, 84, 85, 87; landscaping in, 83; Lower Town plains in, 82, 87; on maps, 11, 85, 87; occupations in, 82, 83, 84; Old Town Historic District in, 83, 84, 86; population of, 83; as port, 82; public education in, 209; and railroads, 82; reconstructions in, 85, 87; roads in, 85; schools in, 83; settlement of, 87; and town planning, 85; and trade, 83, 84, 85–86; Upper Town plateau in, 82, 83, 87; as urban center, 84; as World Heritage City, 12, 79, 82, 88. *See also* Canada; Montreal, Can.; Ontario, Can.
Quimby, George I., 149–50

Race and racism: in Annapolis, Md., 80; archaeology and, 7, 8, 44, 100; Chinese and, 49; and diversity, 192; and historical documentation, 37; Maroons and, 36, 37; in New York City, 193; and residential space, 193; scholarship on, 192; and segregation, 193; and settlement patterns, 193; and social mobility, 193; in 21st-century America, 190, 191; in Virginia, 32

Railroads: African Americans and, 112; in California, 46, 111–12, 116; in Canada, 82, 196; Central Pacific Railroad, 111–12; Chinese and, 16, 45; and environment, 112; immigrants and, 112, 190; and labor, 112; as military targets, 176; and Pullman Palace Car Company, 115; and Rogers Locomotive Company, 141; sites for, 147; transcontinental, 80, 111; and urban archaeology, 196. *See also* Roads; Transportation
Ranches, 11, 118, 119, 122, 123, 124, 126, 127
Ratcliff on the Thames, Eng., 61
Rebolledo, Diego de, 23
Reconstructions and restorations, historical: accuracy of, 151, 152; Alexandria Canal Tide Lock (Va.), 99; of battlefields, 151; computer-generated, 210; Dundurn Castle (Ont.), 197; Fort Michilimackinac (Mich.), 154, 155; Fort Mose (Fla.), 43; Fort Necessity (Pa.), 152; Fortress of Louisbourg (Cape Breton Island), 153; of forts, 151; Fort Stanwix (N.Y.), 157; Fort Ward Civil War Site (Va.), 97; of gardens, 197; of human faces, 70–71; of industrial processes, 143; of landscapes, 85, 197; L'Anse aux Meadows (Newfoundland), 54; living history at, 153, 154; of military sites, 152, 159; of Moser Farmstead plan (Ark.), 121; at Nathaniel Russell House (S.C.), 197; National Park Service and, 152, 157; Parks Canada and, 152, 209; of Penetanguishene naval base (Ont.), 198; in Quebec, Can., 85, 87; Roland Robbins and, 140; of rural industrial sites, 141, 143; volunteers and, 208
Redman, Stewart, 129
Redman (family), 129
Register of Historic Places (Canada), 207
Reitz, Elizabeth, 105
Religion: African Americans and, 34–35; African Methodist Episcopalian, 128; Africans and, 34–35; and archaeology, 34; and ceramics, 35; Chinese and, 49; Christian, 28, 135, 136; and diversity, 192; 18th-century role of, 7; and everyday life, 118; Maroons and, 39, 40, 44; Presbyterian, 128; in rural America, 118; Shaker, 135–37, 138; in Spanish America, 34; and worship, 128, 136. *See also* Catholics and Catholicism

Requa farm (N.Y.), 125
Réseau archéo-Quebéc, 209
Rich Neck Plantation (Va.), 189
Rituals, 43, 49
Roads: in Arkansas, 120; *camino real* (Fla.), 20, 23, 24; in Canada, 85, 153, 196; in Florida, 20, 21, 23, 24; at Fortress of Louisbourg (Cape Breton Island), 153; highways, 131; maps of, 21, 23; and rural historic landscapes, 124; and urban archaeology, 196; wagon, 122. *See also* Railroads; Transportation
Robbins, Roland Wells, 139–41
Robson, Benjamin, 95
Robson, Eliza, 95
Robsons (family), 95
Rogers, Buck (fictional character), 200
Rogers Island, N.Y., 156, 157
Rogers Locomotive Company, 141
Roller, Marie, 83
Rome, N.Y., 157
Rothschild, Nan, 79, 193
Rubertone, Patricia, 124
Ruff, Christopher, 28
Runs After the Clouds (Lakota Sioux warrior), 173
Russell, Mrs., 107
Russell, Nathaniel, 107. *See also* Museums: Nathaniel Russell House (S.C.)
Russell, Tom, 107
Russell (family), 107
Russia, 61
Rutsch, Edward, 96, 141

Sabbathday Lake, Maine, 137
Sage, Francis, 95
Saloons, 113
Salwen, Bert, 95
Sanborn Farm (N.H.), 147
San Francisco, Calif., 111, 112
Santa Catalina de Guale (Ga.), 25–26
Santa Elena (fort site, S.C.), 152
Santa Rosa Island, Fla., 11, 176
Saskatchewan, Ont., 209
Saskatchewan Archaeological Society, 209
Saugus Iron Works (Mass.), 140
Saunders, Rebecca, 26
Sawyer Decision (1884), 76
Schoenbak, Bengt, 54

Schoeninger, Margaret, 26
Scholarship: on African Americans, 183, 192; on Asians, 190; on battlefields, 150; on Battle of Little Bighorn (Mont.), 166, 171, 172, 191; on children, 118; on class, 197; on colonial America, 31; on colonialism and colonization, 149–50, 190–91; comparative, 68; on Delaware historical sites, 125; elitism in, 190; and ethnicity, 192, 198; on farms, 121–23; on forts, 150; and gender, 198; on Guillaume Couillard, 86; and historical archaeology, 195; inclusiveness of, 184, 190, 191, 192, 194, 198; on Indians, 183; on industry, 142; on Jamestown, Va., 203; Kathleen Deagan on, 198; limitations of, 206; on Louis Hébert, 86; on manifest destiny, 191; on minorities, 118; minority perspective in, 127; myths in, 192; on nationalism, 191; on Plymouth, Mass., 203; on pottery making, 146; on race, 192; regional, 146; on Shakers, 135; on shipwrecks, 160; on slaves and slavery, 189, 192; and socioeconomic position, 121–23, 198; stereotypes in, 192; on *Titanic*, RMS, 160; on wars and conflicts, 151; on westward expansion, 127, 190; on women, 118, 127, 190
Science and scientists, 58, 143, 161, 162, 187
Scientific American (periodical), 135
Scientific Revolution, 7
Scientists, social, 160
Scorcese, Martin, 96
Scots, 92
Scott, Doug, 173
Scottish Rite Hospital (Tex.), 70
Segregation, 36, 113, 193
Settlement, 8–10, 122, 193, 196
Settlers, 51, 52, 118, 119, 127
Seventh U.S. Cavalry, 166–71
Seville, Sp., 22
Sexuality, 190
Shakers, 135–37, 138
Shenandoah National Park (Va.), 200–202
Sherwood Farm, 119
Ships and boats: as artifacts, 93, 94; ballast for, 60, 61; brail boats, 142; British, 158; Civil War–era, 160–65; construction of, 69, 93, 161–62, 165; damage to, 57; design of, 161; everyday life on, 164; as gravesites,

160, 161, 178, 179, 182; historical documentation on, 165; ironclad, 150, 161; in landfills, 93; machinery on, 162; and material culture, 164; materials for, 51; merchant, 165; musseling, 142; as National Historic Landmarks, 150; 19th-century, 90; preservation of, 150, 160; recovery of, 161, 162–64; repair of, 60; scholarship on, 160; shapes of, 162; steam-powered, 162; submarines, 162–64; and technology, 161–62, 165; and trade, 129; transport, 164; and warfare, 150, 158; weapons on, 162; wooden, 89. *See also* Railroads; Roads; Transportation; Waterways; *specific ships*

Sierra Nevada (Calif.), 52, 73

Silcott, Wash., 123

Silver Mountain City (Calif.), 73–74

Simoneau, Daniel, 84

"Simple Gifts" (song), 136

Singley, Katherine, 185

Slavery: in Annapolis, Md., 16; and archaeology, 16; Atlantic trade in, 34; challenges to, 36; characteristics of, 16; in Charleston, S.C., 16; and historical archaeology, 7, 8, 30; legacy of, 190; and middle passage, 31; and modern-day tensions, 183; in New York City, 16; power relations in, 32; scholarship on, 192; as social control, 193; in St. Augustine, Fla., 16; in Virginia, 33

Slaves, African and African American: activities of, 31, 33, 102, 104, 189; in Africa, 30; and agriculture, 30, 31, 32; and archaeology, 35; and architecture, 31, 32, 33; and British, 37–38; and cemeteries, 94–95; and ceramics, 31, 107; and choice, 42; and colonialism, 190–91; and craft skills, 31; culture of, 16, 30, 106, 189–90; and diet, 189; and disease, 30; and emancipation, 102; and European goods, 105; and everyday life, 16, 35; in Florida, 30, 37–38; and foodways, 33, 105, 189; health of, 30; in Hispaniola, 9; and Indian labor, 10; and jewelry, 44; labor of, 93; and landscapes, 32; laws governing, 37; living quarters of, 31, 94, 104, 107, 109; and material culture, 32, 35, 104–5, 106, 107; in New York City, 93, 94–95; occupations of, 4; origins of, 34, 95; owners of, 37; and passive resistance, 30; and physical stress, 95; as pioneers, 30, 31; and plantations, 16, 106, 124; population of, 33, 107; and rebellion, 37; and religion, 34, 38; on Rich Nick Plantation (Va.), 189; runaway, 30, 36; scholarship on, 95, 189; and Seminole Indians, 40; skeletons of, 95; in South Carolina, 30, 33, 34, 102, 104–5, 106, 107, 109, 193; Spanish and, 37–38; status of, 32; and tobacco, 32; treatment of, 30; in Virginia, 30, 32; in West Indies, 31; working conditions of, 30, 32. *See also* Maroons

Slaves, Indian, 9, 30, 55

Small Things Forgotten, In (Deetz), 4

Smyrna, Del., 129

Society for American Archaeology, 209

Society for Historical Archaeology (SHA): and archaeological conservation, 187, 188; awards of, 2, 4; exhibits of, 187; and historical farm preservation, 131; John Cotter and, 2; Kathleen Deagan and, 8; publications of, 12, 185, 209, 210; and public education, 209; Public Education and Information Committee of, 210; and *Unlocking the Past* project, 12, 210, 212; Web site of, 12, 209

Soil: and agriculture, 86, 128; analysis of, 104; and artifact disintegration, 43; burned, 64; erosion of, 129; exhaustion of, 129; garden, 154; layers of, 103, 184, 196; at Nathaniel Russell House (S.C.), 107; peels of, 66; plowed, 64; polluted, 76, 110; samples of, 85, 86; specialists on, 63; stains in, 203; study of, 66; and subsoil, 64; zones, 103

Soldiers and officers: African American, 38, 43; archaeology and, 152, 159; and Battle of Gettysburg (Pa.), 184; and Battle of Little Bighorn (Mont.), 166–71; British, 156; in Canada, 82; diaries and letters of, 151; and diet, 159; engineers, 42; in Florida, 23, 36, 38, 43; German, 176–78; households of, 82; huts of, 151, 158, 159; living standards of, 159; in New York State, 156; rangers, 156; skeletons of, 156; Spanish, 19, 23; in Spanish colonies, 19; U.S., 36, 158, 165, 166–71, 174, 175, 184; in Vermont, 158–59

Somersville, Calif., 4

Soto, Hernando de, 21

South, 30, 120, 123

South Africa, 4, 173, 192

South Carolina: and agriculture, 30, 31, 33, 102; archaeological sites in, 11, 30, 34; ceramics in, 32, 33, 34; demography of, 33; economy of, 33; environment of, 33; forts in, 152; Maroons from, 37; migration to, 33; plantations in, 11, 30, 32, 33, 102; political power in, 33; settlement patterns in, 33; shipwrecks near, 162; slavery in, 30, 33, 34, 102; Spanish in, 152. See also Charleston, S.C.

Southeast, 52

Southeast Archaeological Center (National Park Service, Fla.), 208, 210

South Union, Ky., 137

Spain, 8, 9, 15–16, 19–20, 25

Spanish: in the Caribbean, 8, 10; and colonization, 19, 58; as conquistadores, 25; and cultural interaction, 12; cultures of, 10; in Florida, 8, 16, 19–24, 26–28, 58; and Fort Mose (Fla.), 39; and forts, 152; and French, 152; goals of, 28; in Hispaniola, 9, 10; immigration by, 16; and Indians, 10, 25, 28, 57; and religion, 34; in South Carolina, 152; and Texas, 69

Spanishtown (Calif.), 76

Spector, Janet, 126–27

Spencer-Pierce-Little Farm (Mass.), 119, 125, 130, 131

Spencer-Wood, Suzanne, 10

Sprague, Roderick, 5

Stadt Huys (New York, N.Y.), 90

"Standards and Guidelines for the Conservation of Historic Places in Canada," 207

Stanwix, Fort (N.Y.), 157

Starbuck, David, 136, 150, 172, 196

State Historic Preservation Offices, 206

Staten Island, N.Y., 93

Statistical Research, Inc. (Ariz.), 207

St. Augustine, Fla.: archaeology in, 80; archivists at, 40; British and, 21, 38; Kathleen Deagan and, 8; Maroons in, 38; roads from, 20, 23; and slavery, 16; trade with, 19

St. Catherines Island, Ga., 25–26

Stereolithography, 70

Stewart-Abernathy, Leslie C. "Skip," 124

St. Joseph, Fort (Ont.), 11, 144–45

St. Joseph Island, Ont., 144–45

St. Lawrence River valley, 55

St. Louis, Fort, 68

Storehouses, 58

Stores, 118, 129

Sturbridge, Mass., 124, 143, 144

Sumter County, Fla., 36

Surinam, 36

Tablewares, 7, 33–34. See also Ceramics

Tabor, Bill, 98

Tabor, Emmett, 98

Taiwan, 16

Tallahassee, Fla., 21, 208, 210

Tampa Bay, Fla., 21

Target-shooting galleries, 52, 74

Tarrytown, N.Y., 125

Tattoos, 4

Technology: and agriculture, 117, 119, 130; American faith in, 202; and consumer revolution, 5; developments in, 117; English, 57; European, 61; and everyday life, 117; history of, 5; and industry, 117, 147; and ironworking, 145; for landfills, 80, 92–93; lesson plans on, 143; and mining, 72, 75–76; Monitor, USS, and, 161–62; in museums, 80; and National Register of Historic Places, 175; and pottery manufacture, 146; preservation of, 138; on ranches, 123; refrigeration, 121; of rural industry, 134, 138; and ships, 165; and wars and uprisings, 149, 176

Temple, N.H., 140, 141

Tennessee, 11, 144, 145

Terrorism, 149

Texas, 11, 41, 52, 68, 69, 71, 173, 176–78

Textiles, 134

Theaters, 207

Thomas, David Hurst, 25

Titanic, RMS (ship), 160, 165

Tobacco, 42, 115, 119, 136, 137

Tokyo, Japan, 90

Tolle-Tabbs (Md.), 186

Tolomato, Fla., 23

Tools and machinery: agricultural, 125, 132; anvils, 60, 145; as artifacts, 135; awls, 127; backhoes, 91, 104, 196; blacksmith's, 144; boilers, 143; bulldozers, 8, 140; button-processing, 142; catalogs of, 135; corn shellers, 128; crucibles, 140; decoration on,

127; files, 139; fishhooks, 4; fishing tri-
dents, 186; furnace bellows, 144; and gender, 127; grain elevators, 207; grindstones,
39, 139, 143; hammers, 60; handheld, 127;
Indian, 32; iron, 51; maintenance of, 134;
manufacture of, 134; metal, 43; in Michigan, 154; milling, 139; nails, 42, 134;
needles, 55; operation of, 139; parts for,
118, 135, 139; plows, 118; saws and
blades, 121, 143; scissors, 85; for sewing,
55; sewing machines, 114; on ships, 162;
sieves, 73; sorters, 73; steam-powered, 143,
162; stepladders, 4; stone, 1; sugar-grind-
ing, 143; thimbles, 39, 85; turbines, 135;
water-powered, 139; waterwheels, 118,
135, 143; whetstones, 55
Toronto, Ont., 197, 209
Torpedo Factory Art Center (Va.), 99
Toulouse, France, 85
Tour de Digs (Va.), 100
Toxic clean-up, 76
Toys, 5, 48, 87, 103, 115, 128, 160, 200–202
Trade: Alexandria, Va., and, 97; Anglo-Indian,
32, 57; Anglo-Russian, 61; black-market,
86; Canada and, 83, 84, 85–86, 196, 197;
Caribbean and, 89, 153; Chinese and, 48,
49; Delaware and, 128, 129; Dundurn
Castle (Ont.) and, 197; Dutch and, 89, 152,
155; Europe and, 56, 76, 153; French and,
69, 71, 83; fur, 85–86, 89, 126, 154, 196,
197; history of, 5; Indians and, 69, 89, 126;
Jamestown, Va., and, 52; Louisbourg (Cape
Breton Island) and, 153; Maroons and, 37,
39, 44; Michigan and, 154; networks for,
48, 49, 123; New York City and, 89, 93;
New York colony/state and, 89, 155; with
Orient, 128; Philadelphia, Pa., and, 129;
plantations and, 31; restrictions on, 86;
slave, 202; in South, 31; and trading posts,
149, 152, 196; transportation for, 142; Vikings and, 56; West Indies and, 93; worldwide, 129
Trade goods: agricultural, 37, 86–87, 89;
Asian, 129; beads, 68, 85, 86; bottles, 37;
Caribbean 153; ceramics, 5; clothing, 48;
and consumer revolution 5; copper, 57;
corn, 19; cosmetics, 48; in Dorset (Can.),
56; European, 153, 155; on farmsteads,
121; in Florida, 19; foods, 71; forts and,
159; French, 149; furs and hides, 51, 53,
71, 127; George I. Quimby on, 149; and
hunting, 37; imported, 129; Indians and,
149, 155; ivory, 53, 56; at Jamestown, Va.,
52; on La Belle, 71; local, 129; manufactured, 37, 149; mercury, 76; ornaments, 57;
pearls, 142; plants, medicinal, 87; shipment
of, 81, 89, 129, 149; silks, 57, 129; spices,
57; tea, 129
Transportation: and archaeology, 81; in California, 46, 111; canoes, 31; in Delaware,
129; and economy, 111; facilities for, 142;
freeways, 110; of goods, 81; industry and,
140, 146; along Mississippi River, 142; in
New York City, 93; omnibuses, 95; systems
for, 76; of trade goods, 149; and urban archaeology, 110; walking, 93, 95–96; water,
111; West Oakland, Calif., and, 111, 112.
See also Railroads; Roads; Ships and boats;
Waterways
"Treasures from the Sand, Archaeology at
Michilimackinac" (exhibit), 154
Trees, 55–56, 60, 61, 122, 131
Triggs, John, 183, 184, 193
Tucson, Ariz., 207

Ulster Plantation (Ire.), 202–3
Underground Railroad, 30
Unglik, Henry, 144–45
UNESCO, 82, 84, 88
Union Railroad Station (Los Angeles, Calif.),
46
United Nations, 79
United Society of Believers in Christ's First
and Second Appearing. See
Shakers
United States, 76, 139, 154, 156, 165, 176,
188
Unlocking the Past (book, De Cunzo and
Jameson), 12, 210
Unlocking the Past (painting, Pate), 210, 211
Upper Forge (Pa.), 144
Upper Peninsula, Mich., 154
Urbanism and urbanization, 190, 206
Utah, USS (ship), 178, 179
Utensils, 32, 39. See also Ceramics

Valley Forge, Pa., 144, 157
Valley Forge National Historical Park, 2
Valley of the Moon (London), 112
Ventura, Calif., 45, 46

Vermont, 144, 146, 158–59

Vermont Division for Historic Preservation, 158

Vesey, Denmark, 107

Videos, 160, 172

Vikings, 6, 51, 52, 53, 54, 55, 56–57, 205

Vinland, 53, 54, 56, 57

Virginia: African Americans in, 11; agriculture in, 30, 32, 201; archaeology in, 11, 30, 130, 183, 189, 200–202; architecture in, 200; capitals of, 62; ceramics in, 32, 33; consumers in, 130; creolization in, 32–33; English in, 32; environment in, 52; foodways in, 33; and forced migration, 201; industry in, 201; James Deetz on, 4; on maps, 11; militia of, 152; mines in, 201; museums in, 5, 62–63, 93, 99, 155, 162, 188, 200; national parks in, 62, 200–202; plantations in, 4, 11, 30; race and ethnicity in, 32; servants in, 32; slavery in, 30, 32, 33; socioeconomic status in, 201; Tidewater, 4, 52

Virginia, CSS (ship), 150

Virginia City, Nev., 74–75

Volunteers: at Abraham's Old Town (Fla.), 44; activities of, 98, 197, 208, 209; in Alexandria, Va., 97–98, 99, 100, 197; and archaeological conservation, 187; and archaeological education, 207; in Arizona, 208; in Canada, 196, 197, 209; and *La Belle*, 68; at Little Bighorn Battlefield (Mont.), 166; and PIT program, 207–8; at Requa farm site (N.Y.), 125; at Yulee Sugar Mill Ruins State Historic Site (Fla.), 143

Waldbauer, Richard, 124

Wales, 187

Walker, Iain, 5

Wall, Diana, 79, 92, 193

Wallace, Birgitta, 54, 56

Ward, Johnny, ranch (Ariz.), 118

Wars and conflicts: Africans and, 40; American Revolution, 31, 149, 156, 157–58; Anglo-French, 153; Anglo-Zulu, 173; Civil War, 12–13, 97, 102, 124, 145, 149, 150, 152, 160–65, 166, 173, 184; colonial, 11, 12, 151; and colonization, 202; and death, 128; Denmark Vesey insurrection, 107; economics of, 149; Europeans and, 39; Fallen Timbers (Ohio), 173; in Florida, 38, 40; French and Indian War, 152, 154, 156, 157; Indian 149, 152; Irish Rebellion (1641), 203; in Jamaica, 40; Little Bighorn (Mont.), Battle of, 11, 13, 166–73, 174, 191; Louisbourg (Cape Breton Island) and, 153; Ludlow Massacre, 10; Maroons and, 40, 41; memorials to, 149; in New England, 11, 150; paintings of, 40–41; in Palo Alto, Tex., 173; Sand Creek Massacre (Colo.), 173; scholarship on, 150, 151; Seminole War, 40–41; ships and, 150; Spanish-French, 152; strategies for, 149, 168; and technology, 149; Timucua rebellion, 22–23, 24; U.S.–Mexican War, 173; War of 1812, 152, 197, 198; and westward expansion, 152; World War II, 2, 13, 76, 121, 150, 174–82, 205; world wars, 149

Washington, D.C., 80, 97

Washington, George, 121, 152

Water, 72, 76, 122, 123, 135

Waters, Michael, 176–77

Waterways: Atlantic Ocean, 16, 34, 161, 162; Baffin Bay, 60; Baptizing Spring, 20, 21; canals, 89, 97, 99, 117, 134, 141, 147; and cemeteries, 87; Chesapeake Bay, 19; Cooper River, 34; Corrientes River, 20; and drainage patterns, 87; East Bay, 111; East River, 89, 90, 92, 93; Erie Canal, 89; factories along, 138; Factory Pond, 136; and floods, 76; Frobisher Bay, 57, 58, 59; Georgian Bay, 198; Great Lakes, 82; Guacara River, 21; Gulf of Mexico, 52, 68, 69, 70, 176; Gulf of St. Lawrence, 56; Hudson River, 89, 90, 93, 156; and irrigation, 77; Jumper Creek, 41; Lake Champlain, 158, 159; Lake George, 156; Lake Michigan, 154; Lake Ontario, 196; Little Bighorn River, 166, 171; Matagorda Bay, 68, 70; Mill River, 139; mills along, 138; Mississippi River, 11, 68, 142; North Atlantic, 53; Pacific Ocean, 16, 51; in Papua New Guinea, 174; and pollution, 51, 77; Potomac River, 97, 99; Sacramento River, 77; Salt River, 137; San Francisco Bay, 111; San Joaquin River, 77; and slave trade, 34; springs, 87; St. Charles River, 82, 85, 87; St. Johns River, 20, 164, 165; St. Lawrence River, 82, 83; Straits of Mackinac, 154;

Suwannee River, 20, 21, 23, 24, 42; near West Oakland, Calif., 112

Watkins, Lura Woodside, 146

Wayne, Anthony, 173

Wealth, 7, 61, 74, 75, 124, 142, 193, 198

Weapons and ammunition: armaments, 159, 161; arrowheads, 1, 120, 166; at Battle of Little Bighorn (Mont.), 166–71; bayonets, 39; bullets, 28, 166–70, 184; cannons, 68; carbine strap hooks, 166; cartridges and cartridge cases, 74, 75, 166–71; at Fort William Henry (N.Y.), 156; gunflints, 39; gunpowder, 69; guns, 39, 74, 162, 167, 170; gun turrets, 162; historical documentation on, 151; Irish and, 74–75; iron, 51, 166; lead shot, 69; legislation governing, 74; manufacture of, 139, 141; from *Maple Leaf*, 165; missiles, 176; on *Monitor*, USS, 162; mortar bombs and shells, 156, 159; muskets and musket balls, 39, 139; ordnance, 151, 152; ownership of, 74; pistols, 74; rifles, 74; as status symbols, 75; torpedoes, 162; uses of, 69, 74; water mines, 165; weapons, 38

Weik, Terrance, 16, 190, 192

Wenhold, Lucy L., 20–22

West, 11, 16, 40, 52, 72, 119, 122

West Indies, 31

West Oakland, Calif., 11, 80, 110–11, 112–16, 192, 196

West Virginia, 142

Westward expansion, 119, 127, 152, 190, 206

White, William, 129

White Mountains, 124

Whitney, Eli, 139

Whitney, Eli, Gun Factory, 139, 141

William Henry, Fort (N.Y.), 156

Williamsburg, Va., 62, 65, 80, 200

Winthrop, John, Jr., Blast Furnace (Mass.), 140

Wiseman, James, 140

Women: activities of, 55, 113–14, 126, 127; African, 9–10; and agricultural press, 132; Arapaho, 173; as archaeologists, 7–8; and auxiliaries, 112; in Boston, 10; Chinese, 48; and class, 95; and farming, 126, 127, 132; and foodways, 129; at Fortress of Louisbourg (Cape Breton Island), 153; in Hispaniola, 9–10; historical archaeology and, 192; historical documentation on, 72; history of, 10; immigrant, 112; Indian, 9–10, 126, 127, 173; at L'Anse aux Meadows (Newfoundland), 55; in New York City, 95; occupations of, 72; at Penetanguishene naval base (Ont.), 198; and reform movements, 10; roles of, 9–10, 95, 136, 190; in rural America, 118; at Sand Creek Massacre (Colo.), 173; scholarship on, 118, 127, 190; Shaker, 136; and smoking, 136; as subordinates, 15; in West Oakland, Calif., 113–14, 115; and westward expansion, 190

Woodlots, 131

Work roles, 118

World Heritage Cities, 12, 79, 82, 88

World Trade Center (New York, N.Y.), 79, 96

Worth, John, 22

Wyandotte, Mich., 201

Yamin, Rebecca, 96

Yorktown, Va., 62

Young, Hugh, 42

Young, Lisa, 184, 186

Young Mill-Wright and Miller's Guide, The (Evans), 139

Yulee Sugar Mill Ruins State Historic Site (Fla.), 143

Zierden, Martha, 80, 190, 191, 193, 196

Zooarchaeologists, 83, 105, 109

Zulus, 173